GREAT LIVING

The Mirror Image of Shinran Shōnin

(*Kagami no Goei*)

GREAT LIVING

In the Pure Encounter
between Master and Disciple

*A volume of essays and commentaries
on the Shin Buddhist text Tannishō
in a new translation*

KEMMYO TAIRA SATO

THE AMERICAN BUDDHIST STUDY CENTER PRESS

NEW YORK

Great Living: In the pure encounter between master and disciple.
   A volume of essays and commentaries on the Shin Buddhist text Tannishō
   in a new translation

by Kemmyo Taira Sato of The London Shōgyōji Trust,
Three Wheels Temple, London, England

Published by American Buddhist Study Center Press, New York, NY

Printed in the United States of America
Printed on 10% recycled paper with soy ink.

Permission to use the images published in this book was formally obtained from
the Jōdo Shinshū Hongwanji-ha, Kyōto, Japan

Design by Arlene Kato, W. Yokoyama
Body copy set in Gandhari Unicode, designed by Dr. Andrew Glass

Library of Congress Cataloging-in-Publication Data
Kemmyo Taira Sato
Great Living: In the pure encounter between master and disciple.
   A volume of essays and commentaries on the Shin Buddhist text Tannishō
   in a new translation

ISBN 978-0-9764594-7-7

In grateful memory of my late master,
Dharma mother Ekai-ni, whom I first had
the joy of encountering at the age of fifteen.
I am forever in her debt for the wisdom she showed
in sending me to my teacher, D. T. Suzuki,
whose enormous efforts to share the Buddha-dharma
with the rest of the world have always encouraged and
inspired me on my own journey
to the Pure Land.

KEMMYO TAIRA SATO'S translation and commentary is a landmark in the understanding of the *Tannishō* in the English speaking world. The Buddhist Society is pleased to be associated with this important work, which is based on a series of talks given by Professor Sato at the Society.

Dr. Desmond Biddulph
Chair of the Buddhist Society, London
Editor of *The Middle Way*

Rev. Kemmyo Taira Sato has provided us with a comprehensive approach to the *Tannishō* which has not only been a major text for Jōdo Shinshū Pure Land faith, but also a classic of Japanese literature. He draws on his association with Dr. D. T. Suzuki as well as his personal religious experience to interpret the subtle nuances of the writing. The *Tannishō* is a text with great appeal to modern people beyond the Hongwanji institution but also outside of Japan with its focus on personal faith and the significant role of the relationship of the teacher and disciple in spiritual development. The author sets the text on the background of Pure Land Buddhist history in Japan, highlighting the transformation of the *Nembutsu* as a means for attaining salvation to the *Nembutsu* as an expression of gratitude for a salvation already given. He focuses throughout the book on the issue of pure personal faith and the transmission of the faith from teacher to disciple. For Shinran (1173–1263) Hōnen (1133–1212) played a pivotal role in the formation of his faith. As the title of the *Tannishō* indicates, the author Yuienbo discusses deviations from Shinran's understanding of pure Other Power faith among his disciples, particularly after the death of the founder. These deviations were brought about through interaction with other Pure Land interpreters and with believers in other traditions in Japan, based in Self-Power. Viewing the teaching from various angles, Rev. Sato has contributed greatly to the further clarification of what is distinctive about Shinran's faith, as a modern faith with its potentiality to liberate the ego from its entanglements with the modern world, as well as presenting the faith as universal and open to all.

Dr. Alfred Bloom
Professor Emeritus
University of Hawai'i, Mānoa

CONTENTS

GREAT LIVING

PART ONE: THE TEACHING OF SHINRAN SHŌNIN

PART TWO: ON THE DIVERGENCE FROM SHINRAN SHŌNIN'S TEACHING

PART THREE: THE DOCUMENTS APPENDED TO THE TANNISHŌ

FOREWORD

It was 8 December 1993 that Reverend Professor Kemmyo Taira Sato, having set out unaccompanied from Shōgyōji Temple in Japan, first stepped out onto the tarmac at London's Stanstead airport. Sixteen years have passed since that day and now this book, *Great Living: In the pure encounter between master and disciple. A volume of essays and commentaries on the Shin Buddhist text Tannishō in a new translation* has finally been completed.

Over the last hundred years, there have appeared countless books on the *Tannishō* in the form of introductions, commentaries and translations but this work by Reverend Professor Sato is of an entirely different order. Thanks to the author's exciting fresh insights into Buddhist terminology, those wishing to study Pure Land Buddhism by reading the *Tannishō* are certain to find within the pages of this new book clear and distinct spiritual inspiration.

From his middle teens, long before entering Kyoto University, Reverend Sato studied the Buddha-dharma under Dharma mother, Daihi-in Ekai, who was my Master as well. Both of us enjoyed an upbringing bathed in the light of her wisdom and compassion. There is no way to quantify all the inspiration and guidance we received from her as our Master from that time onwards.

In subsequent years Reverend Sato devoted himself to the study of Western religious philosophy and Buddhism in general. It was during his period of intense tutelage under Dharma Master D. T. Suzuki he came to experience at a truly profound level a deep spiritual encounter between East and West.

Reverend Sato spent three years studying with this great Master who, with the spiritual maturity of his own Enlightenment-experience, had grasped the oneness of Zen and *Nembutsu*. In fact, Reverend Sato was to serve D. T. Suzuki until the very end of the great man's life, a witness to his dignity and generosity of spirit.

In his own book, Reverend Sato included a telling line from D. T. Suzuki's work *Japanese Spirituality*, "It is possible to see both Hōnen Shōnin and Shinran Shōnin as one person." Besides demonstrating a profound insight into the relationship between those two sages, the quotation reminds me also of the understanding shared by Reverend Kemmyo Sato and his own Master, Dharma Mother Ekai, and indeed of the spiritual encounter between Dharma-mother Ekai and D. T. Suzuki, where each was mindful of the other, in the way described in the famous phrase from the *Larger Sutra of Eternal Life*, "All Buddhas think of one another."

The strength and integrity that make this book unique emanate from this fountain of spiritual encounter. What should be further emphasised is that, in accord with the sincerest wish of Reverend Sato, a *Nembutsu* Saṃgha, or Buddhist community so longed for in the *Tannishō*, has now come into existence in the U. K.

The series of twenty-two lectures on the *Tannishō*, on which the book is based, was first given by Reverend Sato at Birkbeck College, University of London, in September 1995, and subsequently repeated at the Buddhist Society, the Golden Buddha Centre and also at Three Wheels, the Buddhist Centre of which he is in charge as its residential priest.

The book itself is the fruit of Reverend Sato's steady and tireless efforts that inspired listeners at his meetings to participate in lively encounters and discussions, focusing on the carefully prepared texts.

What underlies this publication is the birth of new *nembutsu* followers through true encounters and re-encounters, amongst those who have been taking part in bimonthly London *Eza* meetings, monthly meetings to read the *Letters* by Rennyo Shōnin, monthly meetings to read the *Shōshinge* by Shinran Shōnin, Japanese Dharma talks, weekly meditation classes and Spring Schools attended by both Japanese and English students.

These meetings, including the *Tannishō Eza*, had developed into a unique form of Buddhist retreat, called '*Shokai* retreat,' that first began in May of 2008. Concerning the word '*shokai*,' the imagery it conveys is that of 'opening [the channel]' (*kai*) 'to let [the water] flow' (*sho*). A 'Shokai retreat' thus is a time for confronting the problems of life rather than fleeing from them, as outlined in Rennyo Shōnin's famous entreaty: "Constantly dredge out the

The Stūpa of Namu-Amida-butsu
Brookwood Cemetery, Surrey

Channel of Faith and let the water of Amida's Dharma flow freely." The *Shokai* retreat is a new form of Buddhist meeting that, until quite recently, did not exist in the U. K. At this type of meeting ten or more participants share time together, listening to the Buddha-dharma by taking part in services to the Buddha, Dharma talks and question-and-answer sessions, while also carrying out minor tasks such as cleaning and gardening for the temple.

Since *nembutsu* followers aspiring for birth in the Pure Land share one and the same path towards their goal, they are called 'Dharma friends on the same way.' In living their lives together in a certain place at a certain time they share a common awareness that 'that place' is their home and the prime source of the *nembutsu*.

Shinran Shōnin described the Buddhist path as *kyō-gyō-shin-shō* (teaching, practice, faith and realisation) and declared that its essence lies in expounding the truth of the Pure Land. What is to be expounded is the truth of the Pure Land and that alone.

Although the worldly path aims at bettering one's life, it is through encounter between self and others that the Buddhist path is followed. Our Saṃgha is a place where, living the *nembutsu*, we create and develop true encounters. In order for such a place of encounter to exist Reverend Sato created the framework of Three Wheels. It was indeed in Buddhist terms the fulfilment of the virtues of the Pure Land adornments: Buddha, Bodhisattvas and Land.

At the beginning of the modernisation of Japan, a willingness on the part of young Japanese students to go and study in England was the first step in the history of the Anglo-Japanese encounter. Students from Chōshu and Satsuma provinces, in particular, made a huge contribution to the Meiji Restoration. Behind their success, however, lay the graves of a number of fellow students who took sick in the alien climate and died young on foreign soil.

Some of these early students went on to brilliant careers while others passed away, their cause unfulfilled. It is a matter Reverend Sato has been at pains not to overlook while busy with the daily activities of the *Nembutsu* Dharma movement. In this, as in so much else, he has been amply assisted by Professor John White (former Vice-Provost of University College London) who, both openly and privately has been an ever powerful force, encouraging Reverend Sato to go forward certain in the knowledge of his generous help and support.

In August 1998, with great sincerity of feeling, Professor White helped erect a monument in Brookwood Cemetery to commemorate the four Japanese students who had died in the U. K. about one hundred and forty years previously.

Subsequently there was an unexpected development. In the grass not too far from the gravesite of the four students a further gravestone was discovered, bearing the names of Professor and Mrs. Alexander William Williamson. Not only had this generous couple undertaken the care of those students from Chōshu and Satsuma, who eventually returned home to pioneer the modernisation of Japan, they had also accepted, looked after, and buried with extreme kindness their unfortunate compatriots who became sick and died young in the U. K. What Professor Williamson and his wife did for those students, indeed for all us Japanese people, is so enormous it defies description.

Reverend Sato, together with a number of English Dharma friends, visited the site and, heedless of the tears of emotion wetting his cheeks, held a service in front of the headstone of Professor and Mrs. Williamson to express our deepest gratitude.

Those young English people who witnessed the ceremony learned to recognise the grave as a stūpa.

A *stūpa* is a place where relics of Buddhas and Bodhisattvas are contained. In this it hardly differs from an ordinary grave. But whereas the main purpose of a Western grave is to honour the memory of the dead, a stūpa is a place where visitors can feel and receive the Buddha's Great Compassion. In this respect the meaning of 'stūpa' differs very much from that of 'grave.'

Based on a bequest left to Three Wheels by his friend Reverend Zenko Croysdale, an English Zen monk, Reverend Kemmyo Sato had the 'Stūpa of Namu-Amida-butsu' erected at Brookwood Cemetery. Ever since the Buddha entered Great Nirvāna, the concept of 'stūpa' has been the primal source of the activities of the eternal life of Buddhism. Now Buddhism, in the form of a stūpa, is rooted in the rich earth of England and faith in the Buddha-name, the mantra (True Word that is, Namu-Amida-butsu) as the source of true encounter between oneself and others, has been established.

The *Tannishō* laments divergence from the true faith and desires all Dharma friends to establish and keep alive the true faith in the light of the teaching of Shinran Shōnin. The Stūpa of Namu-Amida-butsu as a symbol of the true faith, namely the fulfilment of the adornment of the Buddha, has now assumed concrete form before our eyes. This means that we have already been given the adornment of Land, the great earth of faith, here in England, and that it will go on lasting far into the future.

Reverend Chimyo Takehara
Head Priest of Shōgyōji Temple in Japan

INTRODUCTION

There is no religious text like *Tannishō* in the psyche of Japan today. Any Japanese retail bookstore large enough to have a religion section is sure to contain two or three books on the *Tannishō*. As someone born and raised outside Japan who learned to read Japanese as an adult, this appeal has mystified me for years, particularly because until Kiyozawa Manshi's decision to publish the text serially in the late Meiji period journal, *Seishinkai*, the text was only read by Shinshū scholars. The oldest extant manuscript, copied by Rennyo Shōnin (1415–1499), contained a colophon warning against showing it to anyone not well-trained in Shinshū doctrine. I have asked many native speakers why they think this is so but people generally muster only general, generic answers. It is not like the *Tannishō* has a special canonical status, although it was included in the Japanese language printed compilations of Shinshū texts in the Edo period (1603–1867) known as *kana shōgyō*.

It is important to keep in mind that although today the *Tannishō* may be the first and perhaps only book on Shinran's thought that someone at the end of the first decade of the 21st century might read, it was not written by Shinran himself. In fact it has been somewhat of an enigma as to who wrote this work and when, but Satō-sensei does an excellent job of informing his readers what scholars have deduced with some confidence about the book's provenance. Namely, that it was written by Yuien in the second half of the thirteenth century. Now there is more than one person with that name, but the current consensus is that this Yuien was about forty years old when Shinran died, and was related to Shinran's descendants through marriage. His father married Shinran's daughter Kakushinni, and he himself was called to Kyoto to serve as tutor to Kakunyo (1270–1315), Shinran's great grandson. Kakunyo played a major role in the development of a distinct identity for the Shinran lineage outside that of Hōnen's other disciples in producing such biographies of Shinran and essays expressing his own rulings on which interpretations of Shinran's teachings should be considered orthodox such as the *Gaijashō*. We should thus expect to see something of Yuien's perspective in Kakunyo, though how much influence he actually had is hard to know. I mention all this because while the *Tannishō* is in some sense "second-hand" knowledge, it was not written by an outsider with limited exposure to Shinran and his doctrines. What we have in the *Tannishō* is a record of a series of question and answer sessions by someone on intimate terms with Shinran. Perhaps this is one of the appeals of the text to newcomers and Shinran aficionados alike: we see in it an example of how someone in Shinran's community processed what Shinran was trying to communicate, a perspective that in many ways parallels how we, too, must process Shinran's thought, but of course with the major advantage that this "interested party" was able to ask questions directly of the master himself.

From the title *Great Living*, we see that Reverend Satō has chosen to follow the interpretation of Daisetsu Suzuki in translating the Japanese term for praxis, or *gyō*, as "living." Suzuki coined this expression in his translation of Shinran's *Kyōgyōshinshō*, normally rendered "teaching, practice, faith, and realization." We know from extant drafts of Suzuki's translation that he struggled with the term *gyō*, for Shinran's usage is different from most Buddhist thinkers who follow the standard paradigm wherein *praxis* leads to *realization* or liberation. For Shinran, *praxis* leads to faith. Suzuki tried "act" and "practice" for *gyō*, eventually settling on "living." It is impossible to know if he might have changed his mind again, given more time, but his *Kyōgyōshinshō* came at the very end of his life. In any case, understanding *gyō* as "living" is an inspired choice of words, implying that how we live our lives is itself praxis. It replaces the notion that certain activities we normally label "religious" such as ritual or meditation warrant unique valorization because they have special spiritual or karmic significance. In Shinran's view, religious acts bring us to the realization of faith, and it is faith that brings us to the liberation. This begs the question of what is precisely meant by "religious acts" and here Suzuki is suggesting that it is one's entire life that makes realization possible, not merely sitting meditation or reciting the *nenbutsu*. Indeed, if we look at the history of Zen, the vast majority of religious awakenings or enlightenments do not occur during meditation but in the course of interactions between the individual and the world around him, i.e., in living life itself. Indeed, what Shinran seems to be teaching Yuien is *how to live* in the light of Buddhist teachings and experience as found in its canon as discerned and embodied in his own teacher Hōnen.

Among the many dialogs captured in the *Tannishō*, it is undoubtedly the notion of the saving of *akunin* or "people with bad karma" discussed in chapters three and thirteen that have generated the most interest in the *Tannishō*. In the translation here: "Even a good person can attain birth in the Pure Land, how much more readily, then, the person with bad karma." Known as *akunin shōki* in modern Japanese, this doctrine was not unique to Shinran, but it nevertheless stands out as one of the clearest statements of the core of his faith and today is recognized as the signature doctrine of the *Tannishō* itself. In the past, the term *akunin* had been translated as "evil people" or "evil persons" and we still see this phrase used today, but this creates the jarring idea that Buddhism denigrates the humanity of certain individuals of a criminal nature so thoroughly as to exclude them from the rhetoric of spiritual transformation, and then turns around and welcomes them to the salvific Pure Land. This is not what Shinran was talking about, for his appeal was to the human condition as a whole. The term *akunin* was used very broadly in Chinese Buddhist literature to refer to individuals who had committed harmful acts in the past and were therefore in spiritual crisis in some sense. They expected harsh retribution to come to them in the future for their bad behavior or thinking, typically in the form of bad rebirths. In the Pure Land tradition, this was a metaphorical way of referring to the karmic limitations of all living beings, for who has not behaved badly and who can know what the resultant karmic impact of our bad behavior might be?

Reverend Satō correctly understands *akunin* as someone with a bad karmic record; in other words, everyone. Within his analysis of chapter three, he nicely presents the way in which Shinran understood the implications of believing in the nineteenth, twentieth, and eighteenth vows of Amitābha in the *Larger Sukhāvatīvyūha Sūtra* as indicating a developmental process by which the believer moves from a mundane ethico-religious understanding to a purely religious one. In the context of the *akunin* concerns of the *Tannishō*, this means that an individual's past karma is rendered incapable of preventing that individual from realizing the immediate religious goal of birth in the Pure Land. How does a Buddhist move from a karmic orientation to Buddhism to a non-karmic one? Along with emptiness, the nature of buddha, and so on, this is one of what might be termed the "deep themes" of Mahāyāna Buddhism, meaning that it pervades or is characteristic of all forms of Mahāyāna thought. There are many ways to answer this question but in this context of Pure Land Buddhism, the answer is by the power of the Buddha's vows. Some call this faith, some call it entrusting, some call it *shinjin*, but whatever term one uses, the central idea is a personal recognition of the working of the Buddha's commitments, in this case, the eighteenth vow, within oneself. For Shinran, accepting the eighteenth vow as true and real, therefore, *requires* the acceptance of one's own position as *akunin*, not in the sense that "I am evil" but in the sense that "I am karmically handicapped."

These and so many other points are presented with thoughtfulness and care throughout this study. This is the first systematic presentation of the *Tannishō* and its many implications in English, and a work like this is long overdue.

Mark L. Blum
Professor
Department of East Asian Studies
State University of New York, Albany

LEGEND TO ILLUSTRATIONS

[*Frontispiece*] *The Mirror Image of Shinran Shōnin.* Known as the *Kagami no Goei*, this fine-line sketch of Shinran (1173–1262), in his final years was done by portrait painter Sen'amidabutsu, son of Fujiwara Nobuzane (1177–1265), who was also a painter and poet. A note indicates it was repaired by Shinran Shōnin's great grandson Kakunyo Shōnin in November 1310. Designated as a Japanese National Treasure, this photograph is used with the kind permission of the Jōdo Shinshū Hongwanji-ha (Nishi Hongwanji). *34.4 cm height x 30.4 cm width.*

[p. 17] 1. *Tannishō,* Cover. The Rennyo edition of the *Tannishō,* with title words, *Tannishō ittsū,* in the middle and Rennyo Shōnin's signature in the bottom right corner. The manuscript copy is undated but is thought to have been made by Rennyo Shōnin, 1415–1499, around 1460.

[p. 18] 2. *Tannishō,* Yuien's Preface. Sophisticated use of language is seen in Yuien's Preface written in elegant *kanbun,* or classical Chinese, which was part of the education of the day. It employs *okurigana* and *kaeriten* by which the reader can convert the text into Japanese syntax. Notice the four small holes on the right where the book was bound. The first page would have consisted of everything except for the last two lines, which were on the next page.

[p. 91] 3. *Tannishō,* Chapter 3A. One of the key chapters of the *Tannishō,* it boasts extremely high literary qualities that have made the text as a whole a masterpiece of Japanese Buddhist literature. It is written in the Japanese of the day which employed both *kanji* and *katakana.* The text reads vertically from the top right.

[p. 92] 4. *Tannishō,* Chapter 3B. This chapter contains Hōnen Shōnin's paradoxical statement that, if even the good person is saved, then all the more so the person with bad karma. Yuien discusses this further in Chapter 13.

[p. 149] 5. *Tannishō,* Historical Endnote, A. The relation of the historical endnote to the rest of the *Tannishō* has long been the subject of much dispute. This historical note relates the banishment of Hōnen Shōnin and the execution of four of his disciples during a period of *nembutsu* persecution. It is possible that other documents were originally appended as well.

[p. 149] 6. *Tannishō,* Historical Endnote, B. It contains a statement on Shinran Shōnin's decision to use the name Gutoku; the note is written in classical Chinese.

[p. 150] 7. *Tannishō,* Rennyo Shōnin's note and signature, with flourish. The two lines are written in classical Chinese.

GREAT LIVING

THE PURE ENCOUNTER BETWEEN MASTER AND DISCIPLE

An historical background

The *Tannishō* compiles the sayings of Shinran Shōnin (1173–1262), as set down by his disciple Yuien some years after his death. In this record an aged and wise Shinran Shōnin is often heard to reflect on what his master, Hōnen Shōnin (1133–1212), had taught him over half a century earlier. The profound spiritual bond between him and Hōnen Shōnin, that was first forged when Shinran Shōnin was still in his twenties, thus served as one of the great inspirations of his religious life. It was through this pure encounter with Hōnen Shōnin that Shinran Shōnin discovered a guiding light that helped him find his way throughout life, even long after the master had ceased to be. In the *Tannishō*, therefore, we can frequently detect in the words of Shinran Shōnin the voice of Hōnen Shōnin speaking to us just as Hōnen Shōnin had spoken to him. For his role in promoting the Pure Land teaching of his master, Shinran Shōnin may well be regarded as one of the greatest disciples of Hōnen Shōnin.

Hōnen Shōnin is the person who made the declaration that Pure Land Buddhism ought to be recognised as an independent school of Buddhism in its own right. This call to recognise a new school of Buddhism signaled a radical departure from the traditional arrangement of the Japanese Buddhist schools. Understanding more about Hōnen Shōnin's life and thought is needed to help us arrive at a deeper appreciation of what Shinran Shōnin sought to achieve. In order to clarify the background to the Shin Buddhism that Shinran Shōnin developed, we will first examine some historical features of the Pure Land Buddhist practices performed on Mount Hiei, where Hōnen Shōnin and Shinran Shōnin both lived, in the later Heian (794–1185) and early Kamakura (1186–1333) Periods. We will then discuss the nature of Hōnen Shōnin's religious life in relation to his significant declaration to establish Pure Land Buddhism as an independent school of Buddhism in Japan. Finally, we will explore Hōnen Shōnin's experience of Pure Land Buddhist faith, with regard to the advent of the Shin Buddhist teaching of his disciple Shinran Shōnin.

SOME HISTORICAL FEATURES OF THE PURE LAND BUDDHIST PRACTICE PERFORMED DURING THE HEIAN AND KAMAKURA PERIODS

Pure Land practice prior to Hōnen Shōnin

Before Hōnen Shōnin, the main form of Pure Land practice on Mount Hiei was the so-called *jōgyō sammai*, or constantly practicing *samādhi*. It was one of four forms of *samādhi*, based on the Tendai doctrine, which was brought over from China by Saichō (767–822) and put into practice by Ennin (792–862). The four forms of *samādhi* are: 1) *Jōgyō sammai*, or constant-practice *samādhi*, is the *samādhi* attained by continuously engaging in *nembutsu* practice, by reciting Amida Buddha's name while walking round his statue for ninety days. It is also called the *shobutsu genzen sammai*, the *samādhi* in which all Buddhas become manifest. 2) *Jōza sammai*, or constantly sitting *samādhi*, is the *samādhi* practice in which a monk continues to sit in meditation before a Buddha statue for a period of ninety days without engaging in any other religious exercise. Only if troubled by some discomfort, such as fatigue or disease, is the practitioner allowed to call the Buddha's name. These first two forms of *samādhi* are still practiced by the Tendai School on Mount Hiei today. 3) *Hangyō hanza sammai* is the *samādhi* involving both practice and meditation for a specified period of time in order to rid oneself of bad karma. There are two kinds of this particular *samādhi*: one is based on the *Lotus Sūtra* and the other on the *Daihōdō Darani Sūtra*. 4) *Higyō hiza sammai* encompasses all other kinds of *samādhi*, and so it is called the free choice *samādhi*.

The Pure Land practice of reciting Amida Buddha's name, or *nembutsu*, in the Heian Period is believed to have evolved from the first of the four forms of *samādhi*, the *jōgyō sammai*. According to historical research, large buildings called *jōgyō sammai dō*, or constant-practice *samādhi* halls, were constructed especially for this practice in other temples both esoteric and exoteric. This testifies to the rapid spread of the practice of *nembutsu* and its popularity at that time. At this stage in history, however, the practice of pronouncing the *nembutsu* was not for laymen but only for priests.

Being a priest at the Enryakuji temple on Mount Hiei, Genshin (942–1017), the greatest figure in the history of Japanese Pure Land Buddhism before Hōnen Shōnin, was greatly influenced by the practice of *nembutsu*, deeply rooted as it was in the Tendai tradition. Through his main work the *Ōjōyōshū* (The Essentials for Birth in the Pure Land) he demystified the practice, making it much more accessible to ordinary people. Although this is not the place to go into details about his doctrine, the crucial point is that he laid particular emphasis on reciting the *nembutsu* at the very end of one's life. If one pronounced Amida's Name single-mindedly at that point, he declared that one would surely be born into the Pure Land, even if one had not been able to practice the *nembutsu* during one's lifetime as often as the priests might have done. In his opinion the power of a single pure thought at the very end of one's life would far outweigh the karma accumulated over an entire lifetime.

Based on this conclusion of the *Ōjōyōshū*, Genshin organised the *Nijūgo sammai kō*, meetings for groups of twenty-five people to practice the *nembutsu samādhi*. In these religious groups, twenty-five members formed one unit and would help each other practice the *nembutsu*, especially in the last moments of life. When one of them lay on his deathbed, all the others would gather round and, as his good friends, encourage him to pronounce Amida's Name.

In the *Ōjōyōshū* we read:

It may be asked, 'All good practices are virtuous, and each enables one to attain birth in the Pure Land. Why is it then that the teaching of the *nembutsu* alone is encouraged?' In answer, I would say, 'When I now encourage everyone to practice the *nembutsu,* I do not mean to set aside the various other good practices. What I mean to say is that the *nembutsu* is not difficult to perform for either man or woman, whether high-born or low-born, whether walking or staying, sitting or lying, and no matter when, where and under what kind of karmic condition. Moreover, when anyone is on his deathbed and desires to be born in the Pure Land, no practice is more accessible than the *nembutsu*.'[1]

Once Genshin had introduced the idea of *Nijūgo sammai kō* the number of these religious groups multiplied rapidly. One group had their own special house for funerals. When one of them lay dying, he was brought to the house, and a special ritual was held for his birth in the Pure Land. This was available not only to priests but also to ordinary people, women as well as men. In this way Genshin made the practice of *nembutsu* much more popular and widespread than before.

At the beginning of the *Ōjōyōshū*, Genshin says:

The teaching and practice that leads to birth in the Land of Utmost Bliss is the most important thing in this world of defilement during our latter days. Priests and laymen, men high-born and low-born, who will not turn to it? But the scriptures of the exoteric and esoteric teachings are not unanimous in what they say, and the practices that are said to cause one to attain Enlightenment are so diverse, varying in their ritualistic and philosophical aspects. These are not difficult for men of keen wisdom and great diligence, but how can an ignoramus such as I comprehend them? Therefore, solely depending on the teaching of the *nembutsu*, I have collected a number of essential passages [on the *nembutsu*] from the sūtras and commentaries.[2]

This shows how different Genshin's standpoint was from that of the older religious orders, that is, all the older temples of exoteric and esoteric Buddhism, and how potentially damaging to them such a standpoint must have seemed. Indeed, although Genshin's thought expressed in this book is very advanced, his later writings reveal reversals and compromise, no doubt brought about by the antagonism he suffered from these older established orders. Despite Genshin's own personal regression, the new historical movement typified in his book could not be halted and brought forth a large number of liberalists from within the older orders. These liberal priests thought it impossible to remain in the main temples, because the corruption within the religious order was widespread and worsening. Thus, anyone who was a truly sincere priest would have felt obliged to leave behind the stifling atmosphere of the main temples and move out to quieter lodgings, such as a hermitage not far from their original temple, where they could enjoy the religious life in their own meagre surroundings.

When sufficiently large number of such reclusive priests were gathered in one area, it was called a *bessho*. There were several such areas both on Mount Hiei and Mount Koya. Those priests who retreated from their religious orders were called *intonsha* (recluses). Almost all of them became Pure Land Buddhists. The word *inton*, in its usual sense, means a retreat from the world. Here, however, it has the particular meaning of retreating from a religious order. Thus a reclusive priest did not simply mean one who had entered the priesthood by renouncing the world. Reclusive priests were those who had abandoned the traditional religious order itself, finding it defiled by the desire for scholarly achievement, fame, fortune, status, and power.

Reclusive priests as a rule lived in poverty, the better to enjoy the humble religious life style they had chosen and to keep their minds pure and aloof. In this sense they were also called *hijiri*, literally, 'holy men,' who are sometimes described as wandering ascetics. It was in the late Heian Period of the eleventh century that priests began to abandon the main temples in large numbers for the life style of the *hijiri*. This spawned a genre of literature based on the writings they left to posterity in the Heian and Kamakura Periods.

HŌNEN SHŌNIN ESTABLISHES THE INDEPENDENT PURE LAND SCHOOL

Hōnen Shōnin, also known as Genkū, the preeminent founder of the Japanese Pure Land School, comes to fore as one of the leading *hijiri* figures of his age. In the following we will present a brief biography of his life and then explore the contents of his teaching.

Hōnen Shōnin's life

Hōnen Shōnin was born the only son of a warrior lord, Uruma Tokikuni, in 1133. When he was eight years old his father died, after being assaulted in a land dispute, and young Hōnen Shōnin therefore entered the priesthood on his own initiative. On his deathbed, Hōnen Shōnin's father had told him not to avenge his death but to seek the Buddha's teaching of universal deliverance.

At fourteen he was sent to Mount Hiei to study Buddhism, mainly the Tendai doctrine, under the masters Genkō, Kōen (*d.* 1169) and others. Then, at eighteen, he was sent to Eikū (*d.* 1179) at Kurodani by Kōen, who knew the young man's earnest desire to retreat from the order. Living in Eikū's hut, Hōnen Shōnin studied the Pure Land teaching of the Tendai tradition. When Hōnen Shōnin was twenty-five years old, Shinkū (1146–1228) also became Eikū's disciple and one of Hōnen Shōnin's closest friends.

During his stay at Kurodani Hōnen Shōnin started reading the Buddhist Tripiṭaka in a library as a way of seeking his own awakening and liberation. Although he read through the entire work five times, however, he failed to reach his goal. One day, in 1175, at the age of forty-three, he came upon the following passage in *The Exposition on the Meditation Sūtra* by Shandao (jp. Zendō, 613–681), which is said to have led him to convert to Pure Land Buddhism.

> The right ways of practice are divided in two. One of them is to pronounce single-mindedly the Name of Amida alone, whether walking or staying, sitting or lying, whether for a long time or for a short time; to keep pronouncing the Name from moment to moment. This is called the right practice which truly assures one to be born in the Pure Land, as it is in accordance with Amida's Original Vow.[3]

After this awakening of faith in Amida Buddha, Hōnen Shōnin went to see a *hijiri*, named Yūrenbō Enshō (1139–1177), having been told by his friend Shinkū, that this young seeker had already experienced a similar conversion. Hōnen Shōnin would subsequently live and study with the *hijiri* at Hirotani for the next two years.

At the age of forty-five, after the early death of his friend Yūrenbō Enshō, Hōnen Shōnin moved to Yoshimizu in Kyoto. There at Yoshimizu, in the Higashiyama area of Kyoto, Hōnen Shōnin began preaching his message of Pure Land Buddhism, founded on his religious conversion and the warm friendship he had enjoyed with Yūrenbō. This new activity attracted many followers from all strata of society. In a *gātha* known as the *Shōshinge*, or Hymn on the Right Faith [in the *Nembutsu*], Shinran Shōnin praises Hōnen Shōnin, saying:

> Genkū [Hōnen Shōnin], our teacher,
> > was well versed in the teaching of the Buddha.
> Pitying all of us ordinary beings, both good and evil,
> In this lonely land of ours [Japan]
> He promoted the true teaching and its realisation.[4]

We will have to forego a detailed discussion of Shinran Shōnin's relation to Hōnen Shōnin for the time being. More of his views will become apparent in the discussion of the *Tannishō* to follow. For a list of the main events in Hōnen Shōnin's later life in relation to Shinran Shōnin's meeting with him, readers are referred to the Chronology in the Appendix. Let us now turn to Hōnen Shōnin's teaching.

HŌNEN SHŌNIN'S PHILOSOPHY OF PURE LAND BUDDHISM

Problems underlying Japanese Pure Land Buddhism

Hōnen Shōnin's conversion to Pure Land Buddhism was an epoch-making event in the history of Japanese Buddhism. Before discussing his conversion in greater detail, we would like to turn our attention first to certain problems that the Pure Land Buddhists, known as *hijiri*, faced in those days, which arose inevitably from the special stage of development that Pure Land Buddhism had reached at that time. According to a document dating from the middle of the Kamakura Period, it was the professed ideal that all the head priests of the established temples should "turn their disciples into learned scholars every bit as knowledgeable as their predecessors, and thereby bring themselves to the attention of the state government and build themselves a fine reputation in the world."[5] Reclusive priests, on the contrary, wanted to free themselves of the 'desire for fame and wealth' (*myori*), and in fact it was often the main reason for their retreat from the religious order. Generally speaking they aspired to live a serene and simple religious life, and so discarding riches and honour, they sought to attain pure faith in Amida Buddha.

When Kūamidabutsu (1156–1228), who was one such reclusive priest, was asked a doctrinal question dealing with esoteric Buddhism by a visitor who knew he had once been a foremost scholar in the field, Kūamidabutsu replied, "I have forgotten everything, I cannot remember even a single term." Those reclusive priests knew full well that even the most advanced academic study was far removed from pure faith, from Enlightenment or the awakening to truth; it was removed, in other words, from real religious experience. Despite their aspiration for purity and quietude, however, the *hijiri* (reclusive priests) were not without their shortcomings; their 'other-shore-ness', formalism, and aristocratic tendencies, all caused them to maintain a certain sense of aloofness on their part. Moreover, although they had left their established orders, the *hijiri* still took up their abode in huts or hermitages that were often situated not far from their main temples. This shows the contradiction in their elected life style, situated, as it were, halfway between this shore and the other shore.

First, regarding their other-shore-ness, in their attempt to escape from this world, the *hijiri* tended to concentrate all their attention on seeking birth in the Pure Land. The idea of actually contributing to society rarely occurred to them. The more strongly they were motivated to aspire to the other world, the more deeply they were consciously bound to their consciousness of this world. Their consciousness vacillated between this shore and the other shore. Living close to their main temple, they were not completely free from the influence of the established order. Thus their escapist attitude resulted in their placing too great an emphasis on the last moment of life. Pronouncing the Buddha's Name at the very end of their lives, they longed for Amida Buddha to appear to them with the sacred host of bodhisattvas.

Next, regarding their formalism, in order to be born in the Pure Land the reclusive priests firmly believed they needed to follow formal obligatory rituals of *nembutsu* practice. They believed that whether or not they attained birth in the Pure Land depended totally on the efforts they put into the ritual and the amount of *nembutsu* they practiced. This way of thinking led them to lose sight of the most important aspect of the *nembutsu*, namely, 'pure faith.' Such thinking also reveals that the reclusive priests of that age were still under the sway of the old traditionist view—that 'practice' is the *sine qua non*, the absolute condition, for attaining Enlightenment.

This contradiction of religious life is well captured by Shinran Shōnin, one of Hōnen Shōnin's disciples, who says in his *Kyōgyōshinshō*: "True faith is always accompanied by [the practice of pronouncing] the Name, but the Name is not always accompanied by true faith in the power of the Original Vow." [6] This means that, for those who followed Shinran Shōnin, putting effort into the practice of *nembutsu* was no longer believed to be the absolute criterion for attaining faith; saying the *nembutsu* was instead regarded simply as a person's grateful expression of faith in Amida's Original Vow.

In this context I would like to introduce an interesting story from *The Life of Shinran Shōnin* by Kakunyo Shōnin (1270–1351):

> While the Venerable Genkū (Hōnen Shōnin) was still alive, he was always devoted to the propagation of the doctrine of salvation through 'Other Power' and birth in Amida's country, and the entire world was then anxious to listen to his teaching. Not only were Imperial personages ready to pluck the golden-coloured flowers of the Pure Land, but noble lords of the highest ranks were glad to gaze at the silvery moon shining on the Forty-eight Vows of Amida. Nay, even people, remote and humble, were glad to come to the Venerable Teacher and pay him homage. Thus his followers, noble and lowly, coming thick upon him, converted his residence into a sort of prosperous market. Those who were in constant attendance on him numbered about three hundred and eighty. In spite of this, however, those who were personally cared for by the Teacher and who earnestly followed his instructions were not many, hardly numbering more than five or six.
>
> The Zenshin Shōnin (Shinran Shōnin's previous name) once said to his Teacher (Hōnen Shōnin): 'Since my abandonment of the Path of Difficult Practice for that of Easy Practice and my entrance into the Gate of the Pure Land away from that of the Holy Path, I have ever been under your wise guidance whereby I was able to hoard up the good seeds of release and emancipation. If not for you, what would have become of me? For that reason, I do not know how to give vent to my feeling of happiness and gratitude. There are, however, many fellow-believers of mine, all of whom are enjoying the friendship of belonging to the same company under one director, and yet we do not know one another very well as regards our inner faith, whether it is such as to enable us to be born in Amida's Pure Land or not. Besides, I have a desire to know

who amongst us could be real spiritual friends in our coming lives, and also to have a sort of meeting to test our faith while still living here. Will you kindly permit me to say a few words to my fellow-believers on such an occasion as seems proper?'

To this the Teacher replied, 'Your request is most reasonable. You shall speak to them when they all come here tomorrow.'

The next day when they were all assembled, the Shōnin (Zenshin) requested them to arrange themselves into two groups according to their views on what constitutes the stage of steadfastness (nonretrogression), that is, whether it is attained by faith or work (practice). Some three hundred fellow-believers of his, who were present at this meeting, seemed not to comprehend fully the sense of his request. There were two, however, who declared themselves as belonging to the group of those who believed in the all-importance of faith: they were Seikaku, who was a Hōin ranked as Daikashō-i, and Hōren, who was also called Shinkū Shōnin.

Later there came in Hōriki, Kumagai Naozane, a lay-disciple of the Master and asked, 'My venerable Zenshin (Shinran Shōnin), what are you engaged in?' Replied the Shōnin, 'Sir, we are trying to make a distinction between those who believe in the all-importance of faith and those who believe in work as the most essential.' Said Hōriki, 'If this be the case, I must not be left out, for I will join the group of those who believe in the all-importance of faith.' Thereupon, Zenshin took down his name as requested, while the rest of those present, numbering several hundred, had not a word to say concerning the matter in question. Perhaps this silence was due to their inability to free themselves from the bondage of 'self-salvation' and to their minds still being dark as regards the true diamond-like faith. Then, as they remained silent, the Shōnin who was acting as a recorder, put his own name down. After a while, the Venerable Teacher said, 'I also will take a seat with those who believe in the all-importance of faith.' Then amongst his disciples some humbly and devoutly expressed their willingness to follow his example, while others felt dejected over their weakness of faith.[7]

The story quoted here well illustrates the attitude of people towards the problem of faith versus practice before Hōnen Shōnin's day. Compared to the way ordinary people viewed the *nembutsu* at that time, Shinran Shōnin's insight into the *nembutsu*-experience was both original and profound. According to Shinran Shōnin, the core of the *nembutsu* lies in pure faith in Amida's Original Vow for universal deliverance. The *nembutsu* itself—the practice of pronouncing the Name—is then a spontaneous expression of thanks to Amida Buddha springing from the faith engendered by our encounter with his Vow.

Before Hōnen Shōnin, this crucial point had never been clearly articulated. Although the *nembutsu* was taught as being an Easy Practice, the *hijiri*, or reclusive priests, thought of it as being something rather difficult because they were not yet aware that the true content of *nembutsu* was pure faith. Practising the *nembutsu* was for them something difficult that had to be achieved with much effort in order to attain pure faith. In this respect it remained for them a formal obligatory ritual.

Almost all of them thought that they had to pronounce the Name as many times as possible. They stuck to formality, especially as regards the number of times the practice of *nembutsu* had to be carried out. It was not a question of quality but quantity that most concerned them. Genshin, for example, is said to have pronounced Amida's Name two hundred million times during his life.

Some tended to ill-treat their bodies, by fasting, maiming themselves or committing suicide. These self-destructive activities, executed while pronouncing the Name, show the fundamentally escapist attitude of these priests towards the real world. This kind of escape from reality would finally lead to the negation of their own existence, even to the point that they would commit suicide by immolating or drowning themselves. However desperate or hopeless one's situation, such behaviour is not to be condoned, and indeed runs totally counter to the original spirit of Buddhism.

Finally, regarding their aristocratic tendencies, almost all of the priests who were able to receive formal ordination on Mount Hiei or in Nara were from the aristocracy or from the upper warrior class. Those priests who were not highborn usually placed themselves under the patronage of the higher classes. Many reclusive priests who appeared in the last half of the Heian Period maintained an aristocratic way of life. Those reclusive priests from the aristocracy, who came to form the mainstream of the new Buddhism at that time, considered it important to set aside enough funds for their reclusive life of retreat. Those who were too poor to do so, however, could not become reclusive priests without getting financial support from the ruling classes. Their aspiration for birth in the Pure Land on the one hand and their desire for material welfare on the other, created a serious contradiction in their life style.

Hōnen Shōnin's view of the nembutsu

Practice and faith play an important role in Hōnen Shōnin's conversion to Pure Land Buddhism. To Hōnen Shōnin, practice explicitly means 'pronouncing single-mindedly the Name of Amida alone,' and faith implicitly points to Amida's Original Vow. As noted in the biographical sketch above, the source of inspiration for Hōnen Shōnin's spiritual conversion is said to be the following passage, cited above, from Shandao's *Exposition on the Meditation Sūtra:*

> The right ways of practice are divided in two. One of them is to pronounce single-mindedly the Name of Amida alone, whether walking or staying, sitting or lying, whether for a long time or for a short time; to keep pronouncing the Name from moment to moment. This is called the right practice which truly assures one to be born in the Pure Land, as it is in accordance with Amida's Original Vow.[8]

To better understand the meaning of the first sentence in the above quotation, that 'the right ways of practice are divided in two,' a few words of explanation are necessary. In his *Exposition on the Meditation Sūtra*, Shandao said there are five right ways of *nembutsu* practice: 1) reciting the Pure Land sūtras; 2) meditating on Amida Buddha and his Land; 3) paying reverence to Amida Buddha; 4) saying Amida's Name; and 5) giving praise and making offerings to Amida Buddha. It is through these five right ways that people practice the *nembutsu*; that is, it is through these means that people 'think of Amida Buddha' or 'are mindful of the Buddha.'

Shandao goes on to state that, of the five, the fourth, the saying of Amida's Name, is the most important and that the other four are to be called 'supportive practices.' The above phrase that 'there are two things to be distinguished [amongst the five right ways of *nembutsu* practice]' refers to this distinction between the right practice of saying Amida's Name and the other four supportive practices. Shandao insists that, as distinct from the four supportive ways, 'the single-minded recitation of the Name of Amida alone' is of paramount importance because it is 'the right practice that truly assures birth in the Pure Land.' On this point, Hōnen Shōnin follows Shandao's pronouncement as if it were scripture, giving priority to the recitation of Amida's Name as right practice.

Up until the time of Hōnen Shōnin, no one in the history of Pure Land Buddhism had ever made the radical declaration that the simple act of saying Amida's Name was in itself sufficient to enable one to be born in the Pure Land and that the other four supportive ways of thinking of him could be dispensed with. Before his time no one had ever clarified whether the other four supportive ways were really necessary or not. But this is what Hōnen Shōnin did. Hōnen Shōnin's main work, the *Senchaku hongan nembutsu shū*, even has as its subtitle: 'Namu-Amida-butsu, all practice for birth [in the Pure Land] is based on the *nembutsu*.' In this context the *nembutsu* simply means to say the Name. To quote an important passage from the concluding part of the book:

> If one wishes speedily to be free from birth-and-death, there are two excellent ways, of which the teaching of the 'way for holy men' may be disregarded for the while. Let us rather specifically choose the teaching of the Pure Land. There are, again, two ways to enter into the Pure Land teaching: the right way and the mixed way. Of the two let us give up the mixed way and specifically choose the right way. Of the right way and the accessory [supportive] way, the latter is to be set aside. Let us specifically choose the right way and concentrate our efforts upon the right practice that truly assures our birth in the Pure Land. The right practice that truly assures our birth is to say the Buddha-Name. When this is done, one shall assuredly be born [in the Pure Land], on the strength of the Buddha's Original Prayer (Vow).[9]

When we consider the fact that Pure Land Buddhism had hitherto evinced only a marginal existence within the established schools, this declaration appears revolutionary. The culmination of Hōnen Shōnin's philosophy of Pure Land Buddhism was the point where he chose 'pronouncing the Name' as the only right practice and discarded all the others. He encouraged people to pronounce Amida's Name single-mindedly in order to be born in the Pure Land. In his philosophy, choosing just the one practice meant throwing out all the others. Hōnen Shōnin had absolute confidence in universal salvation by Amida just by the one practice of pronouncing Amida's Name, for he had experienced his own salvation through this one pure act.

Hōnen Shōnin urges us just to say Amida's Name, and you will be saved. This teaching is so disarmingly simple as to seem almost insulting to people of intelligence. Hōnen Shōnin resolutely stood his ground on this point, however, and soon a large number of people were following him and all were warmly welcomed by him. While the *nembutsu* is called Easy Practice, faith is said to be difficult to attain. Practice is thus deeply related to faith in Pure Land Buddhism.

Faith in the nembutsu

Hōnen Shōnin's learning in the field of Buddhism was prodigious and he was regarded by his peers as 'first and foremost in wisdom'. There is no doubt that he was one of the most learned scholars of his day. How then did a highly sophisticated person like Hōnen Shōnin come to believe in salvation through such a simple practice as *nembutsu*? In the history of Buddhist philosophy, Hōnen Shōnin's conversion to Pure Land Buddhism can be called a Copernican revolution. Indeed the impact he had is comparable to that of Descartes in the history of philosophy in the West.

In his *Discourse on Method*, which explored the proper way to reach conclusions and seek Truth in science, Descartes introduced the idea of methodological doubt. Rejecting as false whatever allowed the slightest room for doubt and accepting as true only that which was clear and distinct in itself without need of any presuppositions, he finally came to the conclusion, 'I think, therefore, I am' (*cogito ergo sum*). It was an awakening to his own existence. What was indubitably clear and distinct to him was the fact he was thinking in this way, and it is his awareness of the existence of this thinking 'I' that is demonstrated in his phrase '*cogito ergo sum*'.

Descartes' philosophical conversion can be said to amount to a declaration of modern scientific reason, with the 'I' thinking independently of any sort of theology. At this point the thinking 'I' has started to depart from theology and set out on its own independent path. Descartes' ultimate concern was how to establish the foundations of scientific reason. What is odd is the fact that, immediately after this, he felt compelled to make this 'I' demonstrate the existence of God, using the concept of perfection. To my thinking this was a rather misguided move on his part.

By contrast, what Hōnen Shōnin was awakened to in the course of his religious conversion was his own utter ignorance, his irredeemable state of mind.

He consequently used to call himself 'Hōnen the Ignoramus.' For a long time before his conversion Hōnen Shōnin had been struggling to find the truth. Faced with the problem of his ignorance in the light of Buddha's Enlightenment, he had sought something absolute, beyond the shadow of a doubt. It was actually at the very moment of coming into contact with Amida's Love that he was awakened to the wretchedness of his own existence and felt compelled to entrust his whole being to the one single act of saying the *nembutsu*.

Let us now consider the latter part of passage from Shandao's *Exposition on the Meditation Sūtra*. This part is said to have brought about Hōnen Shōnin's conversion: "This (saying of the Name) is called the right practice which truly assures our birth in the Pure Land in accordance with Amida's Original Vow." To my mind, Hōnen Shōnin entrusted himself completely to the *nembutsu* on the grounds that it was 'in accordance with Amida's Original Vow.' In other words, when he encountered this particular passage, faith in the Original Vow was awakened deep within him and this in turn led him to convert to Pure Land Buddhism. Although what the passage itself explicitly emphasises is the importance of practicing the *nembutsu*, what was of particular interest to Shinran Shōnin about his master's encounter with the passage was the way it awakened Hōnen Shōnin to faith in the Original Vow. Amongst Hōnen Shōnin's many disciples, at least one person, Shinran Shōnin, was clearly very aware of this point.

The full title of Hōnen Shōnin's main work, the *Senchaku hongan nembutsu shū*, can be translated as *The Collection of Passages on the Nembutsu Chosen by Amida Buddha in his Original Vow*. By becoming aware of Amida's Original Vow and by basing himself on it, Hōnen Shōnin chose the *nembutsu* as the right practice that would truly assure his birth in the Pure Land, the *nembutsu* being the practice already chosen in Amida's Original Vow, or Prayer. In this context the Original Vow specifically refers to Amida Buddha's Eighteenth Vow in the *Sūtra of Eternal Life*.

Of Amida's forty-eight vows the Eighteenth is the most fundamental. Here, while still at the stage of a bodhisattva, Amida made this prayer manifested as the Eighteenth Vow for universal deliverance through the *nembutsu*, before he finally became Amida Buddha. This Vow, or Prayer, assures us that if one simply said Amida's Name with faith and sincerity, one will definitely be born in the Pure Land.

In this context, to clarify the concept of the Original Vow, the Sanskrit word for this term is *pūrva-praṇidhāna*. Semantically, *pūrva* (Original) means 'before' or 'prior' in both the spatial and temporary sense, and *praṇidhāna* (Vow) means 'application', 'attention', and 'intense energy' in ordinary speech, and 'commitment,' 'wish,' 'will' or 'vow' in Buddhism. In this case, 'Original' refers to the time when Amida issued a deep prayer for universal deliverance while still at the bodhisattva stage. The Original Vow is thus an expression of Amida's Great Will, by which he made a wish for all beings to be born in his Land and attain Enlightenment.

The source of the 'intense energy' or 'commitment', which is the meaning of *praṇidhāna*, is the Buddha's unconditional love. The Original Vow is the expression of Amida's Will or Love which he cherishes towards all beings, with the manifestation of that Love depending on the circumstances in which we find ourselves in the course of our individual lives. Love (*karuṇā*), together with Wisdom (*prajñā*), constitutes the personality of every Buddha: with Wisdom he contemplates the world, perceiving it just as it is, and through Love he emerges out of his state of *samādhi* to live amongst us, and this coming out amongst us is the expression of his Original Vow.

Hōnen Shōnin pronounced Amida Buddha's Name with his whole being when he felt the Buddha's universal love, or Original Vow, actually working within himself. If you will recall what motivated Hōnen Shōnin to enter the Buddhist path and the kind of quest he set out upon before his conversion, you will understand how especially important this concept of equal love for others was for him. On his deathbed Hōnen Shōnin's father told him not to avenge himself on his father's assailant, but to seek the world of equality, beyond the boundaries of petty distinctions. The search for an impartial and equal love was thus the special task that Hōnen Shōnin consequently took upon himself when studying Buddhism. The religious order in which he found himself, however, was beset by discrimination and delusion. Nowhere around him could he find the love he sought. Worse still, in spite of all his hard work and continuous effort, he could not free himself from the world of birth-and-death. He felt himself far removed from both Wisdom and Love, hence that extremely humble and self-deprecating name, 'Hōnen the Ignoramus'.

It was while he was in this desperate and hopeless state of mind that Hōnen Shōnin came across that special passage in the *Exposition on the Meditation Sūtra*. In Amida's Original Vow he discovered what he had long been seeking ever since his father's death. What he found was the Buddha's impartial love for all beings expressed in the Original Vow. It was this, that caused his conversion to the Pure Land teaching. Because he felt his whole being embraced in the Buddha's Love, he was able to devote himself exclusively to the 'Easy Practice' *nembutsu* without reservation, basing himself entirely on the Buddha's Love.

As I have tried to emphasise throughout my commentary on the *Tannishō,* the encounter between Shinran Shōnin and his master Hōnen Shōnin was the foundation of Shinran Shōnin's faith in Amida Buddha and thus of absolutely fundamental importance to his whole life. It was through their encounter that Shinran Shōnin took refuge in Amida Buddha. As mentioned in Chapters 1 and 2, Hōnen Shōnin was for Shinran Shōnin the living manifestation of the Original Vow itself; he was Amida Buddha's great and unconditional love in person.

Although the *Tannishō* is a compilation of the sayings of Shinran Shōnin, in the present essay we have dwelt at length on the life of Hōnen Shōnin because of the profound spiritual relationship that existed between Hōnen Shōnin and Shinran Shōnin. As was the case with the master-disciple relationship between Shinran Shōnin and his disciple Yuien, who compiled the *Tannishō,* Hōnen Shōnin served as the one great source of inspiration for the words and deeds of Shinran Shōnin after his attainment of faith. Always guided by Hōnen Shōnin, Shinran Shōnin, together with his disciples, followed the light of Hōnen Shōnin's teaching of the *nembutsu* on their way to birth in the Pure Land. Throughout the *Tannishō,* therefore, we can clearly make out the voice of Hōnen Shōnin speaking to us through the life of one of his greatest disciples, Shinran Shōnin.

Part One

THE TEACHING
OF SHINRAN SHŌNIN

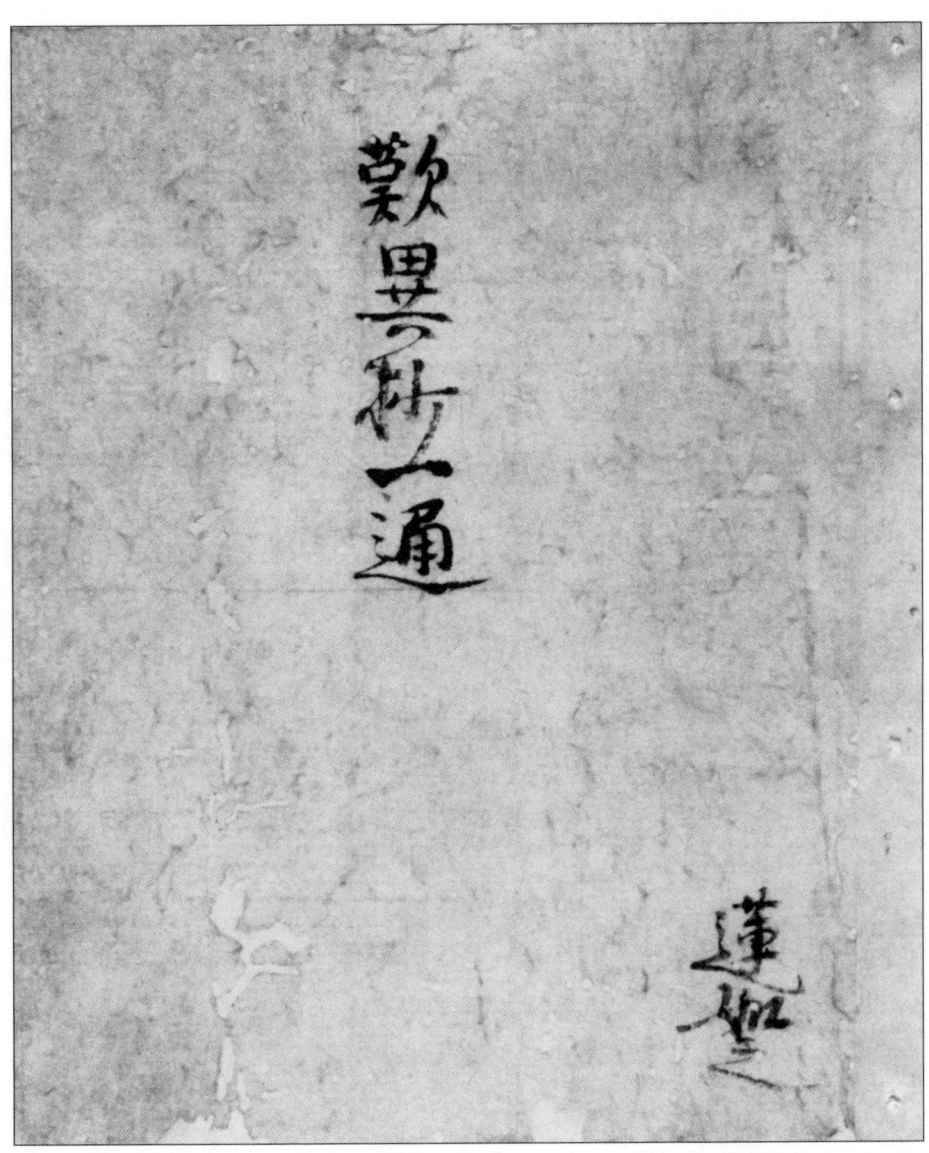

Tannishō, Cover

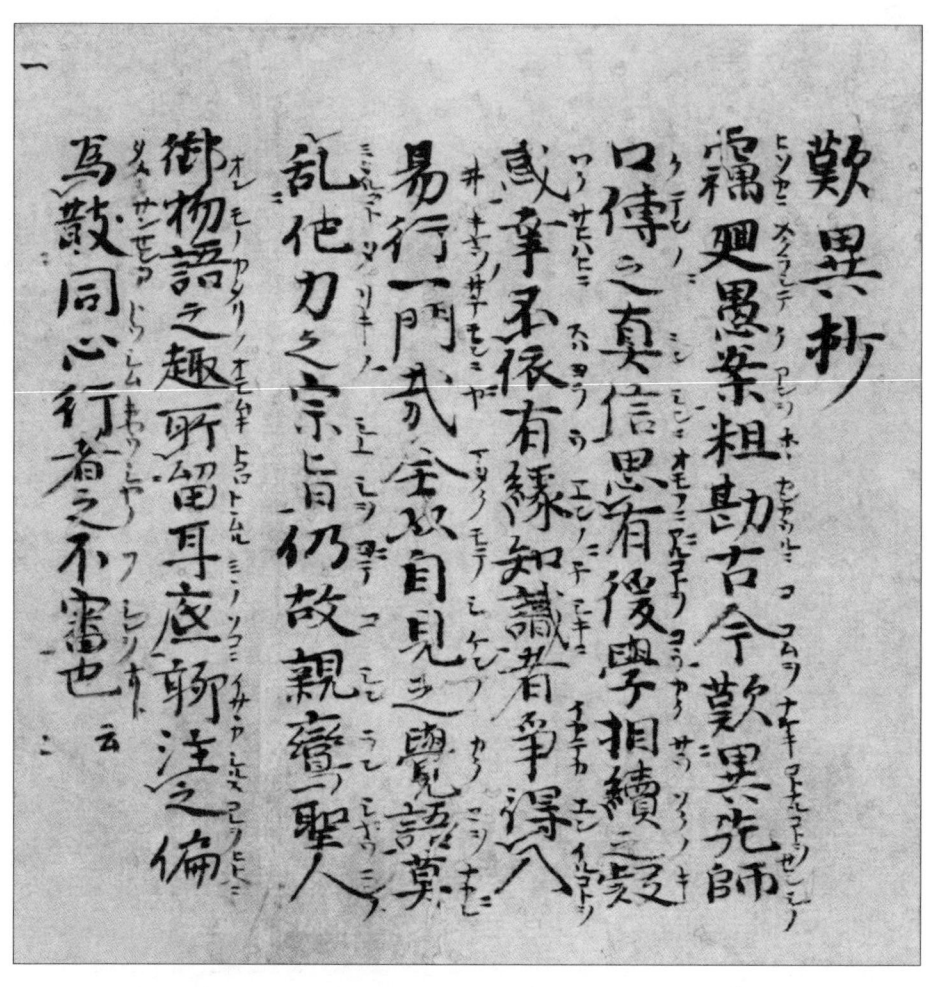

Tannishō, Yuien's Preface

Preliminary Remarks

The *Tannishō* 歎異抄 (*A Record of Lament over Divergence*) is neither an academic work nor a mere historical document; it is, rather, the record of a living encounter that took place between master and disciple in medieval Japan. The master was an aged Buddhist priest named Shinran Shōnin 親鸞聖人 (1173–1262), and his disciple was almost fifty years his junior called Yuien 唯圓 (1222–1289). The remarkable observations the master made on religious life over the years were a source of constant inspiration for the disciple. Even after the master had passed on, the words he had heard him speak remained with him. One day the disciple realised how important it was for him to set them down for posterity. As a result this work represents the direct record of the religious experience related to him by the master. In these pages we thus find reflected the subtle life-giving relationship that was nurtured between master and disciple in their pure encounter as individuals.

Shinran Shōnin, the founder of Shin Buddhism, elucidated the innermost core of Pure Land Buddhism, by making new interpretations of the main concepts of the tradition, firmly based on his own spiritual experience as an individual. Though the unique religious philosophy he articulated first appeared within the narrow confines of Japanese history, paradoxically the trajectory it traces is so deep and broad as to open up a universal dimension of thought which potentially enables it to make a lasting contribution to world culture at large.

In Japan, the *Tannishō* is regarded as one of the greatest Buddhist classics ever produced by that country. Over the last one hundred years in particular the work has enjoyed tremendous popularity, a social phenomenon that is said to have been partly occasioned by the advent of modern printing technology in Japan, and partly by the fact that the Buddhist religious philosopher Manshi Kiyozawa (1863–1903), led the reading public to rediscover this timeless work. In my estimation, however, the main reason for the *Tannishō's* popularity lies in the book itself; that is, it contains a subtle message that has served as a great source of spiritual inspiration for the modern Japanese readership from the time it was rediscovered right up to the present day.

The *Tannishō* has won an especially loyal following amongst the intellectual readers, who comprise the core of Japan's artistic, literary, and philosophical life. The fascination the work has held for this latter group is significant in light of Shinran Shōnin's keen awareness of the problem of intellectual understanding in relation to religious experience. When one awakens to the spiritual dimension of pure faith, one realises the limits of intellectual understanding. Throughout his life Shinran Shōnin was fully aware of the limits of the intellect, where the dualistic way of thinking holds sway.

The vigorous indictment of such thinking detected in *Tannishō* had great appeal for the Japanese readers as they watched their country embark on the sea of modernity. There was much good to be achieved as Japan began to embrace Western ways of thought. At the same time it was also obliged to welcome in the ills of modernity, in particular the scourge of Western nihilism that arose in part from the rise of scientific thought and its inherently dualistic world view. The great influence the *Tannishō* exerted on the modern Japanese reader was due in part to Shinran Shōnin earnestly addressing this very problem of intellectual approach versus spiritual awakening.

The spiritual crisis of modern Japan ran deep, and the despair of the thinking classes was amplified by the incursion of Western nihilism on the one hand and the uprooting of their native traditions on the other. Into this festering wound of society the *Tannishō* cut like a scalpel to the quick. How the book was received, however, varied. Some read it as a work that thrust one ever deeper into despair; to others it pealed out a message of hope and salvation. Even today, as the age of science dawns on Japan the *Tannishō* continues to attract a new generation of readers. Whether it will thrust one into despair or lift one up in hope is not mine to say, but I bring this Shin Buddhist text to the attention of readers fully believing that if one were to devote oneself to a careful reading of this work, it will surely lead one to a tried and true solution to one of the deepest problems of human existence.

TRUE FAITH IS RECEIVED THROUGH
AN ENCOUNTER WITH A MASTER

Yuien's Preface to the *Tannishō*

TRANSLATION

AS I HUMBLY COMPARE, within the limits set by my own ignorance, the time when Shinran Shōnin was alive with the present, I cannot help but lament how much the present followers diverge from the true faith directly expressed by our late Master. I am afraid that those who come after us may thereby fall into doubt and confusion. If I had not had the fortune of meeting my good master, how could I have realised the teaching of Easy Practice? We should not confound the doctrine of Other Power with our own understanding. For this reason, I have committed myself to writing down some of the sayings of the late Shinran Shōnin, which still reverberate in my mind. My sole wish is to dispel any doubts held by our fellow believers regarding our faith.

COMMENTARY

Let us begin with a few brief observations on the compiler's opening remarks above. The key phrase in Yuien's preface is without doubt the term 'true faith' (*shinjitsu shin* 真実信). It was with the sole intention of clarifying the true faith that his master, Shinran Shōnin, had conveyed to him that Yuien set out to compile the *Tannishō*. The true faith we are dealing with here thus is what was transmitted from Shinran Shōnin to Yuien. Yuien was so greatly indebted to the kindness Shinran Shōnin had shown him that, even decades later, he felt compelled to set down his Master's words. True faith in Shin Buddhism thus refers to the transmission of faith that takes place in the pure encounter between two individuals.

Life is a series of encounters; we encounter and re-encounter one another on a daily basis. Encounter can serve as the very source of spiritual light in our lives, provided it is realised purely. To know oneself and to be awakened to oneself, and at the same time to love and respect others just as they are—this is the true meaning of the well-known phrase 'Harmony within diversity'. When you awaken to what you are, you will be so pleased that you cannot help but love others just as they are.

We arrive at this newfound situation through the spiritual light of self-awakening that breaks down the barriers that we have thrown up between ourselves and others. In the *Tannishō* we can sense this taking place in the genuine encounter between Shinran Shōnin and Yuien. All too often, though, we are too full of blind passions and attachments to realise such harmony within diversity, and these obstructions that lie within ourselves impede our ability to encounter one another in a completely pure and open way. This is the reason we need religion in our daily life.

YUIEN AS THE COMPILER OF THE WORK

The content of the *Tannishō* indicates that it must have been compiled by someone who had intimate knowledge of what Shinran Shōnin taught and was acquainted with him over a long period of time, even into his final years. Who that person was, however, was long a matter of speculation and Yuien's role as author not known for a fact. Today, it is well accepted that the compiler of this work was a disciple named Yuien.

Amongst Shinran Shōnin's disciples there were actually two priests by that name. Of the two the compiler of the *Tannishō* is believed to be Yuien of Kawada, in Hitachi Province (present-day Mito City, Ibaragi Prefecture, northeast of Tokyo), where Shinran Shōnin lived for about twenty years. The person called "Yuien of Kawada" was the well-educated son of a Kyoto aristocrat and was probably known in Kyoto literary circles. It was in Kyoto that Yuien first met Shinran Shōnin and seemed to have enjoyed an especially close relationship to Shinran Shōnin. It was only later that Yuien took up residence in Kawada at Shinran Shōnin's request and started a temple there called Senkeiji (present-day Hōbutsuji).

An historical document says that Yuien was exceedingly wise and eloquent, and in his final years, in 1288, some twenty-five years after Shinran Shōnin's death, he successfully transmitted what he had learned from the Shōnin to Shinran Shōnin's great grandson Kakunyo (1270–1351), the third head priest of the Honganji Temple of Shin Buddhism. Though few scholars would venture to say so, the *Tannishō* might well represent a key part of the legacy that Yuien transmitted to Kakunyo.

The person who quelled the great debate that was brewing over the authorship of the *Tannishō* was the Edo period Shin Buddhist scholar Myōon-in Ryōshō 妙音院了祥 (1788–1842), of Mantokuji Temple in Mikawa. He was a graduate of the Shinshū Ōtani-ha academy in Kyoto, but never obtained the highest academic title he felt he deserved. Giving up on a professional career, he returned to his home temple where he continued his research into Shin Buddhist doctrine and history. It was after having undertaken a detailed study of the text and related historical documents that he came up with the Yuien theory which eventually proved that Yuien of Kawada was the true compiler of the *Tannishō*. His most famous work is *Notes Made While Listening to the Tannishō* (*Tannishō monki* 歎異抄聞記).

To prove his theory Ryōshō made two main points: 1) The *Tannishō* is a record of Shinran Shōnin's words, possibly compiled by one of the direct disciples from the Kantō district, and 2) Shinran Shōnin's sayings were addressed to Yuien, whose name appears twice in the text (in Chapters 9 and 13) without the use of any honorific. Regarding the first point let me quote from the first paragraph of Chapter 2, where Shinran Shōnin says, "Having crossed the borders of ten provinces or more, each of you has come to see me at the risk of your life. Your purpose is solely to hear from me how to be born in the Pure Land." These words by Shinran Shōnin were addressed to a group of key disciples who came to see him from the Kantō district having 'crossed the borders of ten provinces or more' to consult him on a serious problem that had arisen within their Shin Buddhist community. Based upon careful study Myōon-in Ryōshō concludes that Yuien, then still a young priest, was amongst the entourage from the Kantō district.

Concerning the second point let me quote two excerpts from relevant chapters:

1) *Tannishō*, Chapter 9: Although I recite the *nembutsu*, I seldom feel like dancing for joy, nor do I desire to hasten to the Pure Land. Why is this so?' I asked.

My Master answered, 'I, Shinran, had the same doubts. O Yuien-bō, you have the same doubts just as I did! ...'

2) *Tannishō*, Chapter 13: The late Master said, 'You should understand that even if it looks as insignificant as a speck of dust on the tip of a single hair from a rabbit's coat or a sheep's fleece, every evil you commit is nothing but the product of your past karma.'

On another occasion he asked me, 'O Yuien-bō! Would you believe whatever I told you?' 'Yes, Master, I would,' was my reply.

Myōon-in Ryōshō conducted detailed research into the grammar and syntax of the *Tannishō* to identify its true author. As some of you may know, the subject of a Japanese sentence is often understood without being clearly indicated and does not always need to be stated explicitly. This sometimes leads to difficulty in understanding a sentence in the flow of conversation and sometimes clarification is needed. When a statement lacks a subject, however, we can tell who the speaker is from the verbal form of the sentence in question. If an honorific is used in the verbal part, the subject of the action is not the speaker; by contrast, if no honorific is used, the subject is the speaker himself. Myōon-in Ryōshō grappled with these grammatical clues to reach his conclusions as to the true identity of the author of the *Tannishō*.

Concerning the English translation of the *Tannishō* as well, we must be very sure that our version is based on a careful linguistic analysis, otherwise we will simply end up with an arbitrary translation of the text based on an unsatisfactory reading. The problem, then, is whether the translator has sufficiently penetrated the complexities of the language of Shinran Shōnin's day to unpack its meaning.

The structure of the work

The *Tannishō* is made up of two parts, each with its own preface. The first preface is a general preface that applies to the entire work, not just to part one. The second preface addresses the problems to be taken up in part two. In part one, Chapters 1-10, Yuien sets down Shinran Shōnin's pronouncements as he recalled them some twenty years after the Shōnin had passed away. Each chapter generally ends with the narrator Yuien's final phrase, 'Thus spoke my Master.' The exceptions are Chapter 3, where Shinran Shōnin cites his master Hōnen Shōnin, and Chapter 10, where Shinran Shōnin cites a key statement by Hōnen Shōnin; in this case, the closing phrase, 'Thus, my Master [Hōnen Shōnin] taught me,' is not the narrative voice of Yuien but that of Shinran Shōnin.

In part two, Chapters 11–18, Yuien gives his critical comments on the serious departures he sees the younger generation of Shin Buddhist followers are making with regard to the genuine tradition. Their facile understanding of the teaching falls far short of the mature religious understanding of Shinran Shōnin, and fails to attain the real joy that religious life embraces.

Each chapter of the commentary deals with a corresponding chapter in the *Tannishō*. This collection is based on a series of talks I gave at the Buddhist Society of London a few years ago. The *Tannishō* translation discussed here is a new one that I made for the occasion. Appended to the *Tannishō* are two separate items: an historical document and Rennyo Shōnin's comment. The nature of these documents will also be discussed.

Yuien as an historical person

As the compiler of the *Tannishō,* Yuien plays an important role in the history of faith-transmission of Shinran Shōnin. The historical details of Yuien's life, however, remain unclear. One person who took an especially keen interest in determining who exactly Yuien was, was the Shinshū Ōtani-ha historian Senkei Ryōga (1720–1797) who mentions Yuien's name three times in chronological entries of the early history of Shin Buddhist temples compiled in his *Ōtani iseki roku*, published in 1779. It would appear, however, that Myōon-in Ryōshō was not acquainted with this important work of research into the history of the Ōtani tradition.

That Yuien was well-educated cannot be disputed, given the excellent literary qualities of the *Tannishō*. It is also from the pages of this work that we learn of Yuien's feelings of spiritual dissatisfaction and how Shinran Shōnin was able to effectively address them. Yuien's fine religious sentiments seem to have made him an excellent receptacle for Shinran Shōnin's teaching. His grasp of what Shinran Shōnin taught may well have earned him a position of importance in the early Shin Buddhist community. It is reasonable to assume that Shinran Shōnin may have assigned him to Kawada to oversee his Saṃgha in the Kantō area. It would account for his having been present at the historical meeting that the close disciples had with Shinran Shōnin as recorded in Chapter 2 of the *Tannishō*. At the same time, it is important to note that Yuien is not one of the so-called twenty-four disciples per se, even though he seems to have held an extremely important position in relation to Shinran Shōnin and his Saṃgha.

One striking detail that we come across is that Yuien's father Zennen, who was then widowed and living with him in Kyoto, married Shinran's youngest daughter Kakushin-ni, who was only two years younger than Yuien. Through this marriage Kakushin-ni later comes into the estate on which she is able to establish the mausoleum in memory of her late father Shinran Shōnin with herself installed as caretaker. Kakushin-ni thus is extremely important historically in laying the groundwork for the origins of the Honganji tradition that has been preserved to the present day.

Kakushin-ni apparently bears Zennen a son named Yuizen, who later goes to live in Kawada with his step-brother Yuien, until he became old enough to marry. Yuien, however, did not remain in Kawada permanently. After moving to what is part of present-day Osaka, he then took up residence in Nara. It is possibly from this location that, a year before his death, he returned to Kyoto to instruct Kakunyo Shōnin as to his great grandfather Shinran Shōnin's teaching of faith. Equally important as the physical location of the mausoleum that Kakushin-ni established is the orientation of Shinran Shōnin's religious philosophy that Yuien manages to transmit to future generations through both Kakunyo Shōnin and the *Tannishō*.

This concludes our brief historical outline of Yuien. For more exact dates, readers should refer to the Chronology of the encounter of Shinran Shōnin and Yuien appended to this volume. It is important to keep in mind, however, that this is merely one theory out of many regarding who the compiler of the *Tannishō* was and, if Yuien, then who exactly Yuien was. Further studies are required to better understand this important though still rather poorly understood aspect of the faith-transmission.

THE CONCEPT OF FAITH IN SHIN BUDDHISM

Chapter 1

TRANSLATION

"At the very moment when the thought that moves you to pronounce the *nembutsu* is awakened within you, believing that your birth in the Pure Land is attained through the inconceivable working of Amida's Original Vow, you instantly receive Amida's compassionate benefit 'that embraces all, forsaking none.' You should realise that Amida's Original Vow never discriminates between old and young, good and bad, and that faith alone is what is essential; for the Vow was originally made for the purpose of saving all sentient beings burdened with the weight of karmic evil and burning with the flames of blind passions. Thus, when you entrust yourself to this Original Vow, no other form of goodness is required because there is no goodness that can surpass the *nembutsu*; nor need you fear any form of evil, because there is no evil powerful enough to obstruct the working of Amida's Original Vow."

Thus spoke my Master.

COMMENTARY

"The chapter on faith in the Vow of Universal Deliverance"
— MYŌON-IN RYŌSHŌ —

The theme of each chapter of the *Tannishō* was first identified by the early modern Shin Buddhist scholar Myōon-in Ryōshō (1788–1842), who is perhaps the most famous *Tannishō* researcher of all time. In his book *Notes Made While Listening to the Tannishō (Tannishō monki)*, he presents a philosophical classification of the work following the categorisation method of traditional Buddhism. In this framework of Shin Buddhist classification this first chapter is called "The chapter on faith in the Vow of Universal Deliverance." To Myōon-in Ryōshō's thinking, faith in the Original Vow lies at the core of Shin Buddhist faith. The Original Vow refers to Amida Buddha's

Vow of Universal Deliverance (弘願 jp. *Gugan*). It is the Vow in which Amida Buddha promises to save all sentient beings out of unconditional love without discriminating amongst them.

The concept of faith in the Original Vow forms the essence of Shinran Shōnin's teaching and the core of his religious philosophy. To characterise exactly what he means by faith or trust in Amida's Vow, Shinran Shōnin masterfully employs a variety of expressions to draw out the sense of what he wishes to convey. In this statement he rounds out this concept using terms that at first may sound foreign to us, such as 'birth in the Pure Land,' or 'the very moment when the thought that moves you to say the *nembutsu* is awakened within you.' He also says that 'no other form of goodness is required' and described 'all sentient beings' as being 'burdened with the weight of karmic evil and burning with the flames of blind passions.' These new terms are not easy for us to understand, but they are essential to his characterisation of Shin Buddhist faith. We need to recognise them and be sensitive to them in the context which they occur.

The process of awakening of faith

Faith, in Shin Buddhism, has two essential aspects: 1) Awakening to Amida Buddha or to Amida Buddha's Original Vow for universal deliverance, and 2) Awakening to oneself or to one's karmically conditioned finite existence; these are two aspects of the same pure faith. Although the connotations of the English word 'faith' are similar to those of the Japanese word *shinjin* 信心, the former cannot entirely encompass the latter. When I use the word 'faith' in the sense of *shinjin*, it would invariably have to include the element of awakening.

Faith (trust in Amida) is said to be attained upon our awakening to Amida Buddha. This awakening to Amida is not separate from an awakening to oneself. In short, in Shin Buddhism, faith is inevitably a process of awakening. Without this experience of awakening, faith could lead us to believe in something totally false, irrational, or arbitrary; this is something we must be careful to avoid.

The process of awakening of faith is accompanied by the purification of the whole mind. The original Sanskrit for the Japanese word *shinjin*, which is from the *Larger Sūtra of Eternal Life* (*Sukhāvatīvyūha*), is *prasāda*, meaning 'an act of purifying the mind' or the resultant purified mind. Through the process of awakening and entrusting oneself to Amida Buddha, one's mind is purified; this is *shinjin* or faith in Shin Buddhism.

According to traditional Shin Buddhist doctrine, there are two phases within true faith: 1) Awakening to the Dharma (Amida Buddha or his Original Vow), 信法; and 2) Awakening to the momentum through which the Dharma works (one's own self or one's karmic existence), 信機. These are but two aspects of the same reality: true faith.

In the *Tannishō*, Amida and his Original Vow are linked to the experience of Awakening to the Dharma, while all beings old and young, good and bad, as well as all sentient beings burdened with the weight of karmic evil and burning with the flames of blind passions, are linked to the experience of Awakening to the momentum.

The Original Vow

The Original Vow of Universal Salvation refers to the most special of the forty-eight vows of Amida, namely, the Eighteenth Vow. It is called the 'King of Vows' or 'Vow of Vows,' precisely because it is the most important Vow of all. The term Original Vow in Pure Land documents nearly always means the Eighteenth Vow. To quote the Eighteenth Vow from the *Larger Sūtra of Eternal Life*:

> If, upon my attaining Buddhahood, all beings in the ten quarters aspiring in all sincerity and faith to be born in my Country [Pure Land] and thinking of me [i.e., pronouncing my Name: *nembutsu*] up to ten times, were not to be born there, then may I not attain the Supreme Enlightenment. Excepted from this are those who have committed the five grave offences and those who slander the Right Dharma.[1]

This vow refers to 'all beings in the ten quarters,' which has traditionally been interpreted to mean that all beings are to be delivered and that there will be no discrimination amongst them whatsoever. This interpretation is reinforced in the text by the phrase, 'Amida's Original Vow never discriminates between old and young, good and bad.' This part of the Vow is traditionally called the 'Gate of Inclusion' (jp. *sesshu mon*).

As regards the latter statement of exception, the vow makes an exception to those who have committed the five grave offences and those who slander the Right Dharma. It is a matter of conjecture whether this statement was a part of this vow from the time that sūtra literature first began during the centuries after the death of Śākyamuni Buddha, or whether it was a later interpolation. There is some evidence that the statement of exception existed in the Sanskrit sūtra literature. However, the modern Shin Buddhist tradition takes no unanimous position on this and generally regards these words as having been added by later compilers as an admonition to subsequent generations to continue to lead moral lives and conform to the social conventions of the day. As this admonition is intended to prevent believers from committing more evil, this latter statement is traditionally called the 'Gate of Deterrence' (jp. *okushi mon*).

Amida Buddha's Original Vow, therefore, retains its absolutely universal quality. It works for the sake of everyone equally, including those who have already committed grave offences.

How did Shinran Shōnin first come across the Original Vow? It was through his encounter with Hōnen Shōnin. Hōnen Shōnin was for him the embodiment of the Original Vow. In the following quotation, Eshin-ni, Shinran Shōnin's wife, relates to her daughter, Kakushin-ni, the story she had heard from Shinran Shōnin himself about his first encounter with Hōnen Shōnin. In *The Letters of Eshin-ni*, Letter 3, she writes:

Surely I received your letter, dated the first day of December last year, shortly after the 20th of the same month. Most definitely your father was born in the Pure Land, and there is no need for me to repeat this.

Leaving Mount Hiei your father remained in retreat for one-hundred days at Rokkakudo, where he prayed for Rebirth [in the Pure Land]. On the dawn of the ninety-fifth day, Prince Shōtoku revealed himself in a vision and imparted a verse to him. Thereupon your father immediately left Rokkakudo early in the morning and visited Hōnen Shōnin in order to be shown the way of attaining birth [in the Pure Land]. And just as he had previously secluded himself for one-hundred days at Rokkakudō, he visited Hōnen Shōnin every day, rain or shine, for one-hundred days, undaunted by any of the serious matters that he had to face. As far as the matter of Rebirth [in the Pure Land] is concerned, your father heard his Master simply teaching the Way of Liberation from the suffering of birth-and-death to everyone in exactly the same manner, no matter whether they were good or evil. He preserved these words carefully in his heart, and whenever people made this or that remark about the *nembutsu* he would say, 'Wherever my Master Hōnen Shōnin goes, I shall follow him, no matter what others may say, even if they said he (Hōnen Shōnin) would be destined to go to the evil states of existence, I would go with him. The reason for this is that I, Shinran, being the sort of person who has been drowning in the world of delusion from time immemorial, would have absolutely nothing to lose by doing so.[2]

When I first came across this letter, I was pleasantly surprised to see the equality and impartiality of Hōnen Shōnin's love for others witnessed by Shinran Shōnin when he first met him. Shinran Shōnin came across Amida's Original Vow through his encounter with Hōnen Shōnin. It led to that extraordinary remark of his concerning his Master: 'Even if they said he (Hōnen Shōnin) would be destined to go to the evil states of existence (the Buddhist hells), I (Shinran Shōnin) would go with him,' without the least hesitation. On meeting Hōnen Shōnin in 1201, Shinran Shōnin immediately 'abandoned the miscellaneous acts [one does to save oneself] and took refuge in the Original Vow.'[3]

In this respect the phrase 'all sentient beings burdened with the weight of karmic evil and burning with the flames of blind passions' is very significant. It is used in the religious sense as an expression of one's self-realisation gained after deep introspection into oneself in the light of the Buddha. When one is illumined by the light of the Buddha, one realises that the moral efforts one makes to embrace good and forsake evil are themselves intrinsically false. This is the 'Awakening to oneself' or 'Awakening to the momentum' through which Amida works within the self, that is an essential element to Shin faith.

The essence of ethics is to love one another. However, since there is no absolute standard for good and bad, all ethical acts are relative. Usually, though, when one makes an effort to achieve some goal, one tends to consider one's efforts as being absolute, rather than relative. When this psychological tendency manifests itself in a self-centred way, our ethical consciousness becomes a cause of strife between people that can lead to the death and destruction of others, which is quite contrary to our original intent as ethical beings. Many a time have we witnessed tragic events in this world where good people on both sides fight and kill one another. This only goes to highlight the importance of the statement, 'Thus, when you entrust yourself to this Original Vow, no other form of goodness is required because there is no goodness that can surpass the *nembutsu*; nor need you fear any form of evil, because there is no evil powerful enough to obstruct the working of Amida's Original Vow.'

Salvation by Other Power faith alone

Lastly I would like to take up another crucial point in Chapter 1: the realisation that salvation is attained by pure faith alone, and never by any special religious practice, not even by the *nembutsu*. The *nembutsu* that flows from one's lips is only an expression of gratitude after the awakening of faith has been attained; as such it is not a special practice aimed at attaining awakening.

Although the use of the English word 'salvation' is perhaps not entirely suitable in the Buddhist context, it is pertinent to use it with regard to the words "you instantly receive Amida's compassionate benefit 'that embraces all, forsaking none'." Salvation takes place 'at the very moment when the thought that moves you to say the *nembutsu* is awakened within you.' Here the awakening of the thought to say the *nembutsu* stands for the awakening of faith, and is one and the same as saying the *nembutsu* 'believing that your birth in the Pure Land is attained through the inconceivable working of Amida's Original Vow.'

Shinran Shōnin does not state that salvation is realised 'when you utter the *nembutsu*,' but 'at the very moment when the thought that moves you to say the *nembutsu* is awakened within you.' The *nembutsu* wells up at the moment that the thought (faith) is awakened, not vice versa. True faith is always accompanied by the *nembutsu*, but the latter is not always accompanied by the former. Shinran Shōnin had a very clear view of faith and emphasised that salvation could only be accomplished through faith in the Other Power (Amida's Original Vow). He thus drew a very sharp distinction between faith and practice.

We should not forget, however, that the *nembutsu* issues forth whenever faith is active within the self. In this respect faith is at one with the *nembutsu*. Paradoxically, they are at once different and the same. In other words, when we hear others pronounce the *nembutsu* through pure faith, such *nembutsu* is called *daigyō*. The Japanese word, *daigyō* 大行, is usually translated literally as Great Practice, since '*dai*' means 'great' or 'absolute' and '*gyō*' means 'practice.' However, we must be careful to note that the expression 'Great Practice' indicates it is not *our* practice, but the working of the Buddha. It is because it is the working of Amida Buddha that it is called 'great.'

The Great Practice of the Buddha appears through "All Buddhas pronouncing the Name". 'All Buddhas' here refers to all Dharma friends who say the *nembutsu* with pure faith. For Shinran Shōnin, Hōnen Shōnin's *nembutsu* was the Great Practice, with Hōnen Shōnin himself representing 'All Buddhas'. In other words, through his encounter with Hōnen Shōnin, Shinran Shōnin found the way to meet all Dharma friends, 'All Buddhas.' It was through this encounter with Hōnen Shōnin that Shinran Shōnin first discovered the living tradition of *nembutsu* as the Great Practice of All Buddhas. Thus, Shinran Shōnin realised the fact that the Great Practice as "All Buddhas pronouncing the *nembutsu*" had a long tradition in the history of Buddhism.

However, if we consider the *nembutsu* to be a practice by which we can effect our birth in the Pure Land by our moral efforts alone, then such a practice would not be called the Great Practice. If we think that doing such a practice is something virtuous in its own right and that our birth in the Pure Land depends upon it, then that is a self-power practice, which is quite distinct from the Great Practice of Other Power.

On Mount Hiei Shinran Shōnin had long been engaged in such self-power *nembutsu* practice as a means to attain birth in the Pure Land. After practicing this kind of *nembutsu* for a long time, however, he encountered Hōnen Shōnin with his pure faith in the Original Vow and his wonderful *nembutsu* of Great Practice that illumined all the people around him equally.

In his English translation of the *Kyōgyōshinshō,* D. T. Suzuki reveals he had an insight into this point when he interpreted Great Practice to mean 'Great Living', which I will elaborate on further in a later chapter.

Shinran Shōnin's notion of time

Finally, I would like to call your attention to Shinran Shōnin's notion of time. His view of time is both exceptionally keen and profound. According to his philosophy, faith is attained instantaneously. Shinran Shōnin states in his *Kyōgyōshinshō*:

> As I reflect on [the significance of] true faith, there is 'one thought' 'One thought' is the shortest possible moment in which faith reveals itself and the feeling of joy, incomprehensively great, is manifested.[4]

This is Shinran Shōnin's interpretation of the term 'one thought' as found in the Pure Land sūtras and commentaries. To give one example from the *Larger Sūtra of Eternal Life*:

> As all beings hear his Name, faith is awakened in them and they are gladdened down to one thought. This comes to them from having been turned-over from Amida's sincere mind. When they desire to be born in the Pure Land, they are born there at that moment and abide in the stage of non-retrogression.[5]

The original Sanskrit for 'one thought' is *ekakśana*, meaning 'one instant' or 'one moment.' D. T. Suzuki says: "As we say in English, 'quick as thought' or 'quick as a flash'; 'one thought' represents in terms of time the shortest possible duration, which is one instant. The one instant of faith-establishment is the moment when Amida's Eternal Light pierces the darkening succession of selfish love and hate which we experienced in our relative consciousness. This event takes place in 'one thought'."[6]

To conclude let me quote another passage from the *Kyōgyōshinshō* concerning the instantaneousness of the faith-experience in Shin Buddhism. This is Shinran Shōnin's commentary on the phrase 'to cut off', an expression found in the *Larger Sūtra of Eternal Life*:

> 'To cut off' means that when the devotee, by virtue of the Original Prayer (Vow), awakens the one mind to be born [in the Pure Land], he is above birth-and-death, and, therefore, has no other kind of birth; nor is there anywhere else for him to be born. All the causes leading to the six forms of existence and the four kinds of birth, as well as their results, are annihilated. As the root of birth-and-death in the triple world is thus instantly cut off, it is said that it is all 'cut off'.[7]

In other words, in the one instant of awakening of faith the root linking us to birth-and-death is 'cut off' forever.

ENCOUNTER AND FAITH

Chapter 2

TRANSLATION

"Having crossed the borders of ten provinces or more, each of you has come to see me at the risk of your life. Your purpose is solely to hear from me how to be born in the Pure Land. If, however, assuming that I know other ways of being born in the Pure Land apart from pronouncing the *nembutsu* or thinking that I may be acquainted with some Buddhist texts that teach those special ways, you are concerned to know some hidden truth, I am afraid you are making a great mistake. If that is indeed your concern, there are many eminent scholars in the Southern Capital [Nara], or on the Northern Mountain [Hiei], whom you would be better off visiting in order to inquire to your hearts' content about the essentials for birth in the Pure Land.

As for myself, Shinran, there is nothing else involved apart from simple faith in the *nembutsu*, according to the instruction of my good teacher, 'Just say the *nembutsu* so as to be saved by Amida.'

I do not profess to know whether the *nembutsu* will really work as the seed that allows me to be born in the Pure Land or whether it may prove the karmic act for which I am condemned to hell. If, however, by pronouncing the *nembutsu*, I were ultimately to find myself misled by my Master Hōnen Shōnin and cast into hell, even then I would have no regrets.

The reason is this: if I were actually capable of attaining Buddhahood by my own endeavours while following other practices but nevertheless simply pronounced the *nembutsu* and so fell into hell, then indeed I would feel regret at having been deceived. But I am quite incapable of any other practice, so hell would have to be my abode in any case.

If the Original Vow of Amida is true, the teaching of Śākyamuni cannot be untrue; if the teaching of Śākyamuni is true, the commentaries by Shandao cannot be untrue; if Shandao's commentaries are true, the teaching of Hōnen Shōnin cannot be untrue; if the teaching of Hōnen Shōnin is true, how can it be possible for me, Shinran, to utter untruth? This being so, it is up to you to choose whether to believe in the *nembutsu* or to reject it."

Thus spoke my Master.

COMMENTARY

"The chapter on pure faith in the *nembutsu*"
— MYŌON-IN RYŌSHŌ —

This chapter is essentially Shinran Shōnin's own expression of pure faith in the *nembutsu*. It is in essence a very earnest personal statement made expressly to show where he himself stood. In it Shinran Shōnin expresses with considerable sternness and vehemence, though not without compassion, the totality and depth of the true faith he held.

His audience is an entourage of disciples who wanted to know whether Shinran Shōnin had anything more to teach them than what he had already taught them earlier when he had been living in the Kantō district. To dispel their doubts they had come to see him after a long journey across more than ten provinces, despite the many dangers that must have lain along the route from the Kantō region to Kyoto at that time. Yuien, the compiler of the *Tannishō*, is believed to have accompanied those disciples.

The disciples' visit would seem to have been a very urgent one, judging by the very serious attitude adopted by Shinran Shōnin toward them and the way he urged them to attain spiritual independence with regard to their faith. Why was it necessary for the disciples to make such a journey and question their teacher on his real standpoint? Here it would be useful to introduce a little background information.

Shinran Shōnin studied under Hōnen Shōnin for the six years that followed their first meeting in 1201. During those six years Shinran Shōnin experienced a religious transformation that he never forgot. Indeed Shinran Shōnin seems to have continued to revere his Master Hōnen Shōnin until the very end of his life, always keeping in mind his Master's words.

The eventual parting between Shinran Shōnin and his Master took place in 1207 when both of them were exiled separately to far-off provinces. Shinran Shōnin went to Echigo, a northern province of Japan. Pardoned in 1211, he left Echigo in 1213 for the Kantō district, where he lived with people from the lower classes, mainly farmers, and taught them how to attain birth in the Pure Land. As a result he gathered numerous followers. After staying in the Kantō area for about twenty years, however, he returned to Kyoto around 1235 and lived there until his death in 1262.

The difficulty of the easy path

The core of Shinran Shōnin's teaching is simply pure faith in the *nembutsu*, which, according to Amida Buddha's Eighteenth Vow, enables all beings to attain birth in his Pure Land. In order to make the message clear, however, he had to employ paradoxes and subtleties in his teaching, because it was too simple and, consequently, too deep an idea for ordinary people to comprehend. For this reason, what had appeared easy to understand while he remained in the Kantō district was now becoming gradually more and more difficult for his disciples to follow, once he returned to Kyoto.

In an attempt to solve this problem Shinran Shōnin dispatched his eldest son, Zenran, to the Kantō district. When Zenran tried to assume the leadership of the diverse Kantō *nembutsu* community, however, he found it was impossible to do so. Perhaps out of desperation, Zenran tried to assert his authority by stressing his personal relationship to his father, Shinran Shōnin. He even went so far as to claim that he, Zenran, knew of a new secret teaching and that what Shinran Shōnin had previously taught was now outdated, like a faded flower. Due to this he ended up misleading people and causing a great deal of confusion amongst them. Around 1256, when a true picture of the situation emerged through correspondence between Shinran Shōnin and his Kantō followers, Shinran Shōnin was sadly obliged to excommunicate his own son; he was 84 years old at the time.

The disciples' journey to Kyoto related in Chapter 2 is believed to have taken place around the year when Shinran Shōnin was forced to disown his eldest son, Zenran. It was for this reason that the visit by the Kantō followers was such a solemn occasion, both for Shinran Shōnin and his disciples. Thus the confusion amongst the Kantō followers at this time seemed to have been caused mainly by Zenran.

However, it is also said that their anxiety was aggravated and deepened by Nichiren's teaching. Nichiren started teaching in the Kantō district in 1253 and criticised Pure Land Buddhism and Zen Buddhism very aggressively, declaring that the *nembutsu* would cause one to fall into hell, and that Zen would cause one to be reborn in the realm of *māras* (demonic beings). Shinran Shōnin's words in Chapter 2, where he declares he cannot be certain the *nembutsu* might not cause him to fall into hell, are considered to have been in answer to the very serious question raised by his disciples who found themselves faced with this problem.

In this chapter there are a few important points which I would like to elucidate in terms of religious philosophy.

The radical difference between knowledge and faith

Firstly, there is a sharp contrast drawn between knowledge and pure faith in Shinran Shōnin's immediate response to the disciples who wanted to know how to be born in the Pure Land. He tells them they are making a great mistake if their concern is to simply understand by intellect alone and if they imagine that he, Shinran Shōnin, knows any other means of salvation apart from the *nembutsu*. The essential point is that the *nembutsu* is not something one should attempt to comprehend logically but something that emanates naturally from within. Faced with his disciples' very intellectual concern, therefore, Shinran Shōnin's answer is simply to reaffirm his own simple faith in Hōnen Shōnin's teaching of the *nembutsu*: "As for myself, Shinran, there is nothing else involved apart from simple faith in the *nembutsu*, according to the instruction of my good teacher [Hōnen Shōnin], 'Just say the *nembutsu* so as to be saved by Amida'." He goes on to declare that if their concern is only intellectual and their sole purpose is "to know some hidden truth" (which is what the original Japanese phrase *kokoronikuku oboshimesu* meant in the Kamakura Period), then it would be better for them to consult the eminent Buddhist scholars in Nara or on Mount Hiei. Faith is not simply a matter of information or even belief if such belief amounts to no more than intellectual assent.

Faith-experience must definitely include an element of transcendence that enables one to go beyond objective knowledge or the intellectual approach. In the Western tradition, for example, Kierkegaard recognises this transcendental aspect. With the aphorism *credo quia absurdum est*, or 'I believe because it is absurd' (which is usually attributed to Tertullian) in mind, Kierkegaard states, 'I believe against my understanding.' These statements epitomise well the transcendental phase of the faith-experience.

Shinran Shōnin is fully aware of this phase, which he calls *ōchō* (横超), or 'leaping over crosswise.' *Ōchō* is a technical term used in Shin Buddhism to describe the attainment of faith in the *nembutsu*. This faith is called 'the great bodhicitta' (大菩提心 jp. *dai bodaishin*), or 'the great mind awakened to Enlightenment'. It is through the great bodhicitta that one attains birth in the Pure Land and Enlightenment. According to Shinran Shōnin, the term 'leaping over crosswise' is contrasted with 'journeying lengthwise'; it is the direct and immediate attainment of the goal, instead of a long, gradual, logical approach. It signifies the Power of Amida's Original Vow that enables sentient beings to 'leap over' the gap which lies between the finite and the infinite.

In contrast to 'journeying lengthwise,' 'to leap-over' refers to the instantaneous transcendence of the realm of birth-and-death. This sudden attainment of birth in the Pure Land stands in opposition to attempting to free oneself by using self-power. The latter implements the various functions at our disposal, such as our senses, intellect, and ego-consciousness. To 'leap-over' means to sever these roots of illusion. In other words, to 'leap-over' indicates the way in which the true faith in the *nembutsu* is imparted from Other Power, enabling the sudden attainment of Buddhahood in the Pure Land.

Various types of spiritual encounter

Secondly, what is particularly evident here is Shinran Shōnin's absolute reliance on his Master Hōnen Shōnin. As I have mentioned before, for Shinran Shōnin Hōnen Shōnin was an embodiment or emanation of Amida Buddha. Therefore, in his experience, there was no contradiction between his faith in Amida Buddha and his reliance on the master.

Encompassed within Shinran Shōnin's pure faith in the *nembutsu*, there are at least four different kinds of encounter taking place in this chapter:

1) First, the encounter between Shinran Shōnin and his disciples.
2) Next, Shinran Shōnin's own encounter with his Master Hōnen Shōnin, which he refers to when addressing his Kantō followers (encounter 1).

This encounter with his Master in turn opens up two further levels:

    3) Shinran Shōnin's encounter with his true self, expressed in the words 'so hell would have to be my abode in any case.'

    4) Shinran Shōnin's encounter with Amida's Original Vow.

At first glance it might appear that Shinran Shōnin was prompted to start talking about Amida's Original Vow as soon as he had put into words his serious self-realisation: 'So hell would have to be my abode in any case.' But such a view would be superficial and misleading. In reality these encounters are one and the same; they should be understood as two aspects of pure faith.

To reiterate my earlier discussion of Chapter 1:

"According to traditional Shin Buddhist terminology, within true faith there are two phases: 1) Awakening to the Dharma (Amida Buddha or his Original Vow) or *shinpō* 信法; and 2) Awakening to the momentum through which the Dharma works (one's own self or one's karmic existence), or *shinki* 信機. These are but two aspects of the same reality: true faith. In the *Tannishō,* Amida and his Original Vow are linked to the experience of Awakening to the Dharma, while all beings old and young, good and bad, as well as all sentient beings burdened with the weight of karmic evil and burning with the flames of blind passions, are linked to the experience of Awakening to the momentum."

Here, it should be clear that when Shinran Shōnin says, "So hell would have to be my abode in any case," he has already encountered Amida's Original Vow. Finding himself embraced in the Original Vow, he is awakened to himself, to the reality of his own existence, and so entrusts his whole being to Amida with absolute faith.

Finally, there is yet another kind of encounter between Shinran Shōnin and his disciples in terms of faith, or at least between Shinran Shōnin and Yuien. The *Tannishō* itself is proof of that. Shinran Shōnin's meeting with the disciples ends with the words: "This being so, it is up to you to choose whether to believe in the *nembutsu* or to reject it." It may sound rather cold-hearted to some, but in fact this is an expression of Shinran Shōnin's true love of others. Shinran Shōnin wants to leave his disciples completely free to choose. He wants each of his disciples to be spiritually independent. By finishing with these words, Shinran Shōnin has, I believe, triggered a new encounter with his disciples in the deepest spiritual dimension.

Shinran Shōnin's view of history

Thirdly, there is something else being referred to in this chapter: Shinran Shōnin's view of history. Shinran Shōnin says, "If the Original Vow of Amida is true, the teaching of Śākyamuni cannot be untrue; if the teaching of Śākyamuni is true, the commentaries by Shandao cannot be untrue; if Shandao's commentaries are true, the teaching of Hōnen Shōnin cannot be untrue; if the teaching of Hōnen Shōnin is true, how can it be possible for me, Shinran, to utter untruth?" This short sentence reveals a Buddhist view of history that is firmly based on the absolute experience of the present.

Shinran Shōnin sounds full of confidence, because he views the whole of history from the viewpoint of the present, from his faith-experience of always meeting Amida Buddha. In other words his historical view is based on his present experience of Dharma, the truth that is always present anywhere and anytime. The Dharma existed even before Gautama Buddha appeared. Gautama Buddha simply realised the Dharma or ultimate truth that was already there. The Dharma is not the Buddha's invention.

In this context the Dharma is present for Shinran Shōnin in the here and now as the *nembutsu* of the Original Vow, the *nembutsu* emerging through his Master Hōnen Shōnin. According to Shinran Shōnin (in the *Kyōgyōshinshō*), pronouncing the Name, the *nembutsu* in other words, is 'the Great Living'. The Japanese term *gyō* for 'living' is usually translated as 'practice'. When D. T. Suzuki was asked to translate Shinran Shōnin's main writing, the *Kyōgyōshinshō*, he opted to use the term 'living'. Shinran Shōnin says, "The Great Living is to pronounce the Name of the Nyorai [Tathāgata] of Unimpeded Light (Amida Buddha). In this living are embraced all good things and all the roots of virtue."[8] 'The Great Living' does not refer to the *nembutsu* as a self-power practice but to the *nembutsu* as the great working of the Buddha or of his Dharma. Through pure faith in the *nembutsu* as the Great Living, in other words the *nembutsu* appearing through Hōnen Shōnin, Shinran Shōnin encountered the *nembutsu* emerging from within and became deeply involved in the history of Dharma or of the Great Living. Indeed he exemplifies the Buddhist perspective that views the whole of history via the standpoint of faith experienced in the present moment.

THE SALVATION OF THOSE
AWARE OF THEIR BAD KARMA

Chapter 3

TRANSLATION

"'Even a good person can attain birth [in the Pure Land], how much more readily, then, the person with bad karma.'

Normally, however, people of the world would say: 'Even a person with bad karma can attain birth, how much more readily, then, a good person.' Although at first sight this latter view appears perfectly reasonable, actually it runs counter to the purport of the Original Vow, Other Power faith. This is because people who rely on doing good through their own self-power fail to entrust themselves to Other Power and are not, therefore, in accord with Amida's Original Vow. If, on the other hand, they discard their reliance on self-power and entrust themselves to Other Power, they will attain birth in the True Land of Enjoyment.

It is impossible for us, fully burdened with blind passions, to free ourselves from birth-and-death through the pursuance of any religious practices whatsoever. Full of sadness at this, Amida brought forth his Vow, the essential purport of which is the person with bad karma's attainment of Buddhahood. Hence those who are aware of their bad karma and so entrust themselves to Other Power are precisely the ones who possess the true key to birth.

Accordingly he (Hōnen Shōnin) said, 'Even a good person can be born [in the Pure Land], so it goes without saying for the persons with bad karma.'"

COMMENTARY

"The chapter on the persons with bad karma
as the right object [of the Original Vow]"
—MYŌON-IN RYŌSHŌ—

This chapter contains at once one of the most striking and one of the most famous of all Shinran Shōnin's statements. It represents his religious philosophy at its very deepest level and gives paradoxical expression to his own religious experience in the clearest

---

See pp. 91 and 92 for photographs of Chapter 3 of the *Tannishō*

possible way. I would like to use the word 'paradoxical' here to describe a statement or teaching that is seemingly contradictory or opposed to common sense (orthodox thought) and yet expressive of truth at the deepest level. In this chapter Shinran Shōnin reveals the paradoxical and radical character of his religious experience and thought.

When he says, 'Even a good person can attain birth in the Pure Land, how much more readily, then, the person with bad karma,' Shinran Shōnin is fully aware of the paradoxical nature of his statement.

He goes on, therefore, to point out, "Normally, however, people of the world would say: 'Even a person with bad karma can attain birth, how much more readily, then, a good person.'" This latter view is widely held and represents the ordinary, common sense approach in this world. Such an opinion is the orthodox view of normal, ethical human beings, and follows the moral law of cause and effect, where good must be chosen and evil abandoned. In our interpersonal relationships we should give careful thought as to how to choose between good and evil in order not only 'to benefit ourselves' but also simultaneously 'to benefit others.' And we should go ahead doing good for the doing, in so far as we are ethical beings.

With this in mind Shinran Shōnin himself declares that 'at first sight this latter view appears perfectly reasonable.' Because it is an ethical view based on the karmic law of cause and effect, it seems 'reasonable' and appeals to people's common sense. It is, however, not a religious view in the true sense, but rather a sort of admixture of morality and religious aspiration. So Shinran Shōnin goes on to observe, 'Actually it runs counter to the purport of the Original Vow, Other Power faith.'

The ordinary view of salvation is ethico-religious. It understands religion from an ethical standpoint, limited by a relativistic interpretation of the world. In other words it borders on the religious and yet is still not free from the constraints of dualistic morality. Such religious belief is imbued with ethics at every turn, and is in fact quasi-religious and at sharp variance with true religion and the true intent of the Original Vow.

For Shinran Shōnin, the essence of Buddhism (the Buddha's teaching), and true religiosity, is pure faith in Other Power, the power of the Original Vow. He draws a very clear distinction between it and ethical effort based on one's self-power.

Shinran Shōnin continues, "This is because people who rely on doing good through self-power fail to entrust themselves to Other Power and are not, therefore, in accord with Amida's Original Vow." When we read these words, we should not forget that the ultimate concern here is how to be born in the Pure Land. The whole sentence concerns one's birth in the Pure Land, one's religious salvation. He who relies on self-power cannot entrust himself whole-heartedly to Other Power. Even if he claims to entrust himself to Other Power, as long as he relies on his own self-power, his faith is not pure. He has yet to become fully aware of his being embraced by Amida's Original Vow.

This being so, Shinran Shōnin goes on to say, "If, on the other hand, they discard their reliance on self-power and entrust themselves to Other Power, they will attain birth in the True Land of Enjoyment."

'A good person' in the first statement of this chapter refers to the person who relies on doing good through self-power with regard to his birth in the Pure Land or his religious salvation. The word 'good' in this context is used in a strictly ethical sense, where one has the power to achieve such good. By contrast, the word 'bad' (or evil) is used in contradistinction to it in a purely religious sense, wherein one realises the powerlessness of one's ability to do anything to bring about one's own salvation; this is the religious awareness of the finiteness of one's existence that is realised through one's encounter with the Light of Amida Buddha.

One who has come in touch with Amida Buddha realises the finiteness of one's power to save oneself, and when illumined by the Buddha's Light, has an insight into the true nature of one's existence as ridden by bad karma or karmic 'evil'. As far as religious awareness goes, one finds one's whole existence to be an 'evil' mass of bad karma, no matter whether one has been living a good life in the ethical sense or not. In short, we come to see the karmically 'evil person' (jp. *akunin*) in ourselves. This awareness of ourselves as being karmically 'evil' issues from the realm of religious consciousness; such religious insight goes far beyond all thought of ethical discrimination between good and evil.

When one is embraced by the infinite Wisdom and unconditional Love of the Buddha, one is awakened to the whole of one's karmic existence as a wretched mass of bad karma; this awareness transcends the ethical consciousness of good and evil. One's ethical consciousness of wrongdoing may oblige one to remain imprisoned by doubt and guilt. However, when one has been illumined by the Buddha's unimpeded Light, the stronghold of one's ethical consciousness falls away when a religious awareness of oneself as a mass of karmic 'evil' emerges in its place.

If you still do not feel yourself free from suffering in spite of actually meeting the Buddha or his Dharma, your ethical consciousness of wrongdoing will start to take on a religious significance. If you are in a dynamic religious setting where the Buddha's teaching is truly alive, your ethical consciousness of wrongdoing will turn into a sense of karmic evil. If you are still suffering while standing before a Buddha, you will gain a growing awareness of your karmic evil, that is, evil as it is understood in Buddhism.

In the *Larger Sūtra of Eternal Life* this matter is addressed in profound detail employing the three most important vows made by Amida Buddha: the Nineteenth, the Twentieth, and the Eighteenth Vow. In existential terms the seeker who is still at the ethical stage of life falls under the purview of the Nineteenth Vow. Here, the *nembutsu* is regarded as just one out of a number of possible good deeds that one can do. By the Twentieth Vow the seeker is at the ethico-religious stage. At this stage one concentrates exclusively on the recitation of Amida's Name, abandoning all attempts at any other good deeds, having already despaired of ethical life. All ethical efforts are concentrated on something purely religious, namely, on pronouncing Amida Buddha's Name. Thus I call this stage the ethico-religious.

The existential stage of the Eighteenth Vow is the purely religious, and goes beyond all ethical discrimination between good and evil. Its sheer reality is such that when one has pure faith in Amida Buddha, one is awakened to his loving kindness filling one's whole being, embracing one just as one is, with one's bad karma proving no hindrance to Amida Buddha. On attaining true faith in Amida Buddha one becomes filled with joy and is assured of attaining Enlightenment in his Pure Land.

Human life is ethical and should be governed by ethics. Shin Buddhism in no way sets out to denigrate ethics. On the contrary it pays great attention to moral considerations and Shin Buddhists are so taken up by ethical considerations that they in fact have a heightened awareness of the various problems in the moral sphere. Shinran Shōnin too could solve such problems only by taking refuge in Amida Buddha.

Ethical goodness in this world is relative. The fundamental problem in the existential realm of ethics is the consciousness of one's own righteousness, or one's strong insistence on justice. But everyone has their own individual standard of justice, and so if they insist that only they are right, they are brought into conflict with one another, leading inevitably to tragic consequences. To overcome such an existential situation full of suffering, people should come to take refuge in religion. As far as Pure Land Buddhism goes, their initial reaction, given the situation, is simply to want to practice the *nembutsu* to the exclusion of all else; that is, they evince an ethico-religious consciousness.

Regarding the problem the ethico-religious consciousness entails, Shinran Shōnin says in his main work the *Kyōgyōshinshō*:

> Indeed, whereas the teaching [of the True Gate or the exclusive recitation of the Name] is one of sudden deliverance, the followers [who pursue practice with mixed mind] are only capable of obtaining gradual deliverance. Although they practice assiduously, they engage in inter-mixed ways of practice, hence theirs is 'a mind intermixed.' 'The meditative and non-meditative exclusive minds' refers to those who turn to the Power of the Original Vow with a belief in the karmic retribution of both evil and good; hence they are called 'exclusive self-power minds.'[9]

Shinran Shōnin also says,

> How sad it is that ordinary and ignorant followers with defilement and hindrances, from time immemorial right up to the present day, have had no opportunity for emancipation because of their tendency to perform the right practices and the miscellaneous practices as well as the meditative good and the non-meditative good in an inter-mixed way. When we reflect upon our cycle of transmigration, we find it difficult, even with the passage of infinite kalpas, to take refuge in the power of the Buddha's Vow and enter the sea of great faith. We should indeed lament and deeply deplore this fact. As long as the sages

of the Mahāyāna and Hīnayāna and all good followers everywhere take the recitation of the auspicious Name of the Original Vow to be their own good, they cannot attain faith nor realise the Buddha's wisdom. As they are unable to realise the [Buddha's] establishment of the cause for birth [in the Pure Land], they cannot enter the Land of Enjoyment.[10]

When one does what one does purely for the doing, no impurity will remain within one's mind. If one can act in such a way, it would be truly wonderful. However, it is easy enough to say but very difficult to achieve. We cling to what we have done for our own benefit as well as for the benefit of others. Somewhere deep in the heart of this tragic life of ours filled with contradictions and conflict, one always finds this tenacious clinging to ethics that is the cause of all our suffering. If we present ourselves before the Buddha in this miserable state and are still conscious of his Wisdom and Love, we feel false and evil by comparison. All that we can do is to take refuge in the Buddha, throwing away all attachment to our own deeds. This indeed is faith.

This development of religious consciousness is similar in process to Kierkegaard's philosophy of 'The Three Stages of Life': aesthetic, ethical, and religious. According to Kierkegaard, one is 'deceived into' a deeper stage by going through the present stage. What is particularly interesting is the transition from the ethical stage to the religious stage. In the ethical realm, subjectivity (the inwardness to become oneself) is truth. But this ethical subjectivity turns into untruth (sin) once it passes into the religious realm, or, more accurately, into Religiosity B. Religiosity A is religion in general. Religiosity B is Christianity with the paradox of the Incarnation. Kierkegaard said that true faith is to believe in this paradox in defiance of understanding (ger. *gegen den Verstand*). If this faith is attained, subjectivity again becomes truth. This subjectivity is, for Kierkegaard, absolutely individual. He said that, in the religious realm, individuality is higher than universality, whereas in the ethical realm, universality is higher than individuality.

Needless to say, because the philosophical foundations of Shinran's faith are very different from that of Kierkegaard's, it is impossible to say that their understanding of faith is the same. What interests me here, however, is the striking similarity in their process of attaining religious faith despite the differences in their spiritual background.

The source of the Buddha's compassion

The condition of 'being fully burdened with blind passions,' in this chapter of the *Tannishō,* refers simply to the common lot of ordinary people. Buddhism has always described our existential condition as being enmeshed in ignorance and delusion. This basic human condition gives rise to greed and anger of a self-centred kind and is in fact the underlying source of all forms of human suffering. For a long time, however, Buddhists believed they could attain Enlightenment through self-discipline and their own ethical efforts, after the manner of Gautama Buddha. They believed this, I think, because Gautama's daily acts were so pure in the ethical sense. Gautama was completely free of the slightest shred of attachment. Every action he performed in his daily routine was quite beautiful in itself. But what Gautama's followers failed to appreciate was that those purely ethical actions of his all had one special source: his Enlightenment and his love for others which together formed the essential core of his life.

With the development of Mahāyāna Buddhism the emphasis on love for others became much more pronounced. The ideal of benefiting not only oneself but others too, at one and the same time, is essential in Mahāyāna Buddhism and expressive of the altruism inherent in that movement. All Buddhas and bodhisattvas are expected to benefit themselves and others simultaneously, in other words, to be enlightened themselves and to help others to become enlightened. To love oneself and to love others are considered to be two sides of the same coin. The Original Vow can be said to symbolise Amida's altruistic love for all sentient beings, a love entirely free of any trace of discrimination.

We are 'fully burdened with blind passions' and, as such, wretchedly self-centred. In order to avoid harming others, therefore, we try to be good, to love others as they are, going beyond the limitations of selfish attachment, but the basic self-centredness of ours cannot be overcome even in the ethical stage, despite the best efforts to do so. Even if one attains the religious stage, in so far as one is proud of one's practice, one cannot be free of self-centredness. Shinran Shōnin was very aware of the limitations of our existence in this respect.

As can be seen from passages quoted previously, Shinran Shōnin was well aware of the problem of emancipation from self-centredness through his own personal experience of having gone through various levels of ethical consciousness. Shinran Shōnin recognised the fact that good deeds tend to become rather poisonous and obstructive to birth in the Pure Land or attaining Enlightenment when they are performed deliberately in the knowledge that they are good. Ethical good turns into evil in the realm of religion. According to Shinran Shōnin's religious philosophy, self-righteous people become aware of themselves as 'evil' when they are illumined by the Buddha's Infinite Light, perhaps through an encounter with a good teacher. At that point the only way to be freed from such deep consciousness of one's 'bad karma' or 'wrong-doing' is through pure faith in the Original Vow. Thus one entrusts oneself to the Other Power of Amida's Original Vow.

This awareness of oneself as 'a person filled with bad karma' belongs to the realm of religion, which lies at the deepest level of human consciousness. It does not belong to the realm of morality. Thus Shinran Shōnin concludes: "Accordingly he (Hōnen Shōnin) said, 'Even a good person can be born [in the Pure Land], so it goes without saying for the person with bad karma'." The source of this quotation is believed to be Shinran Shōnin's Master, Hōnen Shōnin, a view substantiated by a biography, written by Hōnen Shōnin's disciple Genchi (*Daigo-bon Hōnen Shōnin denki*):

[Hōnen Shōnin once said:] 'Even a good person attains birth [in the Pure Land], how much more so persons with bad karma.' This is an oral transmission. I [Genchi] understand that Amida's Original Vow was not made for those good people who have the means to free themselves from birth-and-death by self-power, but rather it was made out of his sorrow for the vilest people laden with bad karma who would have no other means [of liberation from birth-and-death]. Despite this, even bodhisattvas and sages aspire to be born [in the Pure Land]. Even good people amongst the ignorant can attain birth [in the Pure Land] by taking refuge in this Vow. How much more so should persons with bad karma amongst the ignorant entrust themselves to this Other Power![11]

Throughout our study of the *Tannishō* we will find that Shinran Shōnin relied faithfully on Hōnen Shōnin all of his life.

As long as we live in this world we are inevitably ethical beings as well as religious ones. Shinran Shōnin lived his ethical life in a very pure way and always with an immense sense of gratitude. Objectively speaking, he helped people to lead happy lives on their way to the Pure Land. Not only did he love his followers, he even revered them as Buddhas or bodhisattvas. Through pure faith in Amida Buddha, he was free from any sort of attachment to ethical values. He did good deeds, but always forgot about them in his gratitude to others. As he helped others without a trace of pride, everything he did was accompanied by pure faith, like a pure fresh wind blowing through a clear blue sky.

LOVE AND FAITH

Chapter 4

TRANSLATION

"Concerning the practice of love (慈悲 jp. *jihi*) there is a distinct turning point from the Path of Sages to the Path of the Pure Land Buddhist.

Love in the Path of Sages means pitying, loving and nurturing all beings. It is extremely difficult, however, to accomplish the work of saving others in exactly the way one wishes.

Love in the Path of the Pure Land Buddhist means quickly attaining Buddhahood by pronouncing the *nembutsu* so that, through the mind of Great Love and Compassion, one is able to save all beings in exactly the way one wishes.

However much love and pity you may feel for others in this life, it is hard indeed to save them in the way you would wish; hence such love can never be perfect. Only the pronouncing of the *nembutsu* can manifest the mind of great unconditional love."

Thus spoke my Master.

COMMENTARY

"The chapter on the difference in compassion between
the Path of Sages and the Path of the Pure Land Buddhist"

— MYŌON-IN RYŌSHŌ —

Here I would like to compare the rendering above with that of Dennis Hirota, below, whose version is typical of all other existing translations.

"Concerning compassion, there is a difference between the Path of Sages and the Pure Land Path.

Compassion in the Path of Sages is to pity, commiserate with, and care for beings. It is extremely difficult, however, to accomplish the saving of others just as one wishes.

Compassion in the Pure Land Path should be understood as first attaining

Buddhahood quickly through saying the *nembutsu* and, with the mind of great love and great compassion, freely benefiting sentient beings as one wishes.

However much love and pity we may feel in our present lives, it is hard to save others as we wish; hence such compassion remains unfulfilled. Only the saying of the *nembutsu*, then, is the mind of great compassion that is thoroughgoing.

Thus were his words."[12]

In his version a subtle philological glitch occurs when translating the Japanese word *kawarime* 変わり目 in the first paragraph. How this particular term is understood has important bearing on our interpretation of the chapter as a whole. Generally speaking, scholars in the field of Buddhist studies have no particular expertise in Japanese linguistics, nor are linguists particularly well versed in Buddhism. Due to these circumstances Japanese academic circles have failed to detect the nuance originally intended by this term and this may well have led to the misinterpretation of the passage, which I would now like to elucidate briefly.

Turning from the Path of Sages to the Path of the Pure Land Buddhist

The word *kawarime* has two meanings: 1) difference and 2) turning point. The latter implies not only a division between spaces but also a point in time when a transition from one period to another takes place. As you can see above not only in Myōon-in Ryōshō's classification but also in the version by Hirota, the word *kawarime* has been interpreted simply as 'difference.' According to my understanding, however, the word should really be translated as 'turning point.' I do not mean that their interpretation is totally wrong; it is partly correct, because turning from the Path of the Sages to the Path of the Pure Land Buddhist does result in a difference. However, the crucial point is the turning point, a spiritual transition of one's existential standpoint from the Path of Sages to the Path of the Pure Land Buddhist. If one assumes that such a difference between the two paths exists even before starting out, one would surely avoid the Path of Sages right from the very beginning. However, this is not at all what Shinran Shōnin was saying.

In his own life Shinran Shōnin experienced such a transition. At first he tried to follow the Path of Sages but turned to the Pure Land Buddhist Path on attaining pure faith in Amida's unconditional love. Thus he says, 'Concerning the practice of love there is a distinct turning point from the Path of Sages to the Path of the Pure Land Buddhist.' The turning point is nothing but pure faith in Amida. If you understand the term simply as referring to a theoretical division between two schools of thought, you are missing the whole point. Such a misunderstanding has been caused in part by the doctrinal studies of traditional scholars overly concerned with the philosophical aspects of the teaching and constrained by the theological framework of the established Shin Buddhist schools.

In short, simply establishing a theoretical distinction was the furthest thing from Shinran Shōnin's mind when he made this statement. We can get a glimpse of his original intention in Chapter 4, when he says, "Love in the Path of Sages means pitying, loving, and nurturing all beings. It is extremely difficult, however, to accomplish the work of saving others in exactly the way one wishes." In the original Japanese 'pitying, loving, and nurturing all beings,' as a definition of love in the Path of Sages, sounds just like a mother's love for her children. Motherly love is something absolutely fundamental in human life; it is the source of all other types of love. Shinran Shōnin himself starts from this natural feeling of love, a general feeling of love for human beings. The act of loving in this sense is the most precious thing amongst all that is in human life.

In his main work, the *Kyōgyōshinshō*, Shinran Shōnin quoted from the *Commentary on the Treatise on the Pure Land* (jp. *Ōjōronchū*) by Tanluan (jp. Donran, 476-542):

> Those who are not awakened to the Supreme Enlightenment mind and yet are desirous of being born in the Buddha-land for the sake of enjoying themselves in the pleasures which they have learned the residents there enjoy uninterruptedly, will never attain birth in the Pure Land. So it is said, 'The bodhisattva does not wish for himself to indulge in the pleasure of support and maintenance, but he just desires to eradicate all of the suffering beings are undergoing in the world.[13]

Seemingly contrary to this, Shinran Shōnin goes on to say in Chapter 4, "It is extremely difficult, however, to accomplish the work of saving others in exactly the way one wishes." Why is it so difficult? The difficulty does not lie outside ourselves but within— in our self-centred consciousness which influences the way we desire to act. Love is just one example; for instance, one may love others, but in a self-centred way. If one does not become aware of this, one's love will always remain selfish to some extent. However small it may be, the selfish element in love always ends up hurting others.

As to how one should love others, the real problem is the quality of one's love, not quantity; once one attains true quality, quantity will follow. To love others truly is very difficult, impossible even, unless one learns to discard one's selfishness or egoism completely. In Buddhism it has been taught that selfishness comes from the greedy attachment to self that is deeply embedded in one's way of being. It is the cause of all suffering to which Gautama Buddha is said to have awakened. *That* was his Enlightenment. Enlightenment is the only way of eliminating it.

Once we are enlightened, all the suffering caused by our selfishness is gone. Thus it is impossible for unenlightened people to love others truly. Shinran Shōnin wanted to love others, but he saw himself as an unenlightened being. He never claimed to have been enlightened. In this respect he was very harsh on himself.

Buddhism is the teaching of Enlightenment. Almost all Buddhist monks who approached the Buddhist teaching were confident that the various practices of traditional Buddhism could and would bring about Enlightenment. Shinran Shōnin also strove to attain Enlightenment by following traditional practices. In his case, however, upon encountering his master, Hōnen Shōnin, he was awakened by Amida's light shining upon him through Hōnen Shōnin, and illumining the reality of his own existence: the greedy attachment to self embedded within him and his own sheer ignorance. He at once abandoned the practices he had been engaged in and immediately took refuge in Amida's Original Vow.

Shinran Shōnin says in the *Kyōgyōshinshō*, "Thus, I, Gutoku Shinran Shōnin, disciple of Śākyamuni, abandoned miscellaneous practices and took refuge in the Original Vow in the year of *kennin kanoto no tori* (1201)."[14] That was the turning point when he went from the Path of Sages to the Pure Land Buddhist Path, his experience of breaking through the darkness of ignorance. Some might call it Enlightenment, but Shinran Shōnin himself never did. He says in the same book:

The mind-light that embraces us always illumines and protects us.
Though the darkness of ignorance is already broken through,
The clouds and mists of tenacious greed and repulsive hatred
Still continue to cover the sky of true faith.
It is as if, though the sunlight is veiled by clouds and mists,
Below the clouds and mists brightness reigns and there is no darkness.[15]

This passage is from his famous hymn called *Shōshinge* 正信偈 (Hymn of True *Nembutsu* Faith), and well expresses the way he lived life each day after taking refuge in Amida Buddha.

As a result of his religious conversion (his experience of entrusting himself to Amida Buddha) Shinran Shōnin found another way of living and loving others quite different from that found in the Path of Sages. "Love in the Path of the Pure Land Buddhist means quickly attaining Buddhahood by pronouncing the *nembutsu* so that, through the mind of Great Love and Compassion, one is able to save all beings in exactly the way one wishes."

The *nembutsu* in this passage is to be considered as the working of Amida Buddha, emerging through pure faith in the Buddha. We usually think of someone pronouncing the Name of Amida Buddha by his own volition. But in reality, when a religious conversion takes place, it is Amida's working made manifest through that person's faith. Shinran Shōnin says in the *Kyōgyōshinshō*:

As I reverently reflect on the outgoing *ekō*, I find therein the Great Living and the great faith. The Great Living is to pronounce the Name of the Nyorai (Tathāgata) of Unimpeded Light. In this living are embraced all good things and all the roots of virtue. They are instantly perfected [as soon as the Name is pronounced]. The Name is the treasure-ocean of the virtues accruing from the absolute reality of Suchness. Therefore, it is called the Great Living.[16]

'The Great Living' is D. T. Suzuki's interpretation of the Japanese term *daigyō* (大行). Although *daigyō* is usually translated as 'great practice' or 'great act', D. T. Suzuki's interpretation is the perfect epitome of Shinran Shōnin's notion of the *nembutsu*.

In Shinran Shōnin's religious philosophy, through pronouncing the *nembutsu* one lives the eternal life of Amida; at the same time, Amida's eternal life lives through one's individual life of *nembutsu*. While it is an individual person saying Amida's Name, at the same time it is Amida's great universal working manifesting itself through the individual. Through faith there emerges the pure act of *nembutsu*, in which the individual and the Buddha merge into oneness. In that moment there is only the sheer reality of Great Living—Namu-Amida-butsu, Namu-Amida-butsu—with no distinction between subject and object.

The *nembutsu* in this sense is not merely a religious practice, nor is it even the best action one can perform in this world. It is simply the most fundamental way in which to live, a way made possible only by faith.

As seen in the passage quoted above concerning Shinran Shōnin's conversion, taking refuge in the Original Vow means to abandoning all other practices ('miscellaneous acts'), none of which is completely free from selfishness, our greedy attachment to self. The *nembutsu* is the Great Living that issues only from pure faith in Amida Buddha.

Love is an important aspect of this Great Living. Shinran Shōnin describes the unselfish love for others that realises itself through the Great Living:

> Love in the Path of the Pure Land Buddhist means quickly attaining Buddhahood by pronouncing the *nembutsu* so that, through the mind of Great Love and Compassion, one is able to save all beings in exactly the way one wishes.

Those inspired by the Great Living thus say the *nembutsu* in gratitude as they live with the Buddha day in, day out. They love and revere the people they meet as good travelling companions on the same path to the Pure Land, and go through life constantly receiving the support of the Great Love and Compassion of Amida Buddha.

> However much love and pity you may feel for others in this life, it is hard indeed to save them in the way you would wish; hence such love can never be perfect. Only the pronouncing of the *nembutsu* can manifest the mind of great unconditional love.

What is meant by this passage is that ultimately the only way of leading people to the Pure Land, the Land of Enlightenment, is through the Great Living of pronouncing the *nembutsu*.

When Shinran Shōnin spoke in this way towards the end of his life, he very much had his Master Hōnen Shōnin in mind. For Shinran Shōnin it was Hōnen Shōnin's *nembutsu* that was the gateway to the Great Living. Hōnen Shōnin's *nembutsu* had ultimately led him to walk the path to the Pure Land. For him Hōnen Shōnin was representative of all Buddhas who praised Amida Buddha by pronouncing his Name.

Shinran Shōnin says in the *Kyōgyōshinshō*:

> So it is that this great living is born of the Prayer (Vow) of Absolute Compassion, for which reason the Prayer (Vow) is known as that which is praised by all Buddhas, or that in which all Buddhas pronounce the Name, or as that which is heartily applauded by all Buddhas.[17]

This passage is based on the Seventeenth Vow of the *Larger Sūtra of Eternal Life*:

> If, upon my attaining Buddhahood, all the innumerable Buddhas in the ten quarters were not approvingly to pronounce my Name, may I not attain the Supreme Enlightenment.[18]

Concerning the term 'great love,' we find the following statement in the *Commentary on the Treatise on the Pure Land* by Tanluan:

> There are three forms of love: The first one is conditioned by one's personal relations [to family or friends] (衆生縁) and is called of small love (小悲), the second one is conditioned by one's relation to Dharma (法縁) and is called of medium love (中悲), and the third one is not conditioned by any relation (無縁) and is called of great or unconditional love (大悲).[19]

Great love is thus an attribute of the Buddha, not of the unenlightened. It is, however, also given to us ordinary people at the moment of pronouncing the Buddha-name with pure faith. To conclude, Shinran Shōnin composes this verse from his *Shōzōmatsu Wasan*:

> Lacking even a modicum of love and compassion,
> How could I hope to benefit sentient beings?
> Were it not for the ship of Amida's Vow,
> How could I cross the ocean of painful existence?[20]

Here, Shinran Shōnin confesses that neither his ability to truly love others nor the way to save himself was forthcoming until he came across the Path of the Pure Land Buddhist taught by Hōnen Shōnin.

EFFORTLESSNESS

Chapter 5

"I, Shinran have never recited the *nembutsu*, not even once, for the repose of my departed father and mother. The reason is that all sentient beings, without exception, have been my parents and brothers and sisters in their successive past lives, in various states of existence. On attaining Buddhahood at your next birth, you will be able to save every one of them.

If the *nembutsu* were something virtuous to be performed through your own power, then you could direct the virtue of *nembutsu* toward saving your father and mother.

But if, discarding all attempts at self-power, you quickly attain Enlightenment in the Pure Land, then, by means of the miraculous powers which you acquire, you will be able to save first of all those you have the closest karmic relations to, however much they may be suffering due to their previous karma in the six realms through the four modes of birth."

Thus spoke my Master.

COMMENTARY

> "The chapter on the *Nembutsu* of no virtue transference"
> — MYŌON-IN RYŌSHŌ —

Virtue-transference was originally the Buddhist Sanskrit term *parināma* that was translated into Chinese as 廻向 (jp. *ekō*). In Shinran Shōnin's religious philosophy, the term *ekō* takes on special meaning, as he uses it to refer to the virtue transferred from Amida Buddha. I will discuss this point later on.

The subject matter of this passage in the *Tannishō* translated above is closely bound up with the notion of virtue-transference, or the turning-over of virtue, a concept Shinran Shōnin understood in a rather special way, investing it with far deeper meaning than usual. In order to get to the real heart of this passage, I would like to give a short explanation of the virtual sea change that the notion of *ekō* underwent in the context of Shinran Shōnin's religious philosophy.

Mahāyāna Buddhism generally holds that virtue created anywhere by anyone may be transferred toward whoever one wishes or toward the whole society so that everyone there should be enabled to attain Enlightenment. A bodhisattva practices self-discipline not only to perfect his own spiritual qualities but also to increase such qualities amongst his fellow beings. Sometimes he will also willingly suffer pain both in order to save others from doing so and to encourage them to aspire to Enlightenment. Such compassion or commiseration is considered a form of *ekō*, or virtue-transference.

Accordingly, the general understanding of *ekō* in Pure Land Buddhism is that all the virtue that one accumulates through good deeds is transferred to all other beings so that everyone together can turn towards the Pure Land. For Pure Land Buddhists the foremost good deed is the *nembutsu*. Thus it was common for Pure Land Buddhists in Shinran Shōnin's time to transfer the virtue of their *nembutsu* to others; however, this was not so for Shinran Shōnin and his followers.

In Shin Buddhism, Amida Buddha is at once the source and the centre of all such creation of virtue. From Amida alone springs the spiritual activity known as *ekō*, virtue-transference. According to Shinran Shōnin the transference of virtue is from Amida to us, not from our store of virtue to others. The only thing that enables all beings to attain Buddhahood in the Pure Land and then come back to the world to save others is Amida's virtue-transference. When this virtue-transference is understood as originating exclusively in Amida, you can see where the idea of Other Power comes from. It can be said that the structure of Shin Buddhist philosophy is entirely based on Shinran Shōnin's interpretation of the principle of virtue-transference, as outlined by him at the beginning of his main book the *Kyōgyōshinshō*: "As I respectfully reflect on the true doctrine of the Pure Land, there are two forms of *ekō* [virtue-transference]: the outgoing *ekō* and the returning *ekō*." [21]

As mentioned before, Amida at his bodhisattva stage is Dharmākara, a Bodhisattva who is deeply engaged in the work of self-perfection so as to accumulate a stock of virtue on behalf of all sentient beings. This stock of virtue is stored in the Name which has now become the most efficient way of leading all beings to the awakening of Enlightenment. The dynamism of the Name's work is due to Amida's unconditional love for all beings which produces a circular flow, outgoing and returning. The outgoing flow, called *ōsō-ekō*, passes over to all beings and makes them turn towards the Pure Land, while the returning flow, technically known as *gensō-ekō*, is what makes beings, once awakened to Enlightenment, wish to go back to their fellow-beings in this world of limitation and finitude in order to make them attain birth in the Pure Land.

Thus, all these dynamics, not only our outgoing journey to the Pure Land for the attainment of Enlightenment, but also our return to this world for the salvation of sentient beings, are based on Amida's love for us.

The present chapter of the *Tannishō* begins with the words,

I, Shinran, have never recited the *nembutsu*, not even once, for the repose of my departed father and mother. The reason is that all sentient beings, without exception, have been my parents and brothers and sisters in their successive past lives, in various states of existence. On attaining Buddhahood at your next birth, you will be able to save every one of them.

The D. T. Suzuki edition of the *Tannishō* uses the phrase 'for the sake of filial piety' in place of 'for the repose of my departed father and mother' (父母の孝養のため). The original Japanese of that time, however, meant 'for the repose of one's parents.'

The story of the historical Buddha's renunciation of family and social life indicates that the achievement of Enlightenment was, in early Buddhism, more important than any kind of moral virtue or the maintenance of social obligations. The fact that a Buddhist monk is called 'a homeless one' reflects this view.

It goes without saying that in Buddhism, the highest priority must be given to the cultivation of the mind. In the course of its history, however, Buddhism has suffered various distortions. When Buddhism entered China, the Confucianists opposed the spread of Buddhism by criticising it for devaluing social obligations. They claimed Buddhism was socially irresponsible because it encouraged youth to forsake family and society and seek only their own spiritual way. Responding to this critique, Buddhism eventually adapted itself to the Chinese concern for ancestors and family by developing special ceremonies for the departed.

After undergoing this kind of transformation in China, Buddhism came to Japan. Thus, when Pure Land Buddhism was introduced in Japan, it was also very much concerned with salvation in the other world or next life, and, consequently, with the repose of the departed. In Japan, of course, Buddhism encountered Shintoism and strove even further to conform and adapt to the demands of the people. In the Kamakura Period religious reformers such as Hōnen Shōnin, Shinran Shōnin, Zen master Dōgen and Nichiren Shōnin tried to return to the original spirit of Gautama, each in their own way. As you may know, however, the radical attitude they adopted for the attainment of truth was decisively opposed and rejected by the old established order. Hōnen Shōnin, Shinran Shōnin, and Nichiren Shōnin were all exiled to outlying provinces, to Tosa, Echigo, and Sado, respectively, while Zen master Dōgen had to retire to Echizen.

In those days, the expression of filial piety was one of the most important social duties of Confucianism. The Buddhist ceremony for the repose of a person's departed father and mother was considered a reasonable way of conforming to the social demands of the day. As far as the established order was concerned, Buddhism had gotten itself completely bogged down. The words of Shinran Shōnin in Chapter 5 have to be interpreted against this historical background.

Shinran Shōnin says, "I, Shinran, have never recited the *nembutsu*, not even once, for the repose of my departed father and mother." These words imply, as he himself then goes on to say, that, over and beyond the ties of blood, he, Shinran Shōnin, is living in a world where all sentient beings are his parents, brothers and sisters. How can we find such a magnificent, wide open world? It is given us at the moment of attaining faith, 'at the very moment when we are moved to call out Amida's Name.' The *nembutsu* is immediately followed by the awakening of faith. Faith and *nembutsu* are both two and one.

Shinran Shōnin says in one of his letters, dated 28th May, 1256:

> I received your letter dated 7th April on the 26th of May and have read it through carefully. As to the matter you have raised, although the one thought-moment of faith and the one thought-moment of *nembutsu* are two, there is no *nembutsu* separate from faith nor is the one thought-moment of faith separate from the one thought-moment of *nembutsu*. The reason is that the practice of *nembutsu* is to pronounce Amida's Name, maybe once, maybe ten times, on hearing that birth into the Pure Land is attained by saying the Buddha's Name, as stated in the Original Vow. To hear this Vow and not doubt it is the one thought-moment of faith. Thus, although faith and *nembutsu* are two, since faith is nothing but hearing and not doubting that you can be saved by only a single pronouncing of the Buddha's Name (*nembutsu*), there is no faith separate from *nembutsu*. This is what I have heard. You should realise further that there is no *nembutsu* separate from faith. You should get it into your heart that both are Amida's Vow. *Nembutsu* and faith are the manifestation of Amida's Vow.[22]

Nembutsu is not to be understood as a means of doing something by self-power, but as a manifestation of Amida's working of love directed toward us, which is realised only through the awakening of faith. In Shin Buddhism *nembutsu* is not a means of concentration or of bringing about ethical good. *Nembutsu* on our part, that is, the *nembutsu* that comes forth from our mouths, is just an expression of our gratitude for Amida's unconditional love that we meet through faith (the state of mind which has no doubt).

Parting from his parents at the age of nine, if not younger, Shinran Shōnin must have wanted to see his parents again; he must have wished to pronounce the *nembutsu* for the repose of his parents after their death, in so far as that was the highest good deed he could perform. Shinran Shōnin had found, however, something impure within himself when practising the *nembutsu*, however much he might have been concentrating, for such *nembutsu* practice is not the *nembutsu* that comes from pure faith in Amida. This kind of *nembutsu* still includes a degree of doubt, because the *nembutsu* follower still relies on his own efforts to pronounce the Name, expecting some kind of effectiveness from the practice. As long as he believes it has merit, he has not yet entrusted himself fully to the Power of Amida's Original Vow. True practice of the *nembutsu* springs from the well of pure faith in Amida. In this respect the *nembutsu* is the Great Living that comes from pure faith attained by casting aside all doubts and rejecting the whole framework of ego-centred consciousness, including intellectual understanding.

I emphasise pure faith in Amida Buddha in this context for two reasons: 1) because in Shinran Shōnin's religious thought, faith in Amida cannot take place separately from awakening to the self, and 2) because one who has attained faith is somehow already living in the Pure Land while still in this life.

Awareness of our limitations

Awakening to the self includes awareness of the limitations of one's love for relatives or friends. We should realise that our love is formed self-centredly and that we are wrong to be proud of such love. Our state of mind is a fatal obstacle in the path of loving others truly.

Generally speaking, we love others and others love us. We are, however, more conscious of our love for others than of the love that others have for us. It means we tend to forget just how much love and compassion we have received from others, and are too conscious of ourselves, of our own love for others; such love on our part is selfish and impure. Unfortunately this is particularly true of our relationships with our parents, those who love or loved us best. What we know of our parents' love is just one tiny fraction of the love they have given us. A parent's love for their child is ideally huge, boundless, and unconditional, such that my life itself is originally a gift from my parents.

Would you pronounce the *nembutsu* for the repose of your departed parents? If you say you would strive to transfer the virtue of your single-minded recitation of *nembutsu* toward benefiting your parents, are you not then assuming that you yourself are enlightened and have no problems, and that your parents are still in the midst of illusion and suffering? The very reverse is probably true: It is not my parents who are in need of saving but myself, caught in the midst of illusion. For me personally my parents are bodhisattvas already enlightened in the Pure Land. If I tried to achieve 'virtue-transference' for the repose of my parents, it would be most arrogant and presumptuous of me.

All we need is to realise how small and self-centred our love for others is and then take refuge in the Buddha's unconditional Love, just as we learned from Tanluan's *Commentary on the Treatise on the Pure Land* in the previous chapter. Then we will find ourselves in the world where all sentient beings are our parents, brothers and sisters. Only when we go beyond the ties of blood and attain pure faith in the Buddha, can everyone be seen to be very close to us as if they were all our parents, brothers and sisters.

The birth of no-birth

When Shinran Shōnin says, "On attaining Buddhahood at your next birth, you will be able to save every one of them," what does he mean by 'your next birth'? The original word used in the text is 順次生 (jp. *junjishō*). Although this is usually translated as 'the next life', I have translated it as 'your next birth.' If you write 'the next life' in this context, it sounds like one of a successive number of lives you go through. But your birth in the Pure Land means going beyond transmigration, therefore it is called 'the birth of no-birth (and no-death).'

Does Shinran Shōnin mean your work of saving others should be practiced only after death? If so, how could one endure such a delay while faced with those who are really suffering? According to my interpretation, all you can properly do in such a situation is take refuge in Amida Buddha and pronounce his Name. In a sense it is your own birth in the Pure Land, 'your next birth' after the great mental death of the ego-consciousness. While you are still burdened with blind passions, your life after this attainment of faith will be one that you lead under the Light of Amida Buddha, which you are now aware of. It is a new life under Amida's Light of Great Compassion.

If you attain pure faith in the Buddha like this, your new life embraced in the Light of the Pure Land will in some way begin while you still remain within the limitations of this world. Such an alteration in your life will certainly exert considerable influence on those who live around you. In this respect your work of helping others to become enlightened can begin in this life, just as you became aware of your involvement in the Pure Land while still living in this world. Such a life is beyond both birth and death. Hence, once attained it still continues after death, infinitely benefiting oneself and others. Shinran Shōnin goes on to say:

> If the *nembutsu* were something virtuous to be performed through your own power, then you could direct the virtue of *nembutsu* toward saving your father and mother. But if, discarding all attempts at self-power, you quickly attain enlightenment in the Pure Land, then, by means of the miraculous powers which you acquire, you will be able to save first of all those you have the closest karmic relations to, however much they may be suffering due to their previous karma in the six realms through the four modes of birth.

You should not see the *nembutsu* as something good to be performed by your own power. It is originally the Buddha's Name already prepared in his Original Vow so as to be pronounced by us. Once you attain true faith in Amida Buddha, *nembutsu* comes forth naturally so that it needs no effort on your part. It is just an expression of your gratitude for Amida's loving kindness in which you find yourself bathed at the moment of attaining faith. The *nembutsu* of Great Living comes forth so effortlessly and naturally, for it is all due to Other Power.

I Have No Disciples

Chapter 6

TRANSLATION

"It is completely unreasonable for there to be quarrelling amongst our fellow followers reciting the *nembutsu* exclusively, with people saying that such and such are 'my disciples' while such and such are not. I, Shinran, have no disciples.

The reason is this: if a man by his own efforts makes others recite the *nembutsu*, then he may call them his disciples. But it is most presumptuous to claim as 'my disciples' those who recite the *nembutsu* solely as a result of Amida's working within themselves.

It is all due to the karmic condition of things that some follow one master while others leave him. This being so, it would be absurd to say that one who turns from one master to another will not attain birth in the Pure Land. Do people mean to take back the faith given to each person by Amida as if it were something of theirs? Such views are most decidedly unreasonable.

If one follows the truth of reality as it is, one will understand exactly how grateful to be to Amida, and how grateful to be to the master."

Thus spoke my Master.

COMMENTARY

> "The chapter on the admonition against
> engaging in disputes over disciples"
> —MYŌON-IN RYŌSHŌ —

I will discuss this chapter in two stages, looking first at the Master-disciple relationship existing in Buddhism, and then examining Shinran Shōnin's ideas on the same subject as set out in this chapter of the *Tannishō*.

The Master-disciple relationship in Buddhism

How do disciples approach their master and how does the master respond to them? The relationship between Master and disciple varies depending on what school they both belong to. For example, in Zen Buddhism, perhaps the most popular Buddhist school in the West, the patriarchal transmission of truth (Enlightenment-experience), directly from person to person, is an essential part of the relationship between Master and disciple. To attain this transmission Zen Buddhists say they depend not on letters but on the practice of 'just sitting in meditation.' Surrounded by the customary quiet of monastic life the relationship becomes highly charged, sometimes dynamic, at times even violent if it proves necessary for a Master to resort to such means to awaken his disciple. Let me give you an example:

> The Master (ch. Linji, jp. Rinzai, *d.* 867) took the high seat in the hall and said: 'There is a true man of no title in the mass of naked flesh who goes in and out from your facial gates [i.e., sense organs]. Those who have not yet testified [to the fact], look, look!'
>
> A monk came forward and asked, 'Who is this true man of no title?'
>
> Rinzai came down from his chair and, taking hold of the monk by the throat, said, 'Speak, speak!'
>
> The monk hesitated.
>
> Rinzai let go his hold and said, 'What a worthless dirt-stick [literally, excrement-wiping spatula] this is!' Then he returned to his quarters."[23]

This story is from *The Record of Linji* (臨濟録 jp. *Rinzairoku*), a work compiling the sayings of Rinzai, the founder of the Rinzai Sect. To quote another striking passage from a sermon addressed to an assembly of his disciples:

> Followers of the Way, if you want to accord with dharma as it is, just be men of great resolve. If you shilly-shally spinelessly along, you're good for nothing. Just as a cracked jug is unfit to hold ghee, so he who would be a great vessel [of dharma] must not be taken in by the deluded views of others. Make yourself master everywhere, and wherever you stand is the true [place].
>
> Whatever comes along, don't accept it. One thought of doubt, and instantly the demon [*māra*] enters your mind. Even a bodhisattva, when in doubt, is taken advantage of by the demon of birth-and-death. Just desist from thinking, and never seek outside. If something should come, illumine it. Have faith in your activity revealed now—there isn't a thing to do.[24]

As you see from this saying full of love, the master's fierce reproach of his disciple in the previous quotation ('What a worthless dirt-stick this is!') is actually his final way of encouraging his disciple's self-development towards the ultimate attainment of the Way (Enlightenment).

These examples are from the early stage of Zen Buddhism. In today's Zen training this interpersonal relationship between Master and disciple has become somewhat formalised and seems often to be restricted to certain forms of communication. In Shin Buddhism, on the other hand, there are no such formal restrictions regarding the transmission of truth from Master to disciple. The relationship between them is kept much freer and is consequently active within their daily lives, rather than being confined only to their lives within the monastery.

Let me recount you a story from the recent history of Shōgyōji Temple, in Kyushu, the parent body of Three Wheels, our Shin Buddhist centre in London.

> About sixty years ago a young monk (the late Reverend Onrō Uenosono, or Onrō-san as he was less formally known) was working in the garden, when our then Master, Daigyōin-sama, happened to enter the corridor of the Buddha Hall. Our Master spied the monk working and told him to pick a bagworm off one of the trees.
>
> The monk retorted, 'It is not a bagworm, it's a dead leaf.'
> The Master said, 'It is not, it's a bagworm.'
> 'It is not, it's a leaf,' the monk responded.
> The Master insisted, 'No, no, it's a bagworm.'
> The monk contradicted him, saying, 'No, I say it's a leaf.'
> 'It is not,' said the Master.
>
> They continued arguing back and forth like this for a little while longer, until the monk Onrō finally said 'Yes!' most affirmatively and pronounced the *nembutsu*, 'Namu-Amida-butsu', over and over again. At that moment he was filled with the joy of awakening. Our Master too was overjoyed to behold the monk's attainment of faith.

The final great 'Yes!' was an absolute affirmation, transcending the duality between their 'yes's and 'no's. While our ordinary consciousness consists of a heady swirl of dualities of all kinds, such as mind-body, subject-object, self-other, and, in this case, bagworm and leaf, this absolute 'Yes!' meant the monk had at last broken through all of them and attained to the mind of pure faith. It was out of the joy of faith that he uttered the *nembutsu*.

If one seeks to understand this story merely by one's intellect, it might seem to recount the disciple's capitulating to the Master's demands. But even if we adopt the intellectual approach, we should not miss the point that the monk's great 'Yes!' embraced the Master and went beyond all kinds of discrimination.

Looking back at this event that had taken place some sixty years previously, Onrō-san actually confided in me, "The very moment I said that 'Yes!' I felt as if I had embraced my Master." In that pure encounter there was no Master, no disciple; there was only the sheer experience of breaking through all the discriminations of our self-centred world.

I would like to quote another quite interesting myōkōnin story from 'The Records of Shōma's Words and Actions', one of the Shin Buddhist documents which I compiled into a book entitled *Myōkōnin*:

> When Shōma (1800–1872) [an illiterate Shin Buddhist devotee] was staying in a certain temple, the Head priest asked him, 'What is the meaning of the phrase [in the *Meditation Sūtra's*], '[Amida's Light] embraces all beings, forsaking none'?'
>
> Immediately Shōma shot up in front of him, with arms flung wide, shouting loudly. The priest, fearing the fellow had become too worked up by the difficult question, took flight.
>
> But Shōma ran after him. The priest fled from the front of the Buddha Hall to the back. But Shōma went into the back after him. Escaping from the back to the front and again from the front to the back, the priest finally fled into the innermost recesses of the temple and hid himself in the storage cupboard for [paper-covered] lampstands. Pulling the doors closed from inside, the priest thought to himself, 'Dear, dear! I should never have put such a difficult question to Shōma. I hope he won't be able to find me.'
>
> On the contrary, Shōma quickly arrived and threw open the cupboard doors shouting, 'My dear Head-priest! I am here!' Then he stretched his arms out to their fullest extent, and declared, '*This* is the meaning of the words 'embracing all beings and forsaking none'.'
>
> Brimming with joy, the priest declared, 'Now I understand. That which never lets me go after all the desperate attempts to escape I have been making for so long—*that* is the meaning of 'embracing all beings and forsaking none'.[25]

In this amusing story Shōma is shown to be someone who has led a priest to faith or awakening. In Shin Buddhism it happens quite often that a priest will ask a lay devotee to make suggestions as to how to attain faith. In another anecdote, on the other hand, it is said that Shōma always paid respect to his Master Shūten, saying, 'Shūten Tathāgata, Shūten Tathāgata',[26] for Shūten had converted him from errant faith to true faith.

The stories I have just told you, however, are at bottom merely objective descriptions of religious events, each one recorded by a third person. There are relatively few documents that can help us gain an insight into the religious experiences of those actually involved in such events or into their way of thinking. As I am principally concerned with the everyday reality of the relationship between master and disciple, in other words how interpersonal relationships function in our daily life, I would now like to focus on this aspect by returning to Chapter 6 of the *Tannishō*.

Shinran Shōnin's statement that 'I have no disciples'

As mentioned previously, all the sayings of Shinran Shōnin compiled in the *Tannishō* by Yuien are records of what the disciple actually heard from his master at firsthand. Yuien, in his last days, wrote down Shinran Shōnin's words, words that still reverberated in his heart some twenty years after his master had passed away. This means Yuien still continued to listen to his late master speaking to him for the rest of his life. Shinran Shōnin's saying, "I have no disciples," found here in Chapter 6, is extremely important for Shin Buddhists to understand how they should live their faith in the context of their interpersonal relationships with others.

In Chapter 6 there are three important points to discuss. Firstly, Shinran Shōnin claims he has no disciples. If one remembers the objective fact that he may have had thousands of followers (or disciples), what does this statement mean? It means he did not ultimately 'possess' or 'own' any of his disciples. His human relationship with them was not centred on possession. He did not possess anyone and was not possessed by anyone. Possessing and being possessed are two sides of the same coin. He was free from any sort of possessiveness. His followers were basically good friends of his. Usually friendship implies an equal relationship between people. However, Shinran Shōnin's friendship was more than that. He respected his followers as also being his protectors on the same true way, just as he revered his wife as a bodhisattva who would lead him to the Pure Land.

Secondly, Shinran Shōnin's rationale for his claim to have no disciples is, if a man by his own efforts makes others recite the *nembutsu* then he may call them 'his' disciples. "But," said Shinran Shōnin, "it is most presumptuous to claim as 'my disciples' those who recite the *nembutsu* solely as a result of Amida's working within themselves." Religious experiences, such as faith in Amida and saying Amida's Name (*nembutsu*), belong absolutely to the individual. Even if one seems to make another person call Amida's Name, the truth is that a person only serves as a motivational condition to another's spiritual development, just like the midwife in the Socratic method of teaching. As to another's spiritual acts, one should not want to go further than the role of midwife. If one did so, one would end up being 'most presumptuous.' Shinran Shōnin's spiritual sternness thus stems from his way of living, in which he constantly returns to the Buddha again and again, day in, day out. Faith in Amida, which causes one to call Amida's Name, is definitely a most private matter reserved for the individual and the Buddha alone.

Thirdly, based on the spiritual insight mentioned above, Shinran Shōnin makes this point clear: "It is all due to the karmic condition of things that some follow one master while others leave him. This being so, it would be absurd to say that one who turns from one master to another will not attain birth in the Pure Land. Do they mean to take back the faith given to each person by Amida as if it were something of theirs? Such views are most decidedly unreasonable." As faith is awakened through the working of Amida, faith is a gift from Amida; it is not ours to give or take. If one thinks one possesses faith, it is no longer faith.

What then in Shinran Shōnin's teaching is faith exactly? It looks elusive, just like a moment of time, but only if one wants to possess it. Faith is attained instantaneously by coming in touch with the working of Amida. And how does one feel the working of Amida? It is through one's relationship with others.

Shinran Shōnin found Hōnen Shōnin to be not only his Master but also an embodiment of Amida Buddha. On encountering Hōnen Shōnin, Shinran Shōnin was able to meet and take refuge in Amida Buddha through the personality of Hōnen Shōnin. Amida Buddha was what made Hōnen Shōnin what he was. Since Amida Buddha constantly supports all living beings and their world of interdependent relationships, Amida naturally issues forth through them. Hence, Shinran Shōnin's conclusion: "If one follows the truth of reality as it is, one will understand exactly how grateful to be to Amida, and how grateful to be to the master."

One who is awakened to faith knows how to thank Amida, how to thank one's Master and consequently how to thank others. The other people in a person's life are the motivational condition for an individual's religious awakening. Consequently they are those who have done a great deal for that individual's spiritual welfare. As a matter of course, one comes to understand just how grateful one should be to others.

To conclude, concerning the relationship between master and disciple, what is most important of all is friendship without any kind of discrimination. Shinran Shōnin's religious philosophy is, I feel, a natural consequence of such friendship. It is the kind of friendship that ought to be fundamental to all human relations. For Shinran Shōnin, those who surrounded him in his daily life were all good friends who helped lead him to Amida's Pure Land. For that reason he was so grateful to them all for their bodhisattvic efforts to guide him in his spiritual development.

THE ABSOLUTE FREEDOM OF
NO OBSTRUCTION

Chapter 7

TRANSLATION

"The *nembutsu* is the single path that knows no obstruction. This is because the gods of heaven and earth bow down in reverence before one who practices the *nembutsu* with pure faith. No *māras* (demonic beings) or heretics (non-Buddhists) can obstruct such a person. No evil deed can bring upon him karmic retribution, nor can any form of good equal his *nembutsu*. Therefore it is called the single path that knows no obstruction."

Thus spoke my Master.

COMMENTARY

"The chapter on the *nembutsu* of no hindrance"
— MYŌON-IN RYŌSHŌ —

There is an important point with regard to the first line which I would like to call to your attention. Opinion has long been divided as to how to read the Japanese phrase 念仏者は. It has often been translated to denote an actual person, for instance, 'the follower of the *nembutsu*,' 'he who recites the *nembutsu*' or 'the person of *nembutsu*.' But such translations are incorrect both grammatically and semantically. This happens because they read the Japanese words 念仏者は as *nembutsu-sha-wa* ('a person who says the *nembutsu*'). Translators such as Shōjun Bandō and Dennis Hirota are right to translate the phrase simply as 'the *nembutsu*.' In this case the same words are to be read as *nembutsu-wa* (meaning 'the *nembutsu*', not a person saying it).

Grammatically speaking, the Chinese character 者 (jp. *sha*) in this phrase is an auxiliary suffix designating the subject of the sentence. Such usage of this Chinese character is often found in the Japanese literature of the day. Semantically too it would be very odd to say that a *person* [who recites the *nembutsu*] is the *path* [of no obstruction]; thus it makes more sense to say the *nembutsu* is the *path*. The translation "the *nembutsu* is the single path that knows no obstruction" is much more appropriate in the context of Shin Buddhist thought.

The first line of the chapter is, as it were, a distillation of all that Shinran Shōnin has to say in the whole of this rather short chapter. I would like now to examine the textual sources of this line.

Great Practice as Great Living

At the very beginning of the second volume of the *Kyōgyōshinshō,* we find Shinran Shōnin's famous statement: "The Great Living is to pronounce the Name of the Nyorai [Tathāgata] of Unimpeded Light."[27]

This particular quotation is from D. T. Suzuki's English version of the *Kyōgyōshinshō.* As I have stated previously, D. T. Suzuki's interpretation of the term *gyō* 行 as 'living' is unique because the word *gyō* is usually rendered as 'practice.' While the practice refers to the practice of *nembutsu,* the word 'practice' gives it a much narrower connotation than the original term intends; that is, 'practice' makes the *nembutsu* sound like some kind of special religious act aimed at achieving a certain goal. Here, however, the sense of the Japanese word *gyō* in this context is much broader and the word means a devotee's way of living as a whole, the way he lives his life on the path towards the Pure Land after taking refuge in the Buddha of Eternal Life. The devotee's way of living after attaining faith is a manifestation of the working of Amida Buddha, the Buddha of Eternal Life, through his own individual life. In this sense, D. T. Suzuki is entirely correct to interpret the term *daigyō,* or 'great practice,' to mean 'Great Living'.

The 'Great Living' refers to the *nembutsu,* Namu-Amida-butsu. In the Shin Buddhist way of life, the pronouncing of the *nembutsu* is done as an expression of gratitude to Amida Buddha after the devotees have attained faith in Amida Buddha who has vowed to save all beings without discriminating amongst them. Why is this way of living called 'Great Living'? The reason is that it is entirely the manifestation of the working of the Buddha of Eternal Life, and not what belongs to ordinary unenlightened beings. In other words, when the great working of the Buddha manifests itself through the lives of ordinary individuals, it takes the form of the *nembutsu* of Great Living.

To quote again from the same passage of the *Kyōgyōshinshō:*

> This Great Living issues out of the Prayer (Vow) of absolute Compassion. This
> Prayer (Vow) is also known as that in which the Name is praised by all Buddhas,
> or as that in which all Buddhas pronounce the Name, or as that in which the
> Name is heartily applauded by all Buddhas.[28]

If you hear another person pronouncing Amida's Name (the *nembutsu*), this symbolises the saying of the Name by 'all Buddhas.' If the person before you is saying the *nembutsu* with pure faith, that person represents 'all Buddhas.' Thus, all the teachers and friends you meet on your path to the Pure Land are all Buddhas and Bodhisattvas who lead you to trust in Amida Buddha. If, when seeking birth in the Pure Land, you encounter a person pronouncing the *nembutsu* with pure faith, he is a true friend, a good teacher, and a Buddha.

Shinran Shōnin's statement, "The Great Living is to say the Name of the Nyorai [Tathāgata] of Unimpeded Light" is closely related to another slightly longer version of Namu-Amida-butsu, called the Ten-character Name: *Kimyō jinjippō Mugekō Nyorai* 帰命尽十方无碍光如来. It means, "I take refuge in the Tathāgata of Unimpeded Light reaching to the furthest ends of the ten quarters." The Tathāgata of Unimpeded Light is another title for Amida Buddha. In the days of Shinran Shōnin a scroll bearing the Ten-character Name was often used as an object of worship. These days, however, the scroll bearing the Six-character Name, 'Namu-Amida-butsu' 南无阿弥陀仏, which means "I take refuge in Amida Buddha," is widely used.

The way of no-hindrance

Amongst the quotations from the *Avatamsaka Sūtra* (jp. *Kegon-gyō*) that Shinran Shōnin compiles in the *Kyōgyōshinshō,* there is one that may well have been the scriptural source of the first line of Chapter 7 of the *Tannishō*:

> The King of Dharma is Absolute Oneness. The person of no-impediment transcends birth-and-death by means of the One Way. The bodies of all Buddhas are of One Dharma-body, One Mind, One Prajñā.[29]

The One Way of no-impediment or no-hindrance is an idea discussed in more detail in Tanluan's *Commentary on the Treatise on the Pure Land*. Shinran Shōnin also quotes this part in his *Kyōgyōshinshō*:

> 'The Enlightenment (or Way)' is the way of no-hindrance. According to a sūtra [the *Avatamsaka Sūtra*], a man of no-hindrance transcends birth-and-death by means of the One Way. The One Way is no other than the way of no-hindrance, and the way of no-hindrance is to know that birth-and-death is Nirvāṇa itself. Such a non-dualistic teaching as this is an aspect of no-hindrance.[30]

To return to the first statement of Chapter 7: "The *nembutsu* is the single path that knows no obstruction." The Japanese word *muge* 無礙, translated here as 'no obstruction,' is a special term which describes how completely opposite things are brought into harmonious unity in the world of Enlightenment; it is also translated as no-hindrance or no-impediment.

According to the *Avatamsaka Sūtra* the world of highest Enlightenment is called *jiji muge hokkai* 事事無礙法界: the true world in which different entities mutually interpenetrate in an interrelated oneness with no obstruction, that is, without losing that which integrally makes each of them what they are. The single path of the *nembutsu* by which we travel to the Pure Land is also an absolute Way of no obstruction, along which we enjoy encountering and re-encountering others in daily life in a harmonious unity of no-hindrance.

How is such a world possible? The *nembutsu* is the act of pronouncing Amida's Name. Though Amida's Name is originally a gift from Amida Buddha, it is only shown to us through the pure encounter of hearing others pronounce that Name. So, "one who practices the *nembutsu* with pure faith" enjoys a harmonious oneness with others through repeated encounter and re-encounter in daily life. Thus it is said that "the gods of heaven and earth bow down in reverence before one who practices the *nembutsu* with pure faith. No *māras* (demonic beings) or heretics (non-Buddhists) can obstruct such a person."

Concerning the gods of heaven and earth, *māras*, and heretics, my first Master, Ekai-ni, said in her essay entitled "On the Way to the Land of Happiness":

> Now, in the light of Buddha's teaching, I know that the gods of heaven and earth, *māras* (demonic beings) and heretics (non-Buddhists) stand for all the blind passions that lie latent in my mind."[31]

You might have your own ideas as to what those beings symbolise. As for me I have little to add to what my master Ekai-ni had to say in her essay. Supernatural beings such as gods and demons are, to my way of thinking, the manifestation of latent potentials that lie hidden deep in our consciousness. Those that stand by our side and help us pursue our true goals in life are considered 'good spirits,' while those that are against us and hinder us are looked upon as 'our demons.'

As a further example of the idea of 'the harmonious unity of no-hindrance,' I would like to relate what I learned from one of my own teachers when I went to inquire after his health while he was hospitalised at Kyoto University Hospital. Professor Kō Hirasawa, a former Provost of Kyoto University, was ninety-five years old at the time. After exchanging greetings in his hospital room we began discussing how it was possible for our spiritual side to continue to develop throughout our lives.

"We can develop our spiritual side to the very end of our lives, as long as our minds are intact," he said. "For example, how we savour a word changes, its meaning becoming richer for us with time."

"Yes, indeed," I said, "I believe you are quite right. While living with D. T. Suzuki during the last three years of his life, I witnessed how lively his spiritual life was. Advancing step by step he always had some new project in mind for the next five years. The last of those projects was his translation of *The Blue Cliff Record* which he was never in fact able to finish."

Professor Hirasawa continued to make his point. "Last autumn I climbed the Higashiyama Mountains in Kyoto and came upon a pine tree and a maple tree standing side by side. It was a beautiful sight. Had I chanced on it previously, what I would probably have found beautiful was the contrast between the green of the pine and the red of the maple. But I did not feel that way now. Instead I was struck by the beauty I saw in the way the green of the pine and the red of the maple melted into one another without either one being lost. As soon as I returned home I composed a piece of calligraphy on a sheet of Japanese paper: *tairitsu muge* 対立無礙 (literally, 'no-hindrance between opposites'). It was the beauty of the opposition of no-hindrance."

"Your words have moved me very much," I said in response. "Though I have yet to reach that state of mind, in the *Avatamsaka Sūtra* it is said that the world of deepest Enlightenment is *jiji muge hokkai* 事事無礙法界, the true world in which different individual entities fuse into oneness without any obstruction, all being interrelated and none losing that which integrally makes them what they are." Both of us immensely enjoyed our re-encounter that day. I still remember that meeting; it was quite simply like meeting a Buddha for me.

The harmonious unity of no-hindrance again became evident to me a few years ago during a meeting prior to a talk Professor John White, former Vice-Provost of University College London, was to give at Shōgyōji's annual summer training assembly in Kyushu, Japan. At that time my present master observed, "The content of his talk is truly excellent. As the meaning of our encounter becomes ever more profound, constantly deepening with the passage of time, the organic and the inorganic are finally merging into one, are they not? If our encounter continues to deepen like this, it will impart people with a profound sense of peace and tranquillity."

By 'the inorganic' apparently he meant the stones of the Zen garden at Three Wheels, which Professor White had designed, and by 'the organic' our fellow human beings. As the meaning of his words slowly dawned upon me I felt incredibly moved.

My master then was, and still is, the Venerable Chimyo Takehara, Head Priest of Shōgyōji Temple. For me the encounter I had with him on that occasion was something inexplicably profound and made a lasting impression on me. It was an encounter with the Dharma-body of my master living in the world of Enlightenment of no-hindrance.

I have often talked about how happy I am to find 'harmony within diversity' at Three Wheels, not only with reference to the way all the different stones in our Zen garden interrelate, but also in terms of the warm human relationships that link together all our many disparate friends into one big happy family. I was extremely moved when I realised how strongly I had been supported in the process of creating Three Wheels by the deep good wishes of such wonderful friends, both British and Japanese.

What I discovered through that conversation with my master was that in our garden these two groups, the organic and the inorganic, or being and non-being, had already merged into the oneness of absolute tranquility, Nirvāṇa. Professor John White, who has become my dearest of friends and strongest of allies, observes in one of his poems,[32]

This
is the garden

of being
and not being,

of rocks
and no rocks.

Here,
when you enter
and are,

is and is not
are equal.

NEMBUTSU AS THE WORKING OF OTHER POWER

Chapter 8

TRANSLATION

"For the devotee, the *nembutsu* is neither a religious practice nor a good deed. Because the *nembutsu* is not a religious practice carried out intentionally, it is called non-practice,' and because the *nembutsu* is not a good act performed intentionally, it is called 'non-good.' Since the *nembutsu* comes entirely from Other Power and is quite beyond self-effort, the *nembutsu*, for the devotee, is neither a religious practice nor a good deed."

Thus spoke my Master.

COMMENTARY

"The chapter on non-practice and non-good"
— MYŌON-IN RYŌSHŌ —

The first line of this chapter, 'For the devotee the *nembutsu* is neither a religious practice nor a good deed,' is once again highly paradoxical. It appears enigmatic and baffling at first because quite obviously the *nembutsu* is a holy practice and is a virtuous act.

If we pay special attention to the words 'for the devotee,' however, they provide a clue towards solving the riddle. The expression 'for the devotee' shows Shinran Shōnin's awareness of the pride 慢心 (jp. *manshin*) deeply embedded in the consciousness of the person who performs religious practices such as *nembutsu* or *zazen* (sitting in meditation). Usually such pride lies hidden deep in the recesses of the devotee's mind.

One who pronounces the *nembutsu* tends to become puffed up with pride, as if his doing so were a matter of personal merit. In so far as one is making a personal effort to practice the *nembutsu*, it is understandable that this mental attitude should form. However, unless one becomes aware of this pride and goes beyond it, one can never be truly humble, however many times one pronounces the Buddha's Name. Pride is egocentric and often poisonous. Unless all pride is abandoned, no religious act can ever be pure. But how can we get rid of such pride embedded in the depths of our religious consciousness? The only way is to know it for what it is and be aware that such pride has no foundation in reality; in other words, we must be awakened to the reality of the *nembutsu*.

Shinran Shōnin thus says, "Because the *nembutsu* is not a religious practice carried out intentionally, it is called 'non-practice,' and because the *nembutsu* is not a good act performed intentionally, it is called 'non-good'. Since the *nembutsu* comes entirely from Other Power and is quite beyond self-effort, the *nembutsu*, for the devotee, is neither a religious practice nor a good deed."

The Chinese compound for Other Power 他力 (jp. *tariki*) was first used in Tanluan's *Commentary on the Treatise on the Pure Land*, to denote the power of Amida's Original Vow. The essence of the Original Vow, in which Amida Buddha vowed to help all beings be enlightened in his Pure Land without any discrimination, lies in the unconditional love of the Buddha. In short, Other Power is Amida's love working within all of us.

When we are awakened to Other Power, due to Amida's unconditional love working within us, we call out his Name with joy and gratitude. This is the *nembutsu* of Shin Buddhism, where 'The *nembutsu* comes entirely from Other Power.'

The living expression of Other Power

The *nembutsu* is the working of Other Power through the individual. As an example of this, I would like to present an account of a myōkōnin called Saichi Asahara (1850–1932), who composed poems based on his religious experience in daily life.

After listening to the Dharma for more than forty years Saichi came to look at himself in the mirror of truth and realised his own 'monstrously evil karma'. In Shin Buddhism this is the realisation of "those who are aware of their bad karma and so entrust themselves to Other Power" (in Chapter 3 of the *Tannishō*), a term which implies a turning away from the self-centred performance of good, and replacing it with complete dependence on Other Power. Saichi says:

> In Other Power
> There is no self-power, no Other Power.
> All around is Other Power.
> Namu-Amida-butsu, Namu-Amida-butsu.[33]

In the first line 'Other Power' is Saichi's experience of absolute Other Power. In the second line he alludes to the relative, dualistic 'Other Power' that stands opposed to 'self-power.' The true experience of 'Other Power' is the experience of absolute Other Power that transcends our conceptual thinking and in which there is no conceptual discrimination between self and other. 'The person who entrusts himself to Other Power' discovers his true self in the midst of Other Power, as expressed in the third line, 'All around is Other Power.'

The whole of the first three lines of the poem could easily have been written by any religious philosopher, for it is simply the result of Saichi's reflection on his own experience of Other Power. However, as D. T. Suzuki pointed out to me with the deepest insight, "The essence of the poem lies in the last line: 'Namu-Amida-butsu, Namu-Amida-butsu.' Having enjoyed giving expression to his own personal experience, Saichi is simply returning to Amida Buddha by pronouncing the *nembutsu*, 'Namu-Amida-butsu, Namu-Amida-butsu'. This is the living expression of Other Power working through the poet."[34]

I would like to introduce here an interpretation of Other Power given in the *Buddha of Infinite Light* by D. T. Suzuki. Of the many interpretations by various scholars I like this one the best. Concerning the interesting comparison he makes between 'synergism' and 'monergism,' I think he might have gotten the idea from Rudolf Otto's book, *India's Religion of Grace and Christianity Compared and Contrasted*,[35] which he used as a textbook for a course on religious philosophy at Ōtani University in 1932.

> Other Power is opposed to what is known in Christian theology as synergism. This means that in the work of salvation a person must do his or her share just as much as God does his. In contrast to synergism, the Shin school may be characterised as monergism, which means working alone in the sense that Other Power works alone, without any self-power being involved. Salvation is all Amida's work. The relative existence which we ordinary people lead has nothing to do with effecting our birth in the Pure Land. Birth in the Pure Land is none other than attaining supreme enlightenment.
>
> What I term monergism, the singular working of Other Power, may be illustrated by the behaviour of cats. When the mother cat carries her kittens, she grasps the neck of each kitten with her mouth and carries it from one place to another. That is monergism because the kittens just let their mother carry them. In contrast, monkeys carry their offspring on their backs. This means that the baby monkeys grasp their mother's body with their limbs or tails, so the mother is not doing all the work by herself. The baby monkeys do their share. This is the way of synergism, in contrast to the way of monergism illustrated by the behaviour of cats.
>
> In Shin teaching we can say that it is only by the power of Amida that our liberation and freedom are assured. We do not add anything to Amida's working. This doctrine of Other Power, or monergism, is based on the idea that humans are relative beings, and as long as we are so constituted there is nothing in us which enables us to cross the stream of birth and death. Amida comes from the Other Shore, carries us on the ship of the Original Vow, and delivers us on to the Other Shore.
>
> A deep chasm exists between Amida and ourselves. We are so heavily burdened with karmic hindrances that we cannot shake them off by our own

power. Amida must come and help us, extending the arms of help from the other side. This is what is generally taught by Shin people. But from another point of view, unless we exhaust everything we have in our efforts to reach the ultimate end, however ignorant and helpless we may be, we will never grasp Amida's arms.

It is all right to say that Other Power does everything by itself. We just let it accomplish its work. Nevertheless, we must become conscious of Other Power doing its work in us. Unless we are conscious of Amida's doing work in us, we shall never be saved. We can never be sure of the fact that we are born in the Pure Land and have attained our enlightenment. To acquire this consciousness, we must exhaust our efforts. Amida may be standing and beckoning us to come to the Other Shore, but we cannot see Amida until we have done all we can do. Self-power is not what is really needed to cross the stream of birth and death, but Amida will extend his helping hand only when we realise that our self-power is of no account.[36]

In order to explain the notion of Other Power, D. T. Suzuki employs a comparison between the monergistic behaviour of a mother cat and the synergistic behaviour of a mother monkey. Several years ago an old friend of mine told me how moved he was to see D. T. Suzuki talking about the unconditional love of the mother cat with actual tears in his eyes.

What is important in D. T. Suzuki's interpretation is his observation that Other Power is solely concerned with our crossing the stream of birth-and-death to the Other Shore. D. T. Suzuki seems to be focusing on how to attain faith or awakening. He says that Amida (Other Power) will extend his helping hand only when we realise that our self-power is of no account. To reach this realisation we must first exhaust our self-power and experience the ineffectiveness of our own efforts to save ourselves; only then do we attain an awakening of faith.

Returning to the text, the *nembutsu* that is described here arises wholly from Other Power, as is recognised by the devotee once he has attained faith. What then is the relationship between Other Power and self-power, after the attainment of faith?

Effortlessness and non-practice

It goes without saying that even after the attainment of faith or enlightenment we must continue to make every effort to lead better lives in this wholly relative world. In this respect nothing has changed. The devotee lives his life in Other Power while making every effort to live in this world. But if that is so, what difference is there before and after the attainment of faith? The point is the devotee who has attained faith makes great efforts without appearing to do so. He looks as though he is living his life effortlessly. Even while making an effort he forgets all his efforts. Forgetting what he has already done he constantly moves forward, seeking to live better, seeking to love both himself and others. He lives in this world, doing for the doing, without any attachment to his efforts, and just lets Other Power work within himself. All he need do is just to thank Amida Buddha for enabling him to live in this way.

He knows well the reality of this world and is fully aware how self-centred people are, himself included. But because of his faith in Amida Buddha, he is beyond the reality of the world. His mind is soft and free as a child's. Even while making every effort, he appears to do so effortlessly.

D. T. Suzuki is a good example of this effortless effort. Erich Fromm says in his essay entitled 'Memories of D. T. Suzuki':

> I have often wondered about the unique quality of Dr. Suzuki. Was it his lack of narcissism and selfishness, his kindness, and his love of life? It was all of these, but often I have thought of still another aspect: the child-like quality in him. This needs some comment. The process of living hardens the heart of most people. As children we still have an open and malleable heart: we still have faith in the genuineness of mother's smile, in the reliability of promises, in the unconditional love which is our birthright. But this 'original faith' is shattered sooner or later in our childhood. Most of us lose the softness and flexibility of our hearts; to become an adult is often synonymous with becoming hardened. Some escape this fate; they keep their heart open and do not let it harden. But in order to be able to do so, they do not see reality fully as it is. They become as Don Quixote, seeing the noble and the beautiful where they are not; they are dreamers who never awaken fully to see reality including all its ugliness and meanness. There is a third solution, but an exceedingly rare one. The persons who take this road retain the softness of a child's heart, and yet they see reality in all clarity and without illusions. They are children first, then become adults, and yet they return to being children without ever losing the realism of adulthood. This is a difficult way, and that is why it is so rare. I believe it was this that characterised Dr. Suzuki's personality. He was hard as rock and soft as wax; he was the realistic, mature man, who was able to look at the world with innocence and faith of the child.[37]

To conclude this chapter I would like to comment on one further point: that the *nembutsu* as non-practice or non-good goes far beyond the usual notion of religious practice or discipline. One who pronounces the *nembutsu* as non-practice enjoys absolute freedom and is in touch with Amida Buddha (Other Power) day in and day out. Whatever he does, through everything he is in contact with, a manifestation of the working of Other Power is his to enjoy; he is always in touch with the Dharma-world.

The word 'non-practice' reminds me of the traditional Tendai discipline known as the Four Forms of *Samādhi*, long practiced on Mount Hiei: 1) The *samādhi* in the constant practice of the *nembutsu* called *jōgyō sammai*, 2) the *samādhi* in the constant sitting in meditation called *jōza sammai*, 3) the *samādhi* half in the practice of the *nembutsu* and half in sitting in meditation called *hangyō hanza sammai*, 4) the *samādhi* in non-practice and non-sitting called *higyō hiza sammai*. This is originally based on the *Mohe zhiguan* 摩訶止観 by Zhiyi (538–597). The last of the four, non-practice and non-sitting, or *higyō hiza*, is said to be the highest stage of *samādhi* wherein one enjoys absolute freedom in everything one does. I cannot go into historical details here, but these four forms of *samādhi* were carried out in different halls two of which still stand to this day on Mount Hiei.

As you may know the founders of the new Buddhist schools in the Kamakura era all came from Mount Hiei. Pure Land Buddhism is in some way related to *jōgyō sammai* 常行三昧, the *samādhi* in the constant practice of the *nembutsu*, Zen Buddhism to *jōza sammai* 常坐三昧, the *samādhi* in the constant sitting in meditation, and the *Lotus Sūtra* school to *hangyō hanza sammai* 半行半坐三昧, the *samādhi* half in the practice of the *nembutsu* and half in sitting in meditation. Each school, especially Zen Buddhism and Pure Land Buddhism, seems to have as their highest stage something akin to *higyō hiza sammai* 非行非坐三昧, the *samādhi* in non-practice and non-sitting. I think this highest stage can be defined as the absolute freedom of 'As-it-is-ness', to use D. T. Suzuki's term, and is one of the most salient characteristics of Japanese Buddhism as a whole.

THE SALVATION OF THOSE BESET BY DOUBT

Chapter 9

TRANSLATION

"'Although I recite the *nembutsu*, I seldom feel like dancing for joy, nor do I desire to hasten to the Pure Land. Why is this so?' I asked.

My Master answered:

'I, Shinran, had the same doubts. O Yuien-bō, you have the same doubts just as I did! But when you reflect on the matter more deeply, you will find that your birth in the Pure Land is all the more assured just because you cannot rejoice at what should make you feel like dancing for joy on earth and in the air. It is the effect of blind passions lying heavily on one's heart and preventing one from rejoicing. Knowing this fact beforehand, the Buddha called us 'ignorant beings filled with blind passions.' Thus I realise that the Compassionate Vow of Other Power is for the benefit of such ignorant beings as ourselves and I find it all the more to be trusted.

'Furthermore, not being desirous of hastening to the Pure Land, we feel very much dejected when we become ill, however mild the illness, at the thought of our possible death. This is likewise caused by the effect of blind passions. We feel reluctant to abandon this old home of pain and suffering, where we have been transmigrating from time immemorial right down to the present day, and we feel no longing for the Land of Peace and Happiness, where we have yet to be born. This is again due to our blind passions, so fierce and powerful. But when our karma in this *sahā* world expires and we have no choice but to leave it behind, then, however reluctant we may feel, we will nevertheless proceed to the Pure Land. Amida especially pities those who are not desirous of hastening to the Pure Land. When you consider all this, you may realise all the more clearly how trustworthy the Great Compassionate Vow is and how firmly your birth in the Pure Land is assured.

'If, on the contrary, you felt like dancing for joy and wished to hasten to the Pure Land, you might wonder if you had any blind passions at all.'"

Thus spoke my Master.

COMMENTARY

> "The chapter on no joy and no happiness"
> — MYŌON-IN RYŌSHŌ —

Chapter 9 is the first of two chapters in which the compiler's name, Yuien, appears, indicating that the *Tannishō* is in fact the record of a dialogue between Yuien and his Master, Shinran Shōnin.

At first glance their conversation may seem rather sombre and melancholy. It starts with an all-important question posed by Yuien who asks, "Although I recite the *nembutsu*, I seldom feel like dancing for joy, nor do I desire to hasten to the Pure Land. Why is this so?" This is immediately followed by Shinran Shōnin's kindly words, "I, Shinran, had the same doubts. O Yuien-bo, you have the same doubts as I did!" Although Shinran Shōnin's words are indeed warmly spoken, if you do not understand the exact nature of their encounter, you might take their exchange to be a rather gloomy one.

At this time Yuien had abandoned all worldly ambitions and was evidently living in the Buddhist community led by his Master, Shinran Shōnin. Despite his sincere efforts to live a religious life, Yuien found himself unable to call up a feeling of joy in the Dharma. Saddened by this fact, Yuien went to his Master to ask why he could no longer find any contentment in religious life, whereupon Shinran Shōnin, identifying with his disciple, declared, "I, Shinran, had the same doubts. O Yuien-bo, you have the same doubts as I did!" Could such a response have been merely a gesture of sympathy towards a troubled disciple? Even if that were the case, the story can be seen as a beautiful instance of human affection between Master and disciple, which is all the more poignant because it is taking place in the religious world.

Hyakuzō Kurata's famous play, *A Priest and his Disciple*,[38] was based on just such an interpretation of this chapter. When I read the play at the age of sixteen, however, I did not come away entirely satisfied with Kurata's interpretation. His way of thinking may have been influenced by Taishō Romanticism. At the same time Kurata's interpretation is typical of the view held by those outside the religious community.

In order to understand the text properly I would like to draw your attention to several points. Firstly, we should bear in mind that Yuien himself was a person who had already attained faith (awakening); to think otherwise would be a great mistake. Having been awakened to the Buddha's love and compassion, Yuien had experienced joy in the Dharma and knew how important joy was for spiritual life. When you entrust yourself to Amida Buddha, you are awakened to the fact that you are already cradled in Amida's arms. If this is the case, why then should you not be happy? Surely this is cause for you to be filled with supreme joy!

In the volume of the *Kyōgyōshinshō* that deals specifically with the subject of the awakening of faith Shinran Shōnin says, "As I reflect on [the significance of] true faith, there is 'one thought.' 'One thought' is the shortest possible moment in which faith reveals itself and the feeling of joy, incomprehensibly great, manifests itself."[39] Shinran Shōnin thus points out that the moment faith emerges it manifests itself as joy. In the same work he also states that "being filled with feelings of joy" is one of the ten benefits resulting from faith. He writes:

> Further, while living in this world, they [the devotees] will surely be the recipients of the following ten benefits:
>
> 1) They will be protected by spiritual powers.
> 2) They will be provided with the highest virtues.
> 3) They will be able to convert evil into good.
> 4) They will be well thought of by Buddhas.
> 5) They will be praised by Buddhas.
> 6) They will always be [bathed] in the protective
>   light radiating from the mind of Amida.
> 7) Their minds will be filled with feelings of joy.
> 8) They will know what it is to be grateful and how to requite favours.
> 9) They will be able to practice the great compassionate heart all the time.
> 10) They will attain to the group of the right definite assurance.[40]

Faith expresses itself in joy. As a disciple of Shinran Shōnin, Yuien knew just how important joy was to one's faith, yet found it very difficult to maintain a joyful state of mind. What Yuien failed to see is that joy is a result of faith (awakening) and not vice versa, and because he was unable to call up a feeling of joy Yuien came to doubt his own faith-experience and consequently his ultimate salvation. This situation was caused by his blind passions. As we will see Shinran Shōnin helped him to resolve his impasse.

Blind passions

The term 'blind passions' (jp. *bonnō*) used in this chapter comes from the original Sanskrit Buddhist term *kleśa*. It can be rendered in various ways: delusions, mental afflictions, etc. After having thought about it for some time, I have decided to use the term 'blind passions', which covers a wide range of feelings mental, emotional, and physical. These feelings are said to be blind because they basically arise in a self-centred way. In this respect they can also be called 'delusions.' When such blind passions afflict harm on self and others, they may be called mental afflictions, or afflicting passions.

Broadly speaking, when we experience this world, we reconstruct that experience through our intellect (mind) and our senses (body). The world-view we thus form as human beings is self-centred, because we are not fully aware of the limitations of our intellect and sense organs. Usually we consider our views to represent the truth and that this truth is absolute, and so we remain strongly and selfishly attached to our views.

Unless we become aware of our selfish attachment, such an attitude leads to untold suffering and affliction in our lives.

The Four Noble Truths

The tenacious selfish attachment embedded in our world-view becomes the cause of all our suffering. According to Gautama Buddha's teaching of The Four Noble Truths, this blind selfish attachment is the cause of all suffering. The Four Noble Truths are:

1) Life is suffering, the suffering of birth, ageing, sickness and death.
2) Suffering has a cause, which is selfish attachment.
3) All forms of suffering will cease once we realise the cause of suffering.
4) There is a way to extinguish suffering.

As long as we live in this world of intellect and senses, the blind passions will continue to arise again and again, regardless of whether we are enlightened or not. This is because our selfish attachment (or clinging), the root cause of suffering, lies embedded at the centre of all these blind passions. Only when we become aware of that cause will all suffering cease; this is Enlightenment or awakening.

Several years ago I visited St. James and St. Michael's, a primary school for refugee children in London, to introduce Buddhism to a class of seven and eight year olds. Just before I started my talk, the teacher told me that he had taught the children The Four Noble Truths. After chanting a very short sūtra, I wanted to find out how much they had actually understood of this profound teaching. I therefore asked if they knew The Four Noble Truths or not. About ten children raised their hands. They seemed to have understood something of what they had been taught. I was particularly pleased to hear what one eight year old girl had to say about her understanding of The Four Noble Truths: 'Professor! In our life there is some badness and this badness has its cause. When we know this cause, that badness disappears.' I was so surprised at what a good grasp she had of something so profound.

Just as the little girl had seen, what is most important for us is to become aware of the actual cause of suffering in our lives. Only if you know your selfish attachment to be the cause of all your suffering can your suffering disappear. When the eternal Truth releases you from the citadel of self-centred consciousness, its infinite Light comes flooding in and you will find yourself being embraced in this infinite Light just as you are. This awakening will bring you inner peace, or if you like, peaceful awareness, an awareness of yourself just as you are, resting in the great compassion of the Buddha.

Inner peace or Nirvāna is one of the Three Seals of Buddhism: impermanence, selflessness, and Nirvāna. From its very start in India, Buddhism has been foremost in its emphasis on inner peace. To quote from a talk of mine, entitled 'My Journey to India: On Our Audience with His Holiness the Dalai Lama':

Of all the great spiritual contributions His Holiness has made to the world, this, I think, is one of the two greatest. Inner peace is the source of world peace. Without attaining inner peace our peace movement will only be accompanied by further fighting. It is absurd in Buddhism for us to speak about world peace without first attaining inner peace in our relationship with those around us. His Holiness has always been emphasising this point. Incidentally, his other major spiritual contribution is, I believe, the way he has clarified the fundamental principle that every human being desires happiness—a great proposition usually hidden behind the truth that life is suffering. Without insight into the nature of true happiness, we will never really feel life is suffering. In Buddhism the essence of happiness lies in the extinction of selfish attachment.

In Buddhism true happiness or joy comes from the extinction of suffering, Nirvāṇa or Enlightenment. In the sense that every human being can be enlightened, in other words can become a Buddha, they are all considered to be capable of attaining true happiness. Only those who have experienced true happiness can realise how important the true meaning of happiness is. As I mentioned in the above quotation, the principle of happiness lies behind the teaching of The Four Noble Truths.

In Shin Buddhism we become aware of the reality of our selfish attachments, through Amida's Light. By entrusting ourselves to Amida Buddha, in other words through faith, we break through the darkness of self-centred consciousness caused by our selfish attachment.

To quote the *Shōshinge* composed by Shinran Shōnin:

The mind-light that embraces us always illumines and protects us.
Though the darkness of ignorance is already broken through,
The clouds and mists of tenacious greed and repulsive hatred
Still continue to cover the sky of true faith.
It is as if, though the sunlight is veiled by clouds and mists,
Below the clouds and mists, brightness reigns and there is no darkness.[41]

As mentioned before, Yuien had already attained faith-experience. For him "the darkness of ignorance was already broken through." However, surrounded by "the clouds and mists of tenacious greed and repulsive hatred" which "still continued to cover the sky of his true faith" Yuien had lost the feeling of joy, hence his famous question.

Something else I would like to mention here is the very deep level of spirituality that Shinran Shōnin himself had by now attained. As you can see in the lines quoted above, despite "the clouds and mists of tenacious greed and repulsive hatred" Shinran Shōnin is quietly enjoying Amida's light penetrating those clouds, and affirms that "below the clouds and mists, brightness reigns and there is no darkness."

Even so we are all burdened with blind passions and cling to our selfish world-view. Shinran Shōnin laments in the *Kyōgyōshinshō*:

Now I can truly realise how wretched I am! I, [Shin]ran, the stupid baldheaded one, deeply submerged in the wide ocean of desires and cravings, confusedly lost amongst the huge mountains of worldly fame and interests, have no aspiration for being counted amongst the elite of the definitely assured group and feel no pleasure in approaching the really true experience. How deplorable! How heart-rending![42]

In light of this awareness Shinran Shōnin says to Yuien, "Knowing this fact beforehand, the Buddha called us 'ignorant beings filled with blind passions.' Thus I realise that the Compassionate Vow of Other Power is for the benefit of such ignorant beings as ourselves and I find it all the more to be trusted." Aware that his whole being is embraced by Amida's love and compassion, Shinran Shōnin entrusts himself just as he is to Amida Buddha.

Shinran Shōnin's identification with Yuien, that is, the latter's utter lack of joy and his reluctance to hasten to the Pure Land, was actually his way of embracing Yuien at the deepest spiritual level. Resting quietly within the compass of Amida Buddha's unconditional love, Shinran Shōnin encouraged his disciple to entrust himself to Amida Buddha.

NATURALNESS

Chapter 10

TRANSLATION

"As regards the *nembutsu*, no meaning is meaning, because it is immeasurable, indescribable, and inconceivable.' Thus my Master [Hōnen Shōnin] taught me."

COMMENTARY

"The chapter on the meaning of no meaning"
— MYŌON-IN RYŌSHŌ —

The shortest chapter of the *Tannishō*, it offers keen insight into the naturalness (自然法爾 jp. *jinen hōni*) of the *nembutsu*. In a letter to his disciples from the *Lamp for the Latter Age* collection, Shinran Shōnin gives a detailed interpretation.

INTERPRETATION OF NATURALNESS

'*Ji*' means 'of itself,' or 'by itself.' As it is not due to the designing of man but to [Amida] Nyorai's vow [that man is born in the Pure Land], it is said that man is naturally or spontaneously (jp. *nen*) led to the Pure Land. The devotee does not make any conscious self-designing efforts, for they are altogether ineffective to achieve the end. *Jinen* thus means that as one's Rebirth into the Pure Land is wholly due to the working of Nyorai's vow-power, it is for the devotee just to believe in [Amida] Nyorai and let his vow work itself out.

'*Honi*' means 'it is so because it is so'; and in the present case it means it is in the nature of Amida's vow-power that we are born in the Pure Land. Therefore, the way in which the Other Power works may be defined as 'the meaning of no meaning,' that is to say, it works in such a way as if not working, [so natural, so spontaneous, so effortless, so absolutely free are its workings].

Amida's vow accomplishes everything and nothing is left for the devotee to design or plan for himself. Amida makes the devotee simply say 'Namu-

Amida-butsu' in order to be saved by Amida, and the latter welcomes him to the Pure Land. As far as the devotee is concerned, he does not know what is good or bad for him, all is left to Amida. This is what I, Shinran, was taught.

Amida's vow is meant to make us all attain supreme Buddhahood. The Buddha is formless and because of his formlessness he is known as 'all by himself' (*jinen*). If he had a form, he would not be called supreme Nirvāṇa. In order to let us know how formless he is, he is called Amida. This is what I, Shinran, was taught.

When you have understood this, you need not any more be concerned with *jinen* ['being by itself']. When you turn your attention to it, the 'meaningless meaning' assumes a meaning [which is defeating its own purpose].

All this comes from *buddhajñāna,* which is beyond comprehensibility.[43]

This letter mainly concerns itself with how to interpret the word *jinen* (naturalness), its contents corresponding exactly to that of Chapter 10. From this commentary on *jinen,* we can see how Shinran Shōnin understood Amida's Original Vow to be the working of Other Power.

What Shinran Shōnin wants to express by 'the meaning of no meaning' is the naturalness of the working of Amida's Original Vow of universal deliverance, and how it manifests itself as the devotee's own *nembutsu.*

In the above translation, D. T. Suzuki rendered *mugi igi* as 'the meaning of no meaning' or 'meaningless meaning.' Such a highly paradoxical statement is not easily understood and may be regarded to have no definite contextual clues that can help us grasp what it means. But Shinran Shōnin's intention here is to clarify the natural working of Amida's Original Vow.

Shin Buddhism thus classifies 'naturalness' into three categories: 1) The naturalness of karma; 2) The naturalness of the Noncreated (skt. *asaṃskṛta,* the content of Enlightenment); and 3) The naturalness of the power of the Original Vow. 'The naturalness of karma' describes how things work in this karmic world; this includes not only the karmic law of cause and effect in the field of morality but also scientific truths in the various academic fields. Karma is the energy that informs our lives and the world in which we live. 'The naturalness of karma' is the way in which karma operates in our world. As beings filled with blind passions, we tend to behave selfishly, thus we need to make a moral effort to love others, and ensure that no harm comes to others and ourselves.

In a moral universe, where the karmic law of good and evil prevails, good deeds bring happiness and evil deeds bring suffering. Such moral awareness can sometimes lead us to behave better than we would otherwise. On the other hand, we can make too much of this karmic law, and become fearful of the possible consequences of our present actions. Strong attachment to karmic law can lead people to join quasi-religious movements which are a mixture of morality and religion. Shinran Shōnin says in his

Shōzōmatsu Wasan:

> As proof of not having realised the Buddha-wisdom,
> One doubts the Tathāgata's wisdom
> And relies on one's practice of the root of good,
> believing in the karmic retribution of evil and good.
> As a result one remains in the Borderland.[44]

> Those followers who believe in the karmic retribution of evil and good
> Are doubtful of the inconceivable Buddha-wisdom.
> They remain in the Womb Palace of the Castle of Doubt.
> Hence they are separated from the Three Treasures.[45]

The phrase found in these hymns, 'believing in the karmic retribution of evil and good', refers to our belief in the karmic law of cause and effect in the field of morality. Such moral belief can cause us to suffer terrible anxieties due to our ethico-religious consciousness. Shinran Shōnin effectively rids us of these anxieties by leading us to believe in the inconceivable Buddha-wisdom.

The intuition of the Name

The naturalness of karma also refers to the very natural way that the laws of nature operate in this world. If you sow seeds, they will send forth shoots that grow and bloom in the spring. This biological phenomenon is an example of the teleological process of organic growth. Whether it is biology, physics, sociology or psychology, each science has its own field and employs scientific reasoning to survey the objects within that field. Each science organises the field it has chosen and deals with the realities occurring there in accordance with the concepts it has forged to enable it to discuss and explain the phenomena within its particular field. Every scientific study starts from certain premises and hypotheses and relies solely on the five senses and the intellect when seeking to explain systematically the phenomenon of its own particular field. As long as scientists do not forget this and are aware of these boundaries, there will be no serious problems with scientific studies.

Truths or laws discovered in scientific studies help us to understand our world more systematically, banishing the worries and fears which can make us prone to superstition. Scientific discoveries have the potential to enrich our lives intellectually. If scientists are content to remain within their boundaries and do not seek to extend their conclusions beyond those boundaries, the truths they discover will hold good within their own particular fields. However, scientists should not insist on their way of explaining reality as the only truth.

Indeed, it would be rather arrogant of us if we were to insist that our five senses and intellect exhaust reality, for the reality of life cannot fully be explored by these devices alone. In this context D. T. Suzuki says in the *Buddha of Infinite Light*:

We can say, however, that as far as our five senses and intellect are concerned the world is to be understood, explained, and interpreted in a certain way. But there is no way to deny the existence of something (it may or may not be proper to speak of 'someone') higher or deeper that covers the field more extensively. There may be something beyond the measurement of our five senses and our intellect. We may possess some such thing in ourselves, perhaps largely underdeveloped. If we have another way of coming into contact with reality that is much deeper, more extensive, than our senses and intellect permit, it is too presumptuous of us to deny such an intuition, and claim 'There is no such thing. Nothing exists outside my senses and intellect.'

We are arrogant if we deny this higher and deeper intuition, which in Pure Land Buddhism is the *myōgō*, 'the Name,' [that works as the *nembutsu* in us]. The working of this Name allows us to enter the Pure Land and makes our realisation of the higher reality, a full grasp of ultimate truth. It does not work on our senses and intellect, which are limited and relative. People who hold the intellect to be our only real guide in life will deny that which extends beyond the senses and intellect. They will negate the efficacy of the Name to explore those fields of human life that cannot be grasped by intellection.[46]

The Dharmakāya as compassionate means

What is called 'the naturalness of the Noncreated' is the naturalness of ultimate truth. The term 'the Noncreated' stands for the ultimate truth, the content of Enlightenment or Dharma in itself. It is formless and so Shinran Shōnin says: "The Buddha is formless and because of his formlessness he is known as being 'all by himself' (*jinen*). If he had a form, he would not be called supreme Nirvāna. In order to let us know how formless he is, he is called Amida."

If the ultimate truth or Dharmakāya (Dharma-body) were to remain completely formless, it would be very difficult for us, who live in the karmic world of delusion (*gōdō jinen*), to find a way to reach it. As long as the Dharmakāya remains formless in its own purity, in other words, remains the Dharma-in-itself, there is no activity by which it can be known. It is only when it reveals itself in the karmic world of cause and effect that it can work directly to save all suffering beings. This taking on of concrete form is what is known as *hōben*, skilful means, and is described as '*Dharmakāya* in manifested form' (*hōben hosshin*). It is important to bear in mind that *Dharmakāya* revealed in form and *Dharmakāya* as Dharma-in-itself are inseparable. They are two, yet one; one, and yet two. Shinran Shōnin understood 'the *Dharmakāya* in its manifested form' to be Amida Buddha, who is ultimately based on formlessness.

'The naturalness of the power of the Original Vow' is thus the way in which all beings in the karmic world are able to come into contact with the ultimate reality of Dharma-in-itself known as the Noncreated or As-it-is-ness. When the Dharmakāya took form as Amida Buddha, as described in the *Larger Sūtra of Eternal Life*, Amida made forty-eight Vows, the most important of which is the Eighteenth Vow, or the Vow of Universal Deliverance, which reads:

> If, upon my attaining Buddhahood, all beings in the ten quarters aspiring in all sincerity and faith to be born in my Country, thinking of me [i.e., pronouncing my Name; *nembutsu*] up to ten times, were not to be born there, then may I not attain the Supreme Enlightenment.[47]

According to the philosophy of Pure Land Buddhism, the Vow of Universal Deliverance enables all sentient beings to be born in the Pure Land, without discrimination. There they find themselves in the realm of the Noncreated, the unchanging realm of the ultimate reality of As-it-is-ness that stands for the world of *tathatā* (真如 jp. *shinnyo*). This Vow is the spontaneous outflow of Amida's *mahākaruṇā* (大悲 jp. *daihi*), or his great compassionate heart, which is Amida himself.

The meaning of no meaning

To return to the text of Chapter 10: "As regards the *nembutsu*, no meaning is meaning, because it is immeasurable, indescribable, and inconceivable. Thus my Master [Hōnen Shōnin] taught me." The *nembutsu*, or the pronouncing of Amida's Name, is what connects our existence to Amida Buddha and his Pure Land. This link between Amida and ourselves was originally provided by Amida Buddha himself. Amida produced it for the sake of us helpless karma-bound existences, thoroughly conditioned by space, time, and causation. As long as we are in this state of finitude, we can never attain Nirvāṇa or Enlightenment by our own efforts. This inability to achieve emancipation is embedded in the very nature of our existence. The more we try to escape from our karmic bondage, the deeper we get ourselves inextricably enmired in it. The help we need must come from a source other than this limited existence.

Shinran Shōnin's statement, 'no meaning is meaning' seems quite illogical or paradoxical but what is actually meant by it can be paraphrased as follows: 'When you stop thinking about its meaning, then the true meaning comes to you.' In Shin Buddhism this true meaning comes from outside of our own intellectual calculation, and arises through the aid of Amida Buddha's Vow to save all beings out of great love and compassion. Because the Buddha himself is the Dharmakāya in manifested form, he is originally from the Dharma-in-itself as the ultimate reality of Enlightenment. The Dharma-in-itself has opted to take form as the Dharmakāya in manifested form, i.e., Amida Buddha. This original movement or action, which is 'immeasurable, indescribable, and inconceivable,' is none other than Amida Buddha's universal love for others.

Amida's love for us, manifesting itself as the *nembutsu* through his Original Vow, is so natural and spontaneous that we need not think about it. Our relative way of thinking is, on the contrary, an obstacle that prevents the *nembutsu* from arising from within. Therefore, Shinran Shōnin says: 'As regards the *nembutsu*, when you stop thinking about its meaning, then the true meaning comes to you, because it is immeasurable, indescribable, and inconceivable.'

To quote again from D. T. Suzuki's *Buddha of Infinite Light*:

> Even when our intellect is unable to verify what scientists call objective or scientific truth, there is something in religious faith that somehow we must accept as reality. Although we have yet to experience it, and we probably may never experience it, still it demands our acceptance, whether we will or not. This is the manner in which theologians speak of faith. One must make a decision to accept it or not to accept it. It is a venturesome deed or experience, plunging oneself into unknown regions and risking one's destiny. But I am afraid that people who have such a view of faith are still on the plane of relativity.
>
> The fact is that we are compelled to accept it; it is not a matter of choice that we accept faith. All religions contain a similar element. It is not that Amida enters our life in some way; rather our being is carried away by Amida. That is the way that the Name comes alive in the actual life of a Shin Buddhist. Some people may ask about the significance of the Name and how it can be so efficacious as to carry us to Amida and the Pure Land. As long as a person has such doubt or question or hesitancy in accepting the Name, he or she is not yet in it, and therefore cannot fully experience it.[48]

In his book *Naturalness*, Kenryō Kanamatsu (1915–1986), a professor of philosophy who received part of his higher education in the United States, describes the way we live our lives through faith in Amida Buddha, saying:

> Living on the plane of spiritual consciousness, however, does not mean abandoning or fleeing from so-called worldly life. Spiritual life is not a separate existence of its own apart from everyday life on the intellectual plane. The spirit does not ignore or negate the intellect; what it does is to transcend it, in the sense that it has its own government within the intellectual boundaries; and as long as it keeps this in good order, it knows no outside bounds imposed upon it. True spirituality is calmly balanced in strength, in the correlation or rather in the identity of the within and the without. It is in the world of relativity and duality, and at the same time is above it. The spiritual world is at once of duality and of unity, of distinction and of non-distinction, and for this reason Karma is no-Karma as well as Karma itself.[49]

The true striving in our daily life consists not in the neglect of action but in the effort to attune it closer and closer to the Eternal Harmony. That is to say, the self is to dedicate itself to the Universal Spirit through its activities. This dedication is the song of humanity, in this its freedom. Joy reigns when all work becomes the path to the union with Amida Buddha; when our self offering grows more and more intense. Then there is freedom. Then there is naturalness in our everyday work. We no longer become troubled with Karma, for we identify ourselves with it. We never fall into causality, because we are already it. Indeed suffering is no doubt suffering, but we have absorbed it in our spiritual consciousness where all such things as take place on the plane of sense and understanding find their proper meaning in harmony with the eternal scheme of the Universe. Joy expresses itself through the law of causality. The saving beam of Amida's smile of compassion is seen shining through the night of gloom. The world with all its sufferings, shortcomings and dualities, becomes one with the spiritual world. Then in this world comes the Pure Land of Amida. This is the meaning of *Sukhāvatīvyūha*—the embellishing (*vyūha*) of the Pure Land (*Sukhāvatī*).[50]

This beautiful description of the way we experience 'naturalness' in our everyday life through our encounter with Amida Buddha should help us to arrive at a way of understanding ourselves in the context of Shin Buddhist faith.

In conclusion, I would like to point out that Shinran Shōnin received this teaching of 'the meaning of no meaning' from his master Hōnen Shōnin. Let me quote two of Shinran Shōnin's letters:

The Shōnin [Hōnen Shōnin] said, 'Because Other Power is the Tathāgata's Vow, no meaning is meaning.' What is meant by 'meaning' is [calculative] thinking [on our part]. Because the [*nembutsu*] follower's thinking is self-power it is called 'meaning.' The Other Power is to ensure birth [in the Pure Land] through the joyful faith of entrusting ourselves to the Original Vow, therefore it is said that there is 'no meaning'.[51]

The Great Master, the Shōnin [Hōnen Shōnin], stated that, 'After having entrusted ourselves to Amida's Original Vow, no meaning is meaning.' What I have learned is that as long as we are thinking of the meaning it is not Other Power but self-power. Because what is called Other Power refers to the inconceivability of the Buddha-wisdom it is up to the consideration of the Buddhas alone as to how ignorant beings, burdened with blind passions, will attain supreme enlightenment. It can never be due to thinking on the part of the [*nembutsu*] follower. Therefore it is stated that 'no meaning is meaning.' 'The meaning' refers to the [calculative] thoughts of people who are not yet free from self-power therefore the Shōnin [Hōnen Shōnin] stated that 'no meaning is meaning'.[52]

In short, when our mind of self-power stops, 'When you stop thinking about its meaning, then the true meaning comes to you,' as the mind of Other Power starts working.

Part Two

ON THE DIVERGENCE
FROM SHINRAN SHŌNIN'S
TEACHING

一善人ナヲモテ往生ヲトグ　イハンヤ
悪人ヲヤ　シカルヲ世ノヒト　ツネニ
イハク　悪人ナヲ往生ス　イカニイハンヤ
善人ヲヤ　コノ條　一旦　ソノイハレアルニ
ニタレトモ　本願他力ノ意趣ニ　ソム
ケリ　ソノユヘハ　自力作善ノヒトハ
ヒトヘニ他力ヲ　タノムコヽロ　カケタル
アヒタ　旅隆ノ本願ニアラス　シカレ
トモ　自力ノコヽロ　ヒルカヘシテ　他力ヲ

Tannishō, Chapter 3A

タノミタテマツレハ　真實報土ノ往

生ヲトクルナリ　煩惱具足アツレハ

惣ヒノ行ニテモ　生死ヲハナルヽコト

アルヘカラサレヽヲ　アハレミタマヒテ　願ヲ

オコシタマフ本意　惡人成佛ノ

タメナレハ　他カノタノミタテマツル惡

人　モトモ往生ノ正因ナリ　ヨテ善

人タニコソ往生スレ　マヒテ惡人ハト

オホセ　サフフヒキ

Tannishō, Chapter 3B

Yuien's Concern over Doctrinal Divergence

TRANSLATION

Now, IN DAYS GONE BY, when our Master Shinran was still alive, those sharing one and the same faith and aspiring to the Land of Enjoyment, who journeyed to the distant capital with a common aim, all had the privilege of receiving our Master's instruction at firsthand. Lately, however, I have been informed that amongst the countless numbers of both young and old, who recite the *nembutsu* under the guidance of those older followers, there are now to be found a great many who are spreading erroneous views not taught by the Master himself. Such groundless views will be looked at in detail in the following chapters.

COMMENTARY

In Part Two, Yuien, the compiler of the *Tannishō*, reminisces about the time when he chanced to receive instruction directly from Shinran Shōnin himself, and compares his knowledge of the teaching to the situation in the present day community. Yuien, then a young priest, was present among the group of disciples "who journeyed to the distant capital with the common aim" to have an audience with Shinran Shōnin. The essential elements of the teaching that Yuien gathered from the great Master at the time, as well as over the years, eventually were written up as the chapters of the *Tannishō*.

Yuien was in fact quite an old man when he finally compiled this book. Some twenty years had passed since Shinran Shōnin's had died and it was almost as many years since that historic meeting between Shinran Shōnin and his disciples. On this occasion, working from original notes that Yuien must have taken long ago, the memories of that time came flooding back, as vivid as if he were again in the audience listening to Shinran Shōnin at firsthand.

As Yuien reflected on what Shinran Shōnin had so patiently taught him, it pained him to think how the current community had diverged from what his Master knew to be true. This special preface, inserted between the first and the second half of the work, thus conveys to us the deep sadness that Yuien felt over the present situation, where unfounded heretical views were currently rampant amongst fellow followers and threatened to eclipse the hard-won legacy of Shinran Shōnin's true teaching.

In contrast to Part One, Chapters 1–10, which consist almost entirely of Shinran Shōnin's sayings, Part Two, Chapters 11–18, consist of Yuien's interpretations of important doctrinal themes and his criticism of the heretical views prevailing in those days. In the course of the discussion, he introduces a number of direct quotations from Shinran Shōnin which serve as the basis of his interpretations and criticisms. These latter chapters provide a glimpse into the insights of shared religious experience that must have circulated amongst the disciples while the founder was alive. It is from this abundant resource that Yuien drew his materials to compile the *Tannishō*.

THE INCONCEIVABILITY OF
AMIDA BUDDHA

Chapter 11

TRANSLATION

There are some who, seeing illiterate people reciting the *nembutsu*, frighten them into confusion by asking whether they do so with faith in the inconceivability of the Vow or with faith in the inconceivability of the Name but without clarifying for them what these two kinds of inconceivability mean. This is a serious matter. To understand it clearly needs very careful thought.

By virtue of the inconceivability of the Vow, Amida Buddha devised the Name as something easy to retain and easy to recite and promised to welcome [to his Pure Land] all those who pronounced the *nembutsu*. Thus it is we come to recite the *nembutsu*, first and foremost in the belief that we will be delivered from birth-and-death by the inconceivability of Amida's Vow of Great Compassion. When we realise this, that it is all due to the Tathāgata's benevolent design that we are able to pronounce the Name, then our own way of thinking is not mixed with this at all. For this reason we are, in accordance with the Original Vow, to be born in the True Land of Enjoyment.

If we have pure faith in the inconceivability of the Vow, then do we also in the inconceivability of the Name. The inconceivability of the Vow and that of the Name coalesce into one, allowing no difference between them.

Furthermore if a person makes a distinction between good and evil acts, imagining the former helps, and the latter hinder, birth in the Pure Land and brings his own way of thinking into the matter, such a person is failing to entrust himself to the inconceivability of the Vow. He is working for his birth in the Pure Land depending on his own mind and thinks pronouncing the Name is something he achieves by himself. Such a person does not entrust himself to the inconceivability of the Name either. In spite of his lack of faith, he will still be born in the Borderland, the realm of Indolence and Pride or the Womb Palace of the Castle of Doubt and will eventually attain birth in the True Land of Enjoyment by virtue of 'the Vow that those who have reached this stage may attain birth in the Pure Land.' This is all due to the inconceivable Power of the Name. Since this is also none other than the inconceivability of the Vow, these two are one and the same.

COMMENTARY

> "The chapter on the erroneous view that makes a distinction between
> believing in the inconceivability of the Original Vow and
> believing in the inconceivability of the Name"
> — MYŌON-IN RYŌSHŌ —

The inseparability of the Original Vow and the Name

Thematically speaking, Chapters 1 and 11, which open Parts One and Two, respectively, are closely related in that the inconceivability of the Original Vow is discussed in both. The main subject of Chapter 1 is faith in the inconceivability of the Original Vow. In Chapter 11, however, Yuien compares and contrasts the inconceivability of the Vow to the inconceivability of the Name and concludes that they were really one and the same originally. In Chapter 1 Shinran Shōnin refers to the inconceivability of the Original Vow as a matter of faith, and in Chapter 11 Yuien confirms that the inconceivability of the Original Vow is not separate from the inconceivability of the Name, because the Name is already included in Amida's Original Vow. Thus Amida's Name is actually the outcome of his Original Vow.

What is important when leading the Shin Buddhist life is keeping the right balance between these two points, that is, the inconceivability of the Original Vow and the inconceivability of the Name. Lose this balance and there arise lopsided erroneous views on what comprises faith in the Pure Land tradition. Needless to say a harmonious balance is to be kept through true faith alone, because in true faith the inconceivability of the Vow and that of the Name are originally one and the same.

As explained in the Preface to Part Two, the following eight chapters are concerned with the erroneous views in Shin Buddhist faith. Yuien begins each of those chapters with a short summary of the erroneous view which he is going to deal with in the rest of the chapter. In this case, it is summarised in the opening paragraph.

Myōon-in Ryōshō calls this "the chapter on the erroneous view that makes a distinction between believing in the inconceivability of the Original Vow and believing in the Inconceivability of the Name." What does this mean? According to Myōon-in Ryōshō, who was a person well versed in the study of heretical views in Shin Buddhism, the sort of view that understands the disparity between the Vow and the Name ends up overemphasising faith in the Original Vow at the expense of the practice of pronouncing the Name. This is caused by an incorrect attitude which regards the *nembutsu*, or pronouncing the Name, merely as a practice engendered by self-power and not as the working of Other Power. Out of attachment to the notion of having to abandon one's self-power, one tends to overemphasise the inconceivability of the Original Vow. This is far removed from the attainment of true faith.

The divergence from true faith

Roughly speaking, the eight kinds of divergence from true faith can be classified into two categories:

1) erroneous views that neglect the *nembutsu* as a practice engendered by self-power, instead emphasising the inconceivability of the Original Vow as distinct from the inconceivability of the Name, and

2) those that concentrate exclusively on the practice of the *nembutsu* as the means of birth in the Pure Land and ignore the importance of faith in the Original Vow.

Chapters 11, 12, 15 and 17 refer to the first kind, while Chapters 13, 14, 16 and 18 refer to the latter kind.

Although the heretical views that fall into the first category emphasise the importance of faith in the Original Vow, because they understand the Original Vow to be separate from the Name, the faith in the Original Vow maintained by such views is not perfect. On the other hand, because the views in the second category place such emphasis on the exclusive practice of the *nembutsu* as 'a good deed' or the cause of birth in the Pure Land, so as to fail to appreciate the importance of the Original Vow, their *nembutsu* lacks the characteristic of Other Power, the most important aspect of the Pure Land tradition.

Compared to the first ten chapters of Part One, the last eight of Part Two seem far more complicated, as they not only include many doctrinal reflections but also relate the difficult problems facing the actual religious community. Regarding the details of those complicated problems and the ways of resolving the difficulties, I would like to touch upon them in each chapter as they arise.

As Chapter 11 is the first of the following eight chapters, it has the pivotal role of representing all the others. In this respect Chapter 11 not only refers to the divergence from true faith that falls into the first category but also discusses the crucial point included in the second category: the attachment to the practice of *nembutsu* as something good or as the means of attaining birth in the Pure Land. This Yuien deals with in the long final paragraph of the text.

What is referred to in the last paragraph as 'the Vow that those who have reached this stage may attain birth in the Pure Land' is the Twentieth Vow, which reads as follows:

> If, upon my attaining Buddhahood, all beings in the ten quarters who, hearing my Name, should cherish the thought of my Country (Pure Land) and who, planting the root of all virtues (the Name or *nembutsu*), should turn it over in sincerity to being born in my Country, should fail to obtain the said result (birth in the Pure Land), may I not attain Supreme Enlightenment.[53]

The Twentieth Vow thus declares that, if all beings pronounce the Buddha Name with sincerity, even if they do so with self-power while still discriminating between good and evil, they may eventually attain birth in the Pure Land.

In short, if only you practice the *nembutsu* with sincerity, you cannot fail to attain birth in the Pure Land; this is sure to come about by dint of the inconceivable working of the Name, as vowed in the Twentieth Vow. By virtue of this Vow even those who practice the *nembutsu* by self-power will eventually be born in the Pure Land. So Yuien says, "This is all due to the inconceivable Power of the Name. Since this is also none other than the inconceivability of the Vow, these two are one and the same."

Now, let us turn our attention to this chapter's key word, 'inconceivability'. Granted, to try to 'think on the inconceivable' is a bit of a contradiction in terms. Etymologically, the original Sanskrit word for 'inconceivable' is *acintya*, meaning 'beyond thinking' or 'non-thinking,' and plays an important historical role in Buddhist thought. In the following I would like to briefly elucidate the positive meaning of this key notion in Shin Buddhist spirituality.

Shinran Shōnin refers to the Original Vow for universal deliverance as something inconceivable, and entirely beyond our understanding. But why should it be inconceivable? After all, Amida's Vow to save all beings without discriminating amongst them would appear to be as ideal a Vow as anyone might conceive. Why then is it beyond our ability to conceive? Although it appears very difficult to conceive, it is not in fact so completely irrational as to fall outside the realm of pure reason or objective thinking. Why then does Shinran Shōnin say Amida's Vow is inconceivable?

In fact it is Shinran Shōnin's acute awareness of the irredeemable nature of his own existence that makes him refer to the Original Vow as something inconceivable. The Original Vow is inconceivable because it saves the unsavable, even the grossly evil, loving all beings without discrimination of any sort. When the notion of "awareness of one's own existence" is brought into play, then Amida's Original Vow for universal deliverance is seen as inconceivable. The salvation of the unsavable is thus paradoxical, going beyond the bounds of our common sense.

In other words, the Original Vow is entirely beyond the distinction between good and evil which belongs to the realm of ethical consciousness. When you become aware of the irredeemable nature of your own existence, nothing will sound more incredible than to hear the Original Vow vows to save all beings without any discrimination amongst them, making no distinction even between the good and the evil. The Shin Buddhist experience of faith takes place the moment you entrust yourself 'as you are' to this inconceivable Original Vow. There is no need to make oneself more 'savable'; the Original Vow unconditionally extends its love and salvation to everyone just as they are, bar none. In other words, it is the paradox of the unfailing salvation of the unsavable through the unconditional love of the Awakened.

The Original Vow and the Buddha Name are one. When true faith is awakened and you return to the Original Vow, entrusting your very life to its inconceivable working, you will also find the Buddha Name working from within, embracing the whole of your existence just as it is, in its own inconceivable way. Once true faith is attained, the Name works with absolute freedom throughout the whole individual. The Name begins to well up quite naturally from the depths of true faith, as the pronouncing of the Name, Namu-Amida-butsu, flows out effortlessly, its waters irrigating every corner of your being. In this sense, the Name is the *nembutsu* of Other Power, the natural working of the Original Vow. In true faith, as Yuien correctly points out, the inconceivability of the Original Vow and the inconceivability of the Name are not separate but one and the same.

Concerning the oneness of the Original Vow and the Name, there are a few letters by Shinran Shōnin addressed to his disciples that touch on the subject. Let me quote two of them, from the *Lamp for the Latter Age.*

The Vow and the Name are One

I have read your letter carefully.

I do not really understand how such a question as yours can arise, for although we speak of the Vow and the Name they are not two different things. There is no Name separate from the Vow and there is no Vow separate from the Name. Just saying this will, however, amount to imposing my way of thinking [to the matter]. Once you simply entrust yourself to the Vow as something inconceivable, do so to the Name as well and pronounce the Name in one thought-moment — why do you need to impose your way of thinking to it?

I wonder why you talk about all your attempts to know things distinctively through listening and learning. It seems to me that such attempts of yours have only led you into confusion. It is all utterly wrong. Once you come to entrust yourself [to Amida] as something inconceivable, you should not impose your own way of thinking in this or that fashion. There must be no room for imposing your own way of thinking.

Respectfully.

You should just leave everything to the Tathāgata.[54]

The nembutsu leads you to the Land of Enjoyment

Concerning your question about the *nembutsu*, it is utterly wrong to look down on people who believe in birth [in the Pure Land] through the *nembutsu*, saying that they are destined for the Borderland. Amida vowed to take into the Land of Utmost Bliss those who recite his Name. Thus to recite the *nembutsu* with deep faith is to be in perfect accordance with Amida's Original Vow. Though a person may have faith, if he does not recite the Name, his faith will avail him nothing. And conversely, though he may single-mindedly pronounce the Name, if his faith is shallow again he will not be able to attain birth. Thus it is only the person who both deeply believes in birth through the *nembutsu* and undertakes to recite the Name who is certain to be born in the Land of Enjoyment.

In short, though a person may recite the Name, if he does not believe in the Original Vow, or Other Power, then he will be surely be born in the Borderland. How then can it be that those who do have deep faith in the Power of the Original Vow may also be born there? Please recite the *nembutsu* fully understanding what I have told you above.

My life has reached the fullness of its years. It is certain that I will be born in the Pure Land before you. And it is certain that I will be waiting for you there. Respectfully.[55]

In everyday life you will notice the Buddha Name working through other individuals, such as your teachers or your Dharma friends, in an incomparable, inexplicable, and inconceivable way. This is known in Shin Buddhism as "All Buddhas' pronouncing the Name." The *nembutsu* issuing from true faith in the Original Vow, is called the *nembutsu* of Other Power, or the *nembutsu* as the working of the Original Vow and when you encounter someone else pronouncing the *nembutsu* with pure faith, this person's *nembutsu* stands for "All Buddhas' pronouncing the Name." This wonderful experience of meeting another person calling the Buddha Name with their whole being will become an opportunity for you to start hearing the Pure Land teaching, just as it was in the case of Shinran Shōnin's encounter with Hōnen Shōnin. Let me quote from one of *The Letters* (*Ofumi*), by Rennyo Shōnin:

> 'Hearing that Name' is not simply hearing the Six-character Name (Namu-Amida-butsu) pointlessly and fruitlessly. 'Hearing that Name' actually means that when we meet a good teacher, receive his teaching, and entrust ourselves to the Name that he recites, then Amida Buddha saves us without fail. This attainment of faith is described in the *Larger Sūtra of Eternal Life* as 'rejoicing in the awakening of faith'.[56]

There is also an interesting story with a humorous twist from the *Rennyo Shōnin Goichidaiki Kikigaki* (A Record of the Venerable Rennyo's Sayings and Doings Throughout His Life) that shows Rennyo Shōnin's sharp insight into religious life grounded in his faith. It goes as follows:

> Hōkyō-bō (Rennyo Shōnin's disciple) said to Rennyo Shōnin, 'When the scroll of the Name you had given me was burned, it became six Buddhas. What an inconceivable happening (a miracle) it was!' Then Rennyo Shōnin replied, 'It is not inconceivable at all. It is no wonder for the Buddha's Name to become Buddhas. What is [truly] inconceivable is that an ignorant person with bad karma is [assured of] becoming a Buddha at the moment of entrusting himself to Amida'.[57]

In sum, when one entrusts oneself to Amida Buddha, one's attachment to self-power stops and there is no need to ask whether the inconceivability of the Name and the inconceivability of the Original Vow are one or distinct. It is only by returning to true faith that we can solve this problem.

FAITH IS AN EXPERIENCE
BEYOND LEARNING

Chapter 12

TRANSLATION

Some followers hold that those who do not read and study the Sūtras and commentaries cannot be assured of birth in the Pure Land. This view could not be further from the truth.

All the sacred documents that expound the truth of Other Power clearly show that everyone who believes in the Original Vow and recites the *nembutsu* will become a Buddha [attaining birth in the Pure Land]. What need is there of further learning for birth [in the Pure Land]?

To be sure anyone who has doubts about their birth in the Pure Land should study hard to try and grasp the purport of the Original Vow, but it is a great pity that there are some who fail to understand the true meaning of the sacred texts despite their best efforts to read and study the Sūtras and commentaries.

Because Amida's Name can easily be recited by those who are unlettered and ignorant of what the Sūtras and commentaries mean, such practice is called the Easy Way. Those who consider learning essential belong to the order of the Path of Sages. Their practice is called the Difficult Way. As for those who engage in academic study, mistakenly looking for fame and wealth, there is an authoritative passage [from Shinran Shōnin's letter]: "I am doubtful of their birth in the Pure Land after this life."

At present those that follow the exclusive practice of the *nembutsu* and those who follow the Path of Sages are locked together in doctrinal dispute, each side insisting that its own doctrine is superior and the other inferior. This leads to the emergence of forces inimical to the Dharma and the slandering of the Dharma. Does it not amount after all to the slandering and destruction of one's own Dharma? Even if all the other schools join forces in attacking you and declare that the *nembutsu* is just for worthless people and that this teaching is shallow and vulgar, you should not try and answer their criticism but simply reply, 'As we are convinced that foolish beings of inferior ability such as ourselves, who may not know a single letter of the alphabet, will be delivered through faith alone, this teaching is the supreme Dharma for us, though it may seem base to those of superior ability. No matter how wonderful another teaching may be, we cannot follow it, for it is beyond our capability. Since the basic intention of all Buddhas is simply to free everyone, not just the personal self but others too, from birth-and-death, please leave us alone to go our own way.' If you respond to them in this way without any rancor, why should they harm you?

Moreover, there is an authoritative passage [in the *Shichikajō no kishōmon* 七箇条起請文] which reads, 'Where there are disputes, all kinds of blind passions arise. A person would be wise to stay far away from such disputation.'

The late Master also said, "The Buddha foretold that there would be some who trusted in this teaching and there would be also others who reviled it. I already have faith in the teaching and there are others who slander it. By this fact I know that what the Buddha taught is true. Therefore you should be confident that your birth in the Pure Land is all the more certain. If, by chance, there were none who reviled the teaching, then we would wonder why there were no slanderers whereas there were believers. I do not mean by this that the teaching should necessarily be slandered. I merely talk about the fact that the Buddha, foreseeing there would be believers and slanderers, foretold this so that his followers would not harbor doubts in the future."

Nowadays, however, there appear to be people who study the Buddha's teaching specifically to stop others from slandering it. Are they really content to dissipate their energies in argument and debate? The more one studies, the more clearly one should understand Amida's true intent and realise the boundlessness of his Compassionate Vow. Only if one becomes the kind of scholar who is capable of persuading people that the Original Vow does not discriminate between good and evil, pure and impure and that they are perfectly able to be born in the Pure Land despite their imperfections that might have made them doubt about their birth, only then will scholarly life take on any meaning.

If you insist that learning is essential for birth and consequently intimidate even those who happen to live the *nembutsu* selflessly in accordance with the Original Vow, your behaviour is nothing less than a diabolical obstruction of the Dharma and a hostile act against the Buddha. Those who insist on doing so not only lack faith in the Other Power but also confuse others with false thoughts.

You should humbly stand in awe [of the Buddha-dharma] lest you go against the teaching of the late Master and also lest you are in disaccord with the Original Vow of Amida Buddha.

COMMENTARY

"The chapter that deals with the problem of
trying to understand the *nembutsu* by learning"

— MYŌON-IN RYŌSHŌ —

As mentioned previously, Myōon-in Ryōshō classifies the eight kinds of divergence from true faith into two categories: 1) erroneous views that neglect the *nembutsu* or pronouncing the Name as being a practice engendered by self-power and emphasise instead the inconceivability of the Original Vow as distinct from the inconceivability of the Name, and 2) those that concentrate exclusively on the practice of the *nembutsu* as the means of birth in the Pure Land and ignore the importance of faith in the Original Vow. According to Myōon-in Ryōshō Chapter 12 is one of the chapters that refers to the first kind of erroneous view.

What Yuien, the compiler of the *Tannishō*, wanted to protect from the various erroneous views prevailing amongst the *nembutsu* followers was the tradition of the true faith that he received from his master Shinran Shōnin at firsthand. In the Shin Buddhist 'true faith', faith in the inconceivability of the Original Vow and faith in the inconceivability of the *nembutsu* are harmoniously integrated. In other words, as beautifully expressed in the second paragraph of Chapter 12, it is the awareness that "everyone who believes in the Original Vow and recites the *nembutsu* will become a Buddha." It is simple faith in the inconceivability of the Original Vow in which Amida Buddha vows to save all those who pronounce his Name, without any discrimination amongst them at all. Through this simple faith the *nembutsu* of gratitude wells up from within.

The divergent view that is dealt with in this chapter is the opinion that in order to attain faith it is absolutely necessary for us to study and gain knowledge about the Buddha-dharma. Yuien states at the beginning of the chapter that "some followers hold that those who do not read and study the Sūtras and commentaries cannot be assured of birth in the Pure Land. This view could not be further from the truth." Yuien severely criticises those followers who hold that faith should be based on academic understanding or knowledge. Although they insist on their faith, it is actually nothing but a show of intellectual understanding, entirely different from the Shin Buddhist true faith of absolutely entrusting oneself to the Original Vow. This erroneous view does not realise the *nembutsu* as the working of the Buddha, but takes it instead merely as an object of intellectual concern.

Yuien talks quite a lot on the subject of 'religious experience beyond learning,' but his essential message can be summarised under the following three headings: 1) religious experience is beyond learning; 2) only when you are aware of its limitations will academic study help you to attain religious awakening (faith-experience or Enlightenment); and 3) those who are unaware of the previous two points are very dangerous.

1) *Religious experience is beyond learning.*

Our going beyond understanding is an essential quality of any authentic religious experience. This is specifically expressed with absolute confidence by Zen people. D. T. Suzuki, for example, noticed such a quality in Shinran Shōnin's religious experience. To quote from his book, the *Buddha of Infinite Light*:

> Shinran Shōnin's religious experience deepened during his period of exile. While living in the culturally deprived areas of Japan, he developed a profound understanding of the needs of the common people. In those days Buddhism was basically an aristocratic religion, and the study of Buddhism was confined to the learned class. Their approach was intellectual and rational, but Shinran Shōnin knew that that was not the way to the authentic religious life. There had to be a more direct way, a religious experience that did not require the medium of learning or elaborate rituals. All such things had to be cast aside in order for one to have religious awakening. Shinran Shōnin experienced this for himself, and discovered the most direct way to that awakening.[58]

In this context Chapter 12 reminds us of Chapter 2. These two chapters are closely related to each other. Shinran Shōnin's words in Chapter 2 show how clearly he is aware of the essence of his faith-experience as something different from scholarly knowledge. Chapter 12 can be seen as Yuien's interpretation of Shinran Shōnin's words found in Chapter 2.

> As for myself, Shinran, there is nothing else involved apart from simple faith in the *nembutsu*, according to the instruction of my good teacher, 'Just say the *nembutsu* so as to be saved by Amida'.

2) *Only when you are aware of its limitations will academic study help you attain religious awakening (faith-experience or Enlightenment).*

As clearly expressed in the words, "All the sacred documents that expound the truth of Other Power clearly show that everyone who believes in the Original Vow and recites the *nembutsu* will become a Buddha [attaining birth in the Pure Land]. What need is there of other learning?" All that you need here is just to attain faith-experience. If you are academically inclined to study religion, you might think that your study will take you to the point where you can take the leap to attain religious awakening. However, it is extremely important for you to know how qualitatively different academic study and religious experience are. Even if philosophy has led you to the threshold of religious experience, no amount of philosophical reflection can substitute for religious experience itself.

Academic study is just one of the various conditions that can lead people to religion. On the other hand, if you assume that without academic study one cannot attain religious experience, this is a serious misunderstanding. If you persist in this misunderstanding, it will bring about a great confusion not only in your personal life but also in your social sphere. And so Yuien says:

> If you insist that learning is essential for birth and consequently intimidate even those who happen to live the *nembutsu* selflessly in accordance with the Original Vow, your behaviour is nothing less than a diabolical obstruction of the Dharma and a hostile act against the Buddha. Those who insist on doing so not only lack faith in the Other Power but also confuse others with false thoughts.

3) *Those who are unaware of the previous two points are very dangerous.*

There are those who think that their field of study has covered the entire realm of religion, and who try and use their intellect or reason to control it. This will cause them to use the knowledge they have gained to attain worldly goals such as wealth and fame. Eventually this will lead them to treat religion as another worldly object, and, as a result, they will end up destroying the realm of true religious meaning.

I would like to emphasise that what is most important in our daily lives is to reverently turn our thoughts to the Buddha in constant awareness of the limitations of one's own understanding. As a result of their reverential respect for the Buddha day in and day out, Shin Buddhists remain extremely humble in giving expression to their faith-experience that goes beyond the limits of ordinary understanding. Hence there emerges the somewhat self-effacing attitude that can be unmistakably seen in this chapter of the *Tannishō*. The deep humility shown by these followers of Shin Buddhism is something rather beautiful and worthy of note in the history of human spirituality.

ABSOLUTE RELIANCE ON
THE ORIGINAL VOW

Chapter 13

TRANSLATION

There are some people who insist that those who are not alarmed by their own evil because of [their reliance on] the inconceivable power of Amida's Original Vow are relying too heavily on the Original Vow and will definitely fail to be born in the Pure Land.

Such a view betrays a lack of trust in the Original Vow and a lack of understanding of the way good and evil deeds result from past karma. Good thoughts arise due to the effect of past good [karma] and evil thoughts do likewise under the influence of [past] evil karma.

The late Master said, "You should understand that even if it looks as insignificant as a speck of dust on the tip of a single hair from a rabbit's coat or a sheep's fleece, every evil you commit is nothing but the product of your past karma."

On another occasion he asked me, "O Yuien-bō! Would you believe whatever I told you?"

"Yes, Master, I would," was my reply.

"And are you sure you would not disobey me?"

"Yes, I am sure," I answered.

"Suppose," he went on, "you were asked to murder a thousand men on the understanding that your birth in the Pure Land depended on it."

"Even if it were you giving the order," I protested, "I still would not be able to kill a single person."

"In that case," replied my master, "why did you say you would never disobey my orders whatever they might be? You can see now from this that, if it really were in accordance with your karma and you were required to do so, you would indeed be able to kill a thousand people for the sake of birth in the Pure Land. You yourself would not kill, not because your thoughts are good but because you yourself do not have the karma to kill even one single person. And yet, though you may not wish to injure anyone, it is still possible you might be led to kill a hundred or a thousand people."

The point being made here is that, because we judge simplistically that thinking good thoughts is good for birth in the Pure Land and thinking evil thoughts bad, we are actually failing to realise that it is only the inconceivable power of the Original Vow that enables any of us to attain birth at all.

There was once a man who had fallen into a completely erroneous way of thinking. He taught that, because the Vow was made to save those who had committed evil, one should actually commit evil on purpose as a way of attaining birth. As rumours of this man's evil deeds spread, Shinran Shōnin wrote in one of the letters addressed to his followers, "Do not take poison just because there is an antidote." By this admonishment Shinran Shōnin sought to put a stop to people's erroneous attachment to such a belief. In no way did he mean that evil could obstruct birth in the Pure Land.

Shinran Shōnin also observed, "If the only way we could entrust ourselves to the Original Vow were through observing the moral precepts and upholding the rules of order, how could we ever free ourselves from birth-and-death?" Wretched beings that we are, it is only through our own personal encounter with the Original Vow that we are truly able to rely on it. Indeed how would we come to commit evil acts if there were not some karmic cause within ourselves?

"This holds true," the Master continued, "for those who gain their livelihood by casting nets or fishing in the seas and rivers, for those who support themselves by hunting beasts and fowl in the mountains and fields and for those who pass their lives conducting trade or cultivating the fields. If their respective karma has matured sufficiently they will commit any kind of act."

Despite the Master's statement there are some followers nowadays affecting to be 'seekers for Rebirth', who claim that only good persons are entitled to pronounce the Name. Indeed they sometimes even go so far as to put up notices at places of worship, saying that those who have committed such and such an act are prohibited from entering. Are these not the sort of people who 'while outwardly demonstrating how wise, good and diligent they are, inwardly remain false and deceitful'?

Evil acts committed by people relying too heavily on the Original Vow are also actually caused by their past karma. If we thus acknowledge that all good and evil deeds are the result of our past karma and if we put our trust instead in the Original Vow, then we will find ourselves in accord with Other Power. *The Essentials of Faith Alone* asks: "How can you fathom the extent of Amida's power and claim to see in yourself too much karmic evil to be saved?" It is actually because we are guilty of relying too heavily on the Original Vow that we finally come to attain the faith to entrust ourselves to Other Power.

If we were to attain faith in the Original Vow only after having extinguished all our karmic evil and blind passions, then there would be no need for us to rely on the Original Vow at all. But if we had been able to extinguish all our blind passions like this, we would already be Buddhas and if we were Buddhas, the Original Vow, the fruit of five kalpas of profound meditation, would be of no use to us.

Those who chastise others for relying too heavily on the Original Vow appear themselves to be filled with blind passions and impurities. Do they not rely on the Original Vow? What kind of evil-doing is caused by relying too heavily on the

Original Vow and what kind of evil-doing is caused by not doing so? Is not all their criticism just so much childish talk?

COMMENTARY

> "The chapter that deals with the problem of prohibiting people
> from relying too heavily on the Original Vow"
> — MYŌON-IN RYŌSHŌ —

It is not easy to understand this chapter because Yuien's argument here is not only deeply theological in essence but it also makes use of highly complex terminology from the early stage of Shin Buddhism. In order to understand what Yuien is trying to say in this chapter, we should clarify the historical background of how he developed his argument.

Chapter 13 should remind us of Chapter 3, just as Chapters 11 and 12 remind us respectively of Chapters 1 and 2. These two chapters are very closely related to one another in the way they deal with the salvation of evildoers. In this context the word 'evil' is not used in an ethical sense rather in a religious one, referring to an awareness of one's karmic evil, the state of one's remaining in despair, still inflicting harm upon oneself and others, despite the fact that one finds oneself already embraced by Amida's unconditional love.

In Chapter 3 Shinran Shōnin says, "Even a good person can attain birth [in the Pure Land], how much more readily, then, the person with bad karma" and also, "It is impossible for us, fully burdened with blind passions, to free ourselves from birth-and-death through the pursuance of any religious practice whatsoever. Full of sadness over this impossible situation, Amida brought forth his Vow, the essential purport of which is the person with bad karma's attainment of Buddhahood. Hence those who are aware of their bad karma and so entrust themselves to Other Power are precisely the ones who possess the true key to birth [in the Pure Land]."

However, there were some people who misunderstood what Shinran Shōnin meant and considered his words to mean that they could do anything they wished, whether good or evil. Some of them even declared one should do evil purposely because Amida's Original Vow of unconditional love did not discriminate against anyone. Shinran Shōnin of course admonished them to cast off such wrong-headed views, referred to as 'relying too heavily on the Original Vow.' This matter was a very serious problem at that time.

Let me highlight the problem with a few examples from the *Lamp for the Latter Age*, a collection of Shinran Shōnin's letters to his disciples.

From Letter 16:

I have heard that, despite the fact you know nothing of the scriptures or of the true foundation of the Pure Land teaching, you are telling people who are appallingly self-indulgent and lacking in shame that a person should do evil just as he or she desires. This is absolutely wrong. Were you not aware that I finally had to break off relations with Zenjō-bō, who lived in the northern district, [for propagating a similar view]?

If a person, who justifies himself by saying he is a foolish being, can do anything he wants, then is he also [permitted] to steal or to murder? Even that person who has been inclined to steal will naturally undergo a change of heart if he comes to say the *nembutsu* aspiring for the Buddha Land. Yet people who show no such sign are being told that it is permissible to do wrong; this should never be allowed to occur under any circumstances.

Maddened beyond control by blind passions, we do things we should not and say things we should not and think things we should not. But if a person is deceitful in his relations with others and does what he should not and says what he should not because he thinks it will not hinder his birth, then this is not an instance of being maddened by blind passions. Since he purposely does these things, they are simply misdeeds that should never have been done.

If you say something to stop the wrongdoing of the people of Kashima and Namekata and correct the distorted views of the people in that area, it will be a sign that you are representing me.

It is deplorable that you have told people to abandon themselves to their heart's desires and to do anything they want. One must seek to cast off the evil of this world and to cease doing wretched deeds; this is what it means to reject (renounce) the world and to live the *nembutsu*. When people who may have said the *nembutsu* for many years [continue to] abuse others in word or deed, there is no indication of their having rejected this world. Thus Shandao teaches in the passage on the mind of sincerity that we should be careful to keep our distance from those people who are given to evil. When has it ever been said that one should act in accordance with one's mind and heart, which are evil? You, who are totally ignorant of the Sūtras and commentaries and ignorant of the Tathāgata's words, must never instruct others in this way.[59]

From Letter 19:

Signs of long years of saying the *nembutsu* and aspiring for birth can be seen in the change in the heart that had once been bad and in the deep warmth for friends and fellow-practicers; this is a sign of their rejecting the world. You should understand this fully.

People who look down on teachers and who speak ill of the masters, they commit slander of the Dharma. Those who speak ill of their parents are guilty of the five grave offenses. We should keep our distance from them. Thus, since Zenjō-bō, who lived in the northern district, abused his parents and slandered me in various ways, I had no close feelings for him and did not encourage him to come to see me. Those who belittle the example of Myōhō-bō, even though they hear of his birth, are certainly not his fellow-practicers.

I hear that you urge people who are drunk with the wine of ignorance to become even more drunk and allow those who have been accustomed to dine on the three poisons to partake of even more poison, telling them that they should enjoy it—how painful it is [to hear]! It is sad enough they are drunk on the wine of ignorance, yet [to hear you] tell them to partake with pleasure of the three poisons while the poisons have yet to subside and they have yet to become sober from the drunkenness of ignorance. Please understand this fully.[60]

From Letter 20:

There was a time for each of you when you knew nothing of Amida's Vow and did not say the Name of Amida Buddha, but now, guided by the compassionate means of Śākyamuni and Amida, you have begun to hear the Vow. Formerly you were drunk with the wine of ignorance and had a liking only for the three poisons of greed, anger, and folly, but since you have begun to hear the Buddha's Vow you have gradually awakened from the drunkenness of ignorance, gradually rejected the three poisons, and come to prefer at all times the medicine of Amida Buddha.

In contrast, how lamentable that people who have not fully awakened from drunkenness are urged to become even more drunk, and those still in the grips of poison encouraged to take yet more poison. It is indeed deplorable to give way to the impulses with the excuse that one is by nature possessed of blind passions, excusing acts that should not be committed, words that should not be said, and thoughts that should not be harboured, and to say that one may follow one's desires in any way whatever. It is like offering more wine to a person before he has yet to become sober or urging him to partake of even more poison before the poison has worn off. 'Here is some medicine, so drink all the poison you like'—words like these should never be said.

In people who have long heard the Buddha's Name and said the *nembutsu*, surely there are signs of their rejecting the evil of this world and signs of their desire to cast off the evil in themselves. When people first begin to hear the Buddha's Vow, they wonder, having become thoroughly aware of the karmic evil in their hearts and minds, how they will ever attain birth as they are. To such people we teach that, since we are possessed of blind passions, the Buddha receives us without judging whether our hearts are good or bad.

When, upon hearing this, a person's trust in the Buddha has grown deep, he or she comes to abhor such a self and to lament continued existence in birth-and-death; such a person then joyfully says the Name of Amida Buddha deeply entrusting himself to the Vow. That people seek to stop doing wrong at their heart's whim, although earlier they were inclined to such things and committed them as their minds dictated, is surely a sign of their having rejected this world.

Moreover, our mind of awakened faith that aspires for attainment of birth arises through the encouragement of Śākyamuni and Amida. Once this true mind is made to arise in us, how can we remain as we were, possessed of blind passions?[61]

As can be seen from these quotations, Shinran Shōnin showed his followers the direction they should take, but further serious problems arose due to the misinterpretation of his admonitions. Some leaders prohibited others from relying too heavily on the Original Vow and some wanted to control their followers by issuing religious prohibitions. Their behaviour was totally contrary to what Shinran Shōnin expected from them. To control people by rules, whether ethical or legal, can never substitute for the way of true religious life. This is the main theme of Chapter 13. What is most important is to entrust oneself to the Original Vow, stop all wrongdoing and do for the doing that which is good while keeping oneself free of any attachment.

Buddhism is not determinism

Another point that interests me in this chapter is Yuien's way of understanding the notion of karma. If you look at your present existence while also bearing in mind the past, you can see with hindsight that your present existence is entirely the result of your past karma. As Shinran Shōnin puts it, "You should understand that even if it looks as insignificant as a speck of dust on the tip of a single hair from a rabbit's coat or a sheep's fleece, every evil you commit is nothing but the product of your past karma." In this respect the notion of karma sounds quite deterministic. But Buddhism is not determinism. Every instant that you walk into the future with full awareness, you are adding something new to your karmic existence; it is an act (karma) and has an immediate effect on others. As everything interacts with everything else, you change the world creatively and dynamically.

This creative activity is not actually expressed in the text because Yuien's argument in Chapter 13 is rather defensive. Our faith in the Original Vow is, however, the very portal to such a creative world. As everything changes, everybody is born into a new self at every given instant. This is well expressed by Shinran Shōnin in the last paragraph of the last quotation from the *Lamp for the Latter Age*, where he says,

Moreover, our mind of awakened faith that aspires for attainment of birth arises through the encouragement of Śākyamuni and Amida. Once this true mind is made to arise in us, how can we remain as we were, possessed of blind passions?[62]

Allow me to conclude with a quote from a talk I gave several years ago:

The Shin Buddhist respect for life, awakened through pure faith in Amida's unconditional love, is clearly manifest in their relationships with those around them—their family members, for example, and their Dharma friends in the Saṃgha. 'Respect for life', or the imperative 'Love your life and love others just as they are', should first be practiced in one's relationships with those closest to one. In this respect family life (married life, the parent-child relationship, brotherly and sisterly love, etc.) and Saṃgha life are incredibly important in Shin Buddhism. Indeed, given the title of this talk, 'Shin Buddhism and Ethics,' we might well say that family life and Saṃgha life are the ethical foundations of Shin Buddhism. Love for those around one will then exercise an influence on society as a whole, producing a pattern of wave-like movements, because everything interacts with everything else. As with a room hung with mirrors, each mirror is reflected in the others and one mirror reflects them all. What is important in daily life is to do for the doing what seems good at the time and then instantly forget it, pronouncing instead Amida's Name with the deepest gratitude. As D. T. Suzuki said to me on one occasion, 'Practice the *nembutsu* just like the wind flowing effortlessly through the sky!'"

RECITING THE NEMBUTSU WITH GRATITUDE FOR THE BUDDHA'S BENEVOLENCE

Chapter 14

TRANSLATION

There are those who insist that one should believe that reciting the *nembutsu* just once is sufficient to eradicate the heavy burden of evil karma accumulated throughout eight thousand million kalpas.

Such a view relates to a person who, having committed the ten evils and the five grave offences during their lifetime, without ever once reciting the *nembutsu*, finally on their deathbed comes face to face with a good teacher for the very first time. This teacher tells them that if they recite the *nembutsu* just once, the evil karma of eight thousand million kalpas will be expunged and that if they recite it ten times, the heavy burden of evil karma of eighty thousand million kalpas will be eradicated and they will thus attain birth [in the Pure Land]. This passage [from the *Meditation Sūtra*] about reciting the *nembutsu* once or else ten times would appear to have been included in order to make us aware of the gravity of the ten evils and the five grave offences. Such a way of thinking, while pointing to how beneficial the *nembutsu* is for the dissolution of evil karma, is nevertheless far removed from the tenets of our faith. The reason for this is that, at the very moment when we are truly awakened, having been illuminated by Amida's Light, we are endowed with Diamond-like Faith and join the company of the truly assured [of birth in the Pure Land]. Thus, when our lives reach their end, all our blind passions and evil hindrances are transformed into the recognition that there is no birth [and no death].

How could we, miserable wrongdoers, be delivered from birth-and-death were it not for Amida's Compassionate Vow? Bear this in mind and cherish the thought that the *nembutsu* you keep reciting throughout your life is entirely the expression of your gratitude to Amida Tathāgata for all he has done to save you through his Great Compassion.

To believe that every recitation of the *nembutsu* has the power to extinguish your evil karma will merely lead you to strive to wipe out your evil karma through your own efforts in order to attain birth in the Pure Land. In that case, given that every thought you have throughout the whole course of your life is a fetter binding you to birth-and-death (transmigration), you will only be able to attain birth in the Pure Land if you recite the *nembutsu* without ceasing right up until the very moment you die. We are, however, constrained by the effects of our past karma and so may very well die without dwelling in right-mindedness, for at any time we can meet with an unexpected accident or suffer the agonies of a serious disease. In such circumstances it would be very difficult for us to recite the *nembutsu*, but then how would we eradicate the karmic evil committed during the last fraction of our lives? And if it were not expunged, would it not be impossible for us to attain birth in the Pure Land?

It is quite possible that, through circumstances beyond our control, we may come to commit an evil act and die without ever being able to recite the *nembutsu* in our final hour. Even under such circumstances, if we have entrusted ourselves to Amida's Vow that vows to embrace all and abandon none, then we will still be able attain birth instantly in the Pure Land. Moreover, if the *nembutsu* wells up spontaneously as our time of attaining Supreme Enlightenment approaches, we will find ourselves placing more and more reliance on Amida Buddha and feeling more and more grateful to him for all he has done for us.

Those who desire to eradicate evil karma by reciting the *nembutsu* are relying on self-power. The fact that their basic intent is to maintain a state of right-mindedness when their lives end means they have no faith in Other Power.

COMMENTARY

"The chapter [that criticises the misleading belief] that
one can eradicate evil karma through
a single utterance of the *nembutsu*"
— MYŌON-IN RYŌSHŌ —

According to Shinran Shōnin the true purpose of saying Amida's Name with pure faith in the Buddha is not in fact the elimination of evil karma. It took a long time for this to become clear because of the existence of Pure Land texts that placed great emphasis on the idea of birth in the Pure Land at the moment of death. Shinran Shōnin finally took it upon himself to reinterpret all the Pure Land documents in light of his own faith-experience. What he clarified thereby was the experience of 'salvation through faith alone' while still living one's daily life.

Before Shinran Shōnin appeared on the scene there was a long and varied history of different teachings and ceremonies attached to the belief of birth in the Pure Land at the time of death. One such observance was the deathbed ceremony of the Heian Period. Such ceremonies take their cue in part from the Buddhist Sūtra literature. To quote one of the important passages from the *Meditation Sūtra*:

The Buddha said to Ānanda and Vaidehī, 'Those who attain birth on the lowest level of the lowest grade are the sentient beings who commit such evils as the five gravest offences, the ten evil acts and all kinds of immorality. Owing to such evil karma, a foolish person like this will fall into evil realms and suffer endless agony for many kalpas. When he is about to die, he may meet a good teacher, who consoles him in various ways, teaching him the wonderful Dharma and urging him to be mindful of the Buddha: but he is too tormented by pain to do so. The good teacher then advises him, 'If you cannot concentrate on the Buddha, then you should call [the Name of] the Buddha of Eternal Life.' In this way, he sincerely and continuously says Namu-Amida-butsu (I take refuge in the Buddha of Eternal Life) ten times. Because he calls the Buddha's Name, with each repetition the evil karma of *saṃsāra,* which he has committed during eight thousand million kalpas is dissolved.

When he comes to die, he sees before him a golden lotus-flower like the disk of the sun, and in an instant he is born within a lotus-bud in the Land of Utmost Bliss. After twelve great kalpas the lotus-bud opens. When the flower opens, Avalokiteśvara and Mahāsthāmaprāpta teach him with voices of great compassion the Suchness of all Dharmas and the method of dissolving evil karma. Hearing this, he rejoices and immediately awakens aspiration for Enlightenment. Such a person is called one who attains birth on the lowest level of the lowest grade. These three together are known as the contemplation of the lowest grade of aspirants and the sixteenth contemplation.[63]

Based on this document Buddhist scholars of those days considered it necessary to eliminate evil karma by reciting the *nembutsu* and they regarded the moment of death as extremely important in order to attain birth in the Pure Land.

In point of fact the *nembutsu* (pronouncing the Name of Amida Buddha) is certainly the most virtuous practice in Pure Land Buddhism and is indeed thought to have the power to dissolve evil karma. If when you recite the *nembutsu,* however, you consider it something valuable or virtuous that you are doing by your own efforts and take pride in it as your own personal achievement, then, as far as your frame of mind is concerned, you could not be further from the truth.

On the contrary, says Shinran Shōnin, the *nembutsu* is something that originally belongs to the Buddha because it is the Name of the Buddha and our act of reciting the *nembutsu* is entirely an expression of our gratitude to the Buddha. If you start feeling proud of your practice your pride, however little, will prove to be an obstacle to your spiritual development. Shinran Shōnin was very careful about the pride of self-power.

Chapter 14 deals with one of the erroneous views that concentrates exclusively on the practice of the *nembutsu* as a means of birth in the Pure Land and ignores the importance of faith in the Original Vow. Those who practice the *nembutsu* in the divergent way, as described in Chapter 14, take pride in practicing the *nembutsu* exclusively while ignoring the importance of faith in the Original Vow. They believe that every recitation of the *nembutsu* has the power to eradicate evil karma and will lead them to attain birth in the Pure Land.

The *Meditation Sūtra* in fact says, "Because he calls the Buddha's Name, with each repetition the evil karma of *saṃsāra* which he has committed during eight thousand million kalpas is dissolved." There is nothing wrong with this statement, if it were not for the fact that we mistakenly pride ourselves on our practice of the *nembutsu*. If only we were able to honestly say 'thank you' for such a teaching that assures us our evil karma would be dissolved by pronouncing the Name of the Buddha (*nembutsu*) there would be no problem. The sad truth is, however, we take pride in our every thought and action, and never think to say the Name of the Buddha in complete humility.

Our pride in practising the *nembutsu* is deeply connected with the belief that we can attain birth in the Pure Land by eradicating evil karma through continuous recitation of the *nembutsu*. It is our well-heeled pride that makes us persist in this belief. According to Shinran Shōnin, however, the *nembutsu* we pronounce is actually the working of the Buddha. When we attain faith in the Original Vow the *nembutsu* wells up from within us. The moment we entrust ourselves to the Buddha, forsaking all attachment to self-power, we realise that the *nembutsu* is something that comes directly from Amida Buddha. But as long as we remain attached to self-power and congratulate ourselves on our efforts, our pride will prevent the *nembutsu* from issuing forth spontaneously of itself. Despite the fact that the *nembutsu* comes from Other Power, we tend to see it as belonging to our own self-power.

The two aspects of Pure Land birth

Birth in the Pure Land is usually considered as an event that happens at the time of death. In Shin Buddhism, however, there are two kinds of birth in the Pure Land: firstly, birth in the Pure Land at the moment of attaining faith in one's present life, and secondly, birth in the Pure Land at the actual moment of death. Shin Buddhism contends that if you truly attain the former, it naturally follows you will attain the latter.

A passage in volume 2 of the *Larger Sūtra of Eternal Life* relating to the fulfillment of the Original Vow reads:

> All beings, on hearing that Name, rejoice in the awakening of faith at least for one thought moment. It is indeed from Amida's sincere mind that all this has been transferred to them. Desiring to be born in that land, they are immediately born there at that moment and abide in the stage of nonretrogression."[64]

The moment faith is awakened in someone is a moment of supreme joy for that person. They are born in the Pure Land and abide at the stage of nonretrogression. Abiding in this stage of nonretrogression means joining 'the company of those truly assured of birth in the Pure Land.' This is the source of their gratitude. Concerning the actual moment of death, Yuien says in Chapter 14, "Thus, when our lives reach their end, all our blind passions and evil hindrances are transformed into the recognition that there is no birth [and no death]."

The experience of attaining faith is beautifully summarised at the beginning of Chapter 1 as follows:

> At the very moment when the thought that moves you to pronounce the *nembutsu* is awakened within you, believing that your birth in the Pure Land is attained through the inconceivable working of Amida's Original Vow, you instantly receive Amida's loving benefit 'that embraces all, forsaking none.'

The faith experience of entrusting yourself to the inconceivable working of Amida's Original Vow instantly makes you receive Amida's compassionate benefit that embraces all, forsaking none. This receiving of Amida's benefit that embraces all, forsaking none, means an instantaneous elevation to the stage of nonretrogression where you enjoy joining the company of those assured of birth in the Pure Land. It is by virtue of the Original Vow of Amida Buddha that the experience of birth in the Pure Land as attainment of faith leads you without fail to birth in the Pure Land at the moment of actual death.

The nembutsu of gratitude

After attaining pure faith in Amida Buddha, our recitation of the *nembutsu* is an expression of gratitude to Amida Buddha and all Buddhas and bodhisattvas for leading us to the teaching of 'universal salvation through faith alone' and allowing us to journey together with them on the pathway to the Pure Land of Enlightenment, which all beings are expected to reach without any discrimination whatsoever. As Myōon-in Ryōshō says in his main work, *Tannishō monki*, Rennyo Shōnin's idea of 'reciting the *nembutsu* solely with gratitude' stems from Chapter 14 of the *Tannishō*. The twelfth letter of fascicle five of *The Letters* by Rennyo Shōnin reads:

> There is no need for those who wish to know in detail the meaning of 'peaceful awareness' (*anjin*) in our tradition to have any particular knowledge or wisdom. All that is needed is the realisation that we are but wretched beings, heavily weighed down by evil karma, and that it is Amida Tathāgata alone who saves even such pitiful beings as ourselves. When, without any effort on our part, but simply with the idea of holding fast to the sleeve of this Buddha, Amida, we entrust ourselves to the Buddha, asking him to help us attain Rebirth [in the Pure Land], then Amida Tathāgata rejoices profoundly and, emitting from his body eighty-four thousand great beams of Light, embraces and holds us within that Light. This is clearly set out in the [*Meditation*] *Sūtra*: "[The] Light

shines forth throughout all the worlds of the ten directions, embracing and never abandoning those who practice the *nembutsu*." This should be known.

This being so, there is no worry about our attaining Buddhahood. How splendid is the Original Vow that transcends all the worlds [of illusion]! And how blissful is Amida Tathāgata's Light! Were we not conditioned to see this Light, our dreadful sickness of ignorance, burdened with karmic hindrances since the beginningless past, could never be cured.

Thanks to the working of this Light, however, those whose past good has matured have already attained Other-Power faith, making it immediately clear that this is faith granted by Amida Tathāgata. Thus we now understand clearly that this faith is not something generated by us followers, but is in fact nothing less than Amida Tathāgata's great Other-Power faith. Consequently all of us, once we have attained Other-Power faith with the most generous help [of the Buddha], should reflect deeply on Amida Tathāgata's benevolence and always recite the *nembutsu*, that is, pronounce the Name, to respond to the Buddha with gratitude for what he has done for us.[65]

Since reciting the *nembutsu* with gratitude is the very foundation of the Shin Buddhist way of living, it can be said that Shin Buddhists live their whole life with thanks. Not only the *nembutsu* but every act they perform is an expression of gratitude towards friends and, indeed, nature itself.

The same is true of the practice of sitting in meditation. If you truly make contact with the living earth, your environment, and with other people through sitting in meditation, your whole being will be reconfirmed by everything around you. Given such an experience you may well feel the need to thank everyone and everything for the way they support you just as you are.

When you become an individual, properly independent of others, you will realise all that they have done for you and how much you owe them. If instead you take everything for granted and fail to feel grateful, it signifies you are still dependent on others in a self-centred way. Humbleness and gratitude are thus of utmost importance in spiritual life.

INSTANTANEOUS AWAKENING OF FAITH IN THIS LIFE LEADS TO ENLIGHTENMENT IN THE NEXT

Chapter 15

TRANSLATION

There are some who insist they have already attained Enlightenment even while still maintaining this earthly body full of blind passions.

Such a view really is quite unacceptable. The attainment of Buddhahood while still in this earthly body is the essential teaching of the Shingon School of Esoteric Buddhism and is achieved, they say, by means of the Three Esoteric Practices. The Purification of the Six Senses is the teaching of the One Vehicle *Lotus Sūtra* and is said to be achieved through the Four Peaceful Practices. But these are all difficult practices, only to be followed by those of superior ability, with Enlightenment attainable only through perfect meditation. In contrast to this, in Pure Land Buddhism the essence of the teaching of Other Power is the attainment of Enlightenment in the next life, since this way to Enlightenment is realised through the establishment of faith [in Amida Buddha]. It is the Easy Way, the way to be followed by those of poor ability, the Dharma in which there is no discrimination between good and evil.

As it is extremely difficult to eliminate blind passions and evil hindrances in this life, even the holy monks who practice the Shingon and Tendai disciplines still pray for [the attainment of] Enlightenment in the next life. How much more so, then, should we who are of far lesser ability! Although in our case there is no observance of precepts nor realisation of wisdom to be found, nevertheless when once we have crossed the painful ocean of birth-and-death on board the ship of Amida's Vow and have attained the shores of the Pure Land, the dark clouds of blind passions will swiftly clear away and the moon of Enlightenment of Dharma-in-itself will immediately appear. Having become one with the Unimpeded Light that illuminates all the ten quarters, we will benefit all sentient beings. This is true Enlightenment.

Do those who claim to have already attained Enlightenment in this earthly body freely expound the Dharma to benefit all beings, as Śākyamuni did, by revealing themselves in various transformations of the Dharma-body, endowed with the thirty-two features and eighty characteristics [of the Buddha]? This is what is actually meant by the attainment of Enlightenment in this life. A hymn by Shinran Shōnin tells us:

> At that moment when solid as a diamond
> Faith is first established,
> The Light of Amida's Heart enfolds and protects us
> So that we are forever separated from birth-and-death.

This means that, because, at the moment faith is established, Amida embraces us never to let us go, we shall no longer transmigrate through the Six Realms of Existence. This is why 'we are forever separated from birth-and-death (transmigration).' But how can we confuse this awakening with 'Enlightenment'? How regrettable that there should be such a misunderstanding!

The late Master (Shinran Shōnin) said:

"I have learned that in the true teaching of the Pure Land (浄土真宗 jp. *Jōdo shinshū*) one entrusts oneself to the Original Vow in this present life and one attains Enlightenment in the Pure Land."

COMMENTARY

> "The chapter [that criticises the misconception] that
> one can become a Buddha in one's own earthly body"
> — MYŌON-IN RYŌSHŌ —

Although this chapter appears easy to understand, there are, in fact, a few points that are quite difficult to grasp.

First of all, the ultimate goal of most Buddhist schools is to attain Enlightenment for oneself and at the same time help others to do so. It is the same with Pure Land Buddhism. The goal is to become a Buddha. Hence Shinran Shōnin says that the true teaching of the Pure Land lies in entrusting oneself to the Original Vow in this present life and attaining Enlightenment in the Pure Land.

Secondly, I would like to draw your attention to some rather special aspects of the Shin Buddhist faith-experience. In order to obtain Buddhahood in the Pure Land one has to attain pure faith in Amida Buddha in this life. As we have already learned while studying the preceding chapters of the *Tannishō*, this faith-experience is beyond good and evil and beyond every kind of knowledge. More accurately, when we attain pure faith we go far beyond all attachments to our world of morality and intellect, far beyond all those attachments we usually form so self-centredly, based on our interpretation of immediate experience. When we entrust ourselves to Other Power, there should not be the slightest reservation or calculation on our part. With utmost gratitude we should let Amida Buddha work to save us just as he will.

Let me quote a letter by Shinran Shōnin addressed to Shinbutsu-bō, one of his disciples, compiled as Letter 13 of the *Lamp for the Latter Age*:

> You ask about 'being grasped never to be abandoned.' Shandao's *Hymns [on the Samādhi] of All Buddhas' Presence* states that Śākyamuni and Amida are our parents of great compassion; using many and various compassionate means, they awaken the supreme *shinjin* (faith) in us. Thus the settling of true *shinjin* [faith] is the working of Śākyamuni and Amida. Persons become free of doubt about their birth because they have been grasped. Once grasped, there should be no calculation at all. Since they dwell in the stage of nonretrogression until being born into the Pure Land, they are said to be in the stage of the truly settled.
>
> Since true *shinjin* [faith] is awakened through the working of the two honored ones, Śākyamuni and Amida, it is when one is grasped that the settling of *shinjin* [faith] occurs. Thereafter the person abides in the stage of the truly settled until born into the Pure Land. Other Power means above all that there must not be the slightest calculation on our part.[66]

Shinran Shōnin's way of expressing himself is so natural. Yet what is being talked about in this letter is a huge departure from ordinary consciousness; it points to an extraordinary world beyond our daily routines. Those who attain faith in Amida Buddha are said to dwell in 'the stage of nonretrogression'. According to the above translation this is also called 'the stage of the truly settled'. 'The truly settled' means those who are definitely assured of attaining Buddhahood in the Pure Land in the next life. Such people are also said to be equal to Maitreya Bodhisattva, a bodhisattva who gained the highest stage of bodhisattvaship, standing only one step away from Buddhahood.

For those who have firsthand personal experience of being embraced in the great compassion of Amida Buddha these are no empty words. This being the case, people sometimes mistake such faith-experience for the attainment of Buddhahood itself. Thus at the beginning of the chapter Yuien says: "There are some who insist they have already attained Enlightenment even while still maintaining this earthly body full of blind passions. Such a view really is quite unacceptable." Yuien, the compiler of the *Tannishō*, thus points out the divergent view prevalent in those days that confused the attainment of faith with the attainment of Enlightenment. This kind of divergence from the truth was one of two heretical extremes.

To illustrate the other heretical extreme mentioned above, let me quote a letter by Kyōshin, one of the disciples, addressed to Shinran Shōnin:

> I respectfully submit the following letter. The *Larger Sūtra of Eternal Life* records the phrase, 'the person realises *shinjin* [faith] and joy,' and one of the *Hymns on the Pure Land* [by Shinran Shōnin] based on the *Avatamsaka Sūtra* states:

The person who attains *shinjin* [faith] and joy
Is taught to be equal to the Tathāgatas.
Great *shinjin* [faith] is itself Buddha-nature;
Buddha-nature is none other than Tathāgata.

Nevertheless, amongst the people of single-hearted practice there seem to be some who misunderstand, saying that the statement by fellow-practicers that the person who rejoices in *shinjin* [faith] is equal to Tathāgatas reflects an attitude of self-power and inclines towards the Shingon teaching. I do not wish to pass judgment on others, and so for my clarification I write to you of this matter.

Those who attain true *shinjin* [faith]
Immediately join the truly settled;
Thus having entered the stage of nonretrogression,
They necessarily attain Nirvāṇa.

The statement, 'they attain Nirvāṇa,' means that when the heart of the person of true *shinjin* [faith] attains the fulfilled land (Pure Land) at the end of his or her life, that person becomes one with the light that is the heart of Tathāgata, for his reality is eternal life and his activity is inseparable from infinite light. This seems to be the reason for saying: 'Great *shinjin* [faith] is itself Buddha-nature; Buddha-nature is none other than Tathāgata.' In my understanding, this corresponds to the Eleventh, Twelfth, and Thirteenth Vows. The joy of knowing the wonder and benevolence of the Vow of great compassion that Amida established for us beings of karmic evil is boundless and can never be fully expressed, for it surpasses all thought and words. Nevertheless, distracted by the business of everyday life, I tend to be negligent for hours at a time. Still, whether day or night, it never slips from my mind, and there is only the act of rejoicing in Amida's compassion; there is solely the diamond-like *shinjin* [faith] whether walking, standing, sitting or reclining, without any thought of the priority of time or space; there is only the saying of the Name out of gratitude for the Buddha's profound benevolence and for the joy imparted by the benevolence of the masters. The *nembutsu* is not a daily routine for me. I wonder if this is wrong. As the matter of ultimate importance for my life, nothing surpasses this. Wishing to receive, if possible, your full and detailed instruction, I have written down something of what I have thought. Although I stayed in Kyoto for quite a while, I was constantly rushed without a moment's peace; I regret this now and desire above all to return with no other business but to be with you for at least five days. That I am moved to say this is all due to your benevolence.[67]

As you can see, this letter by Shinran Shōnin's disciple contains a divergent view that criticises Shinran Shōnin's position that a person who rejoices in faith-experience is equal to the Tathāgata. It argues instead that maintaining such a way of position reflects the attitude of self-power and inclines towards the teaching of the Shingon School (attainment of Enlightenment while still in one's earthly body). This tends to neglect the highly mystical aspect of faith-experience, known as the oneness between the believer and Amida Buddha. It adheres rigidly to the division between man and Buddha, assuming a sort of qualitative difference between them. Taken to the extreme, it resembles, I find, the somewhat dualistic God-man relationship found in mainstream Christianity where man can never become God. This dualistic relationship is not found in Shin Buddhism.

The relationship between being human and being Buddha

In the Shin Buddhist faith-experience the relationship between man and Buddha is 'not one and not two (不一不二),' that is, it is 'neither identity nor duality'. To express this subtle relationship Shinran Shōnin uses the word 'equal' (等) and states that a person who has attained faith is equal to Buddhas. To quote yet another of Shinran Shōnin's letters, Letter 18 of the *Lamp for the Latter Age*:

> In answer to your question: at the moment we encounter Amida's Vow—which is Other Power giving itself to us—and the heart that receives true *shinjin* [faith] and rejoices becomes settled, we are grasped, never to be abandoned. Hence, the moment we realise the diamond-like mind, we are said to abide in the truly settled and attain the same stage as Bodhisattva Maitreya.
>
> Since persons of true *shinjin* [faith] are of the same stage as Maitreya, they are equal to Buddhas. Moreover, all Buddhas feel great joy when such a person rejoices in the realisation of true *shinjin* [faith], and they proclaim, 'This person is our equal.' Śākyamuni's words of rejoicing are found in the *Larger Sūtra*: 'The one who sees, reveres, and attains [the dharma] and greatly rejoices that person is my excellent, close companion'; thus he teaches that the person who has attained *shinjin* [faith] is equal to Buddhas.
>
> Further, since Maitreya has already become one who is certain to attain Buddhahood, he is called Maitreya Buddha. By this we know that the person who has already realised *shinjin* [faith] that is Other Power can be said to be equal to Buddhas. You should have no doubt about this.
>
> There is nothing I can do about your fellow-practicers, who say that they await the moment of death. Those whose *shinjin* [faith] has become true, which is the benefit of the Vow, have been grasped, never to be abandoned, and do not depend on Amida's coming at the moment of death. The person whose *shinjin* [faith] has not become settled awaits the moment of death in anticipation of Amida's coming.
>
> I will be happy if you take the name Zuishin-bō. What you have written in your letter is splendid. I cannot accept what your fellow-practicers are saying, but there is nothing to be done about it.[68]

Faith is the instantaneous experience of being awakened to Amida's Great Love and Compassion. It is the great transcendental experience of Oneness. As long as we live in this world, however, the dualistic consciousness of the intellect and the five senses that belong to the body immediately interferes. Thus as Shin Buddhists we do not say that we have attained Enlightenment. Though one who has attained faith is absolutely sure to become a Buddha by attaining Enlightenment in the Pure Land, there is surely no one who would say, 'I am a Buddha'. The fact that one is equal to the Buddhas also means that one does not need to await the death-moment in anticipation of Amida's coming to take one up to the Pure Land. For Shin Buddhists, one's birth in the Pure Land is assured well before that time.

Finally, I would like to draw your attention to the fact that the notion of Enlightenment or the Buddha in Shin Buddhism is both perfect and dynamic. At the end of the chapter, Yuien actually describes how we attain Buddhahood in the Pure Land: "Having become one with the Unimpeded Light that illuminates all the ten quarters, we will benefit all sentient beings. This is true Enlightenment." Thus, while living in this world Shin Buddhists receive the dynamic working of the Buddha with deep gratitude and joy.

In conclusion I would like to quote a letter by Rennyo Shōnin addressed to his followers. It is the fourth letter of Fascicle 1 of *The Letters* by Rennyo Shōnin:

QUESTION: I have learned that in Shinran Shōnin's tradition we are expected 'to complete the act (karma) [that enables us to attain birth in the Pure Land] in daily life' and not to adhere to '[Amida Buddha's] coming to meet us [at the very moment of death].' What do you mean by this? I know very little about 'completing the act in daily life' or about 'not waiting for Amida Buddha to come to meet us.' I would like to listen to your teaching in greater detail.

ANSWER: Your questions do, indeed, touch on matters of vital importance in our tradition. As a basic principle our school teaches that 'with the instantaneous awakening [of faith]' 'the act [that enables us to attain birth] is completed in daily life.' Once we have understood that it is due to the maturity of goodness from the past that we come to be aware, through listening in our daily lives, of the way Amida Tathāgata's Original Vow saves us, then we can also understand that it is not by our own power but by the help of Other Power (Buddha's wisdom), that we become aware of the way Amida's Original Vow works upon us. This is the meaning of 'completing the act in daily life.' Therefore, 'completing the act in daily life' refers to the state of mind of those who by listening have realised the above-mentioned principle and are confident that birth is assured. It is what is meant by such phrases as 'with the instantaneous awakening [of faith], joining the company of those who are truly assured of birth,' 'completing the act in daily life' and 'immediately attaining birth and dwelling at a stage of nonretrogression.'

QUESTION: I have fully understood the notion of 'attaining Birth in the Pure Land with the instantaneous awakening [of faith].' However, I still do not understand the meaning of 'not waiting for Amida to come to meet us [at the moment of death].' Could you kindly explain it for me?

ANSWER: Regarding the meaning of 'not waiting for Amida to come to meet us,' once we comprehend that 'with the instantaneous awakening of faith, we join the company of those who are truly assured of birth,' then we do not need to wait for 'Amida's coming to meet us.' It is the people who perform various other practices that 'wait for Amida to come to meet us at the moment of death.' For those who practice true faith there is no longer any need to wait for 'Amida's coming to meet us at the moment of death,' because we realise that very moment of instantaneous awakening [of faith] we immediately receive 'the benefit of the light that takes in all beings and never abandons them.'

[Shinran] Shōnin teaches, therefore, 'Amida's coming to meet us at the very moment of death is related with the notion of birth in the Pure Land through various other practices. Because followers of true faith are taken in and never abandoned, they live in the company of those who are truly assured of birth in the Pure Land. Because they live in the company of those who are truly assured, they will attain Nirvāṇa without fail. Therefore, there is no need to wait for the moment of death and no need to expect Amida to come to meet us [at that time].' I hope these words have made things clearer for you.

QUESTION: Should we understand [the virtue of] 'being truly assured of birth in the Pure Land' and [the virtue of] 'attaining Nirvāṇa' as being one benefit, or two?

ANSWER: With the instantaneous awakening of faith we join the company of those who are truly assured of birth. This is the benefit we receive in this world of defilement. Following that, we should understand that it is in the Pure Land that we attain Nirvāṇa. We should therefore see them as two benefits.

QUESTION: I see now that birth is assured once we understand matters in the way you have explained. When we are still told, however, that we should go to the trouble of attaining faith, how should we understand that?

ANSWER: This question is indeed of great importance. If you understand matters in the way I have explained above, such understanding is exactly what we mean by 'to have attained faith decisively.'

QUESTION: I have clearly understood through listening that 'having attained faith decisively' refers to 'having completed the act [that enables us to attain birth in the Pure Land] in daily life,' 'not [waiting for Amida to] come to meet us [at the moment of death]' and 'dwelling in the company of those who are truly assured of birth.' However, what I do not yet understand is whether, after attaining faith decisively, we should say the *nembutsu* for the sake of attaining birth in the Land of Utmost Bliss or as a way of expressing our gratitude to the Buddha for all he has done for us.

ANSWER: I think this question, too, is of vital importance for the good reason that we should not indeed think of the *nembutsu* pronounced after the instantaneous awakening of faith as an act carried out for the sake of attaining birth [in the Pure Land]. It should be understood solely as a grateful response to the Buddha for what he has done for us. This is why Shandao (613–681) made the following comment about the *nembutsu*, '[One says the *nembutsu*] spending one's whole life at the upper limit, one thought-moment at the lower.' I understand 'one thought-moment at the lower' to refer to '[the moment of] attaining faith decisively' and 'spending one's whole life' to mean the *nembutsu* pronounced as a grateful response to the Buddha for all he has done for us. Hence, it is extremely important that you really grasp the point.'[69]

ONE'S SPIRITUAL REFORMATION
ONLY OCCURS ONCE

Chapter 16

TRANSLATION

There are some people who insist that, whenever a follower of our faith becomes angry or does something wrong or has a dispute with his fellow-followers, then as a matter of course (自然 jp. *jinen*, literally 'naturally') he should be sure to reform himself (廻心 jp. *eshin*, literally 'to turn the mind').

Do they mean, we should eliminate evil and practice good [in order to attain birth in the Pure Land]? For those who follow the practice of the *nembutsu* exclusively and single-mindedly this spiritual reformation, known as *eshin* ('turning-of-mind'), occurs only once when a person, hitherto ignorant of the true teaching of the Other Power of the Original Vow, comes to realise, through the wisdom bestowed on him by Amida Buddha, that he cannot attain birth in the Pure Land with the thoughts and feelings he has been harbouring until now, and so abandons his old ways of thinking and entrusts himself to the Original Vow. This is what is meant [in our tradition] by *eshin*, 'spiritual reformation.' If it were necessary to reform oneself in every way morning and evening in order to attain birth in the Pure Land, Amida's Vow that embraces all and forsakes none would be proved useless: one might die before one ever had the chance to reform oneself and regain a tender and forbearing attitude, for life is so fragile it can end in an instant, between breathing out and breathing in.

There are some who claim with their lips that they trust in the power of the Original Vow, all the while thinking in their minds that, although Amida's Vow to save even those with bad karma is said to be inconceivably great, the Vow will still save all the good people in particular. Those who by thinking in this way betray their lack of trust in the effectiveness of Amida's Vow are also unable to entrust themselves to Other Power and are thus destined for birth in the Borderland of the Pure Land. How deplorable this is!

Since birth is brought about by Amida's benevolent design, it is obvious that, once faith has been established, there can be no room for our own way of thinking. The realisation that we are evil should make us revere the Power of the Vow all the more. Then quite naturally (自然 jp. *jinen*) we will acquire a tender and forbearing attitude of mind.

Whatever actions we take in connection with birth in the Pure Land, we should never pretend to be wise but should remain reverential and mindful at all times of how deeply indebted we are to Amida Buddha. The *nembutsu* will then well up spontaneously. This is 'natural (*jinen*).' Not imposing our way of thinking is called 'natural.' This is Other Power.

To my regret, however, I have heard that there are those who speak knowingly about 'naturalness' as if there existed some other kind of 'naturalness.' How lamentable this is!

COMMENTARY

> "The chapter [criticising the misconception] that
> as a matter of course [to attain birth in the Pure Land]
> one should be reforming oneself continuously"
> — MYŌON-IN RYŌSHŌ —

There are two very important concepts that appear in this chapter: 1) *eshin*, or spiritual reformation or conversion, and 2) *jinen*, or naturalness. By giving an explanation of these two terms, I would like to discuss exactly what Yuien is trying to say in this chapter. It is not easy, however, because those two key words, *eshin* and *jinen*, are highly technical terms in the field of Pure Land Buddhism and originally had a number of meanings. These two words, incidentally, are rarely used in modern Japanese.

The importance of spiritual reformation (eshin)

The Buddhist word, *eshin* (literally, 'turning of mind'), has several meanings: 1) conversion to Mahāyāna Buddhism, 2) mental reformation through penitence, 3) attainment of faith in Amida Buddha, 4) virtue-transference for birth in the Pure Land and so on. For this particular chapter the definitions 'mental reformation through penitence' and 'attainment of faith' are especially relevant. Most important is the attainment of faith in Amida Buddha. *Eshin* in the sense of 'attainment of faith' occurs in our lives once and only once. This idea is clearly expressed in the second paragraph of this chapter.

The Shin Buddhist faith-experience attained after profound introspection, that is, the experience of 'abandoning one's old ways of thinking and entrusting oneself to the Original Vow', is always accompanied by bitter penitence and supreme joy. Because faith-experience also includes penitence, the word *eshin* at the beginning of the chapter is used there in the penitential sense.

In the first paragraph of this chapter the word *eshin* would appear to be used in an ethical sense. In the divergent view that Yuien is criticising, *eshin* as the act of reforming oneself is a path that entails unceasing moral and ethical effort, no matter whether you call it penitence or repentance. It is totally different from *eshin* as the faith-experience of entrusting oneself to Amida Buddha. Whereas faith-experience is effortless liberation, repentance as the act of penitence and reforming oneself belongs to the realm of ethics and constant moral effort 'to eliminate evil and practice good.' In short it is self-power.

Once you attain faith in Amida Buddha, you have Amida's Original Vow, that is, Other Power, as your foundation for living in this world. *Eshin*, or 'spiritual reformation' in the sense of attainment of true faith in Amida Buddha, is a fundamental awakening to the truth of life. This faith-experience is like the discovery of a harbour on your lifelong journey to the Pure Land. Through faith you will there find peace of mind and inner peace. Amida Buddha is now your true foundation. Resting on this solid base, you can now strive to do your best in this relative world. Your moral and ethical effort is meant to be relative, not absolute. It has nothing to do with the absolute aim of attaining birth in the Pure Land. You just 'do for the doing' what seems good at the time, not only for yourself but also for your family and friends.

There should be no attachment to what you do. If you find there is anything wrong in what you are doing or what you have done, you can change yourself through penitence or remorse. You should definitely strive to break through your self-centred world, but it is not an absolute condition for your birth in the Pure Land. What you need to attain birth is faith alone, the faith to entrust yourself absolutely to Amida Buddha. Under the light of the Buddha's wisdom you will then be able to view things without attachment and thus be able to see them for what they are, far more clearly than before.

Naturalness (jinen)

As already mentioned in my commentary on Chapter 10, there are several meanings for the word *jinen*:

1) The naturalness of karma 業道自然 jp. *gōdō jinen*;
2) The naturalness of the Non-created (the content of Enlightenment), or *mui jinen* 無為自然; and
3) The naturalness of the power of the Original Vow 願力自然 *ganriki jinen*.

In Chapter 16 *jinen* appears twice, first at the beginning of the chapter and again towards the end. Obviously the word *jinen,* or naturalness, is being used in two different senses. One sense of it, 'the naturalness of karma', has moral and ethical implications, while the other, 'the naturalness of the power of the Original Vow', has religious connotations.

The Japanese word *jinen* can be used either as an adverb or as a noun. In the original text the word *jinen* appears as an adverb. I have translated it at the beginning of the chapter by the phrase 'as a matter of course.' In this case the phrase 'as a matter of course' actually has the connotation of 'as a matter of course in the realm of moral law.'

In the divergent view that Yuien is referring to, ethical effort on our part is 'as a matter of course' absolutely necessary in order to attain birth in the Pure Land. Since the foundation of this view is an ethical way of thinking, proponents consider it 'a matter of course (or naturally)' that they should strive to reform themselves.

When Yuien again talks about *jinen* towards the end of the chapter, he describes how naturally Amida's Original Vow works so as to enable us to attain birth in the Pure Land. The word used is *ganriki jinen,* or the naturalness of the power of the Original Vow. *Jinen* in this context refers to the 'naturalness' of the working of the Buddha, and refers to how naturally his Original Vow works to make us aware of self-power and bring about our salvation.

Those unable to break free from their attachment to their self-power maintain that ethical effort on their part is necessary in order for Amida to enable them to attain birth in the Pure Land, and cleave to moral law. They extol the virtues of *jinen*, but the *jinen* they speak of refers to the *jinen* or naturalness of moral law. While they employ the same word, what they are actually referring to is their addiction to self-power, which is something completely different from the true naturalness of Other Power. Yuien therefore states in closing:

> To my regret, however, I have heard that there are those who speak knowingly about 'naturalness' as if there existed some other kind of 'naturalness.' How lamentable this is!

Everyone Living the Nembutsu is Ultimately Born in the Pure Land

Chapter 17

TRANSLATION

There are some who maintain that anyone born in the Borderland will ultimately descend into hell.

Whatever kind of sacred documents are there that make such a claim? It really is quite deplorable that such a false view should have begun to circulate amongst people claiming to be scholars. In what strange way, I wonder, are such people studying the sacred books like the Sūtras and the commentaries?

I have learned [from my Master] that those who lack [pure] faith will indeed be born in the Borderland, because of their lack of faith in the Original Vow, and that after having atoned for their evil karma of doubt [by staying there], they will be born again in the Land of Enjoyment and thus ultimately attain Enlightenment.

Since devotees with pure faith are few in number, many people [who cannot attain pure faith] are led to the Land of Transformation (Borderland). To assert that their birth [in the Borderland] will ultimately prove to have been in vain, however, is tantamount to accusing the Buddha of having led them in the wrong direction!

COMMENTARY

"The chapter [that criticises the false message] that anyone born
in the borderland will ultimately descend into hell"
— MYŌON-IN RYŌSHŌ —

In contrast to the false view discussed in this chapter, the Shin Buddhist tradition, founded by Shinran Shōnin, teaches that those devotees who pronounce the Name of Amida Buddha with true sincerity will ultimately all attain Enlightenment in the Pure Land. This view is well expressed in the following two *wasan* by Shinran Shōnin based on the *Larger Sūtra of Eternal Life*:

Those who aspire to the Pure Land of Peace and Bliss,
Yet, failing to attain the Other Power faith,

Doubt the inconceivability of the Buddha-wisdom,
And remain in the Borderland, the realm of indolence and pride.[70]

Those who pronounce the Name with self-power,
   meditatively or non-meditatively,
By trusting the Vow of accomplishing the ultimate salvation,
Even without being taught,
Spontaneously turn to enter the Gate of True Suchness.[71]

The awakening of faith through the Three Vows

Shinran Shōnin's confidence in ultimate salvation was based on his own personal awareness of how religious consciousness develops. According to his religious philosophy the process has three stages that are expressed by three vows:

1) The Nineteenth Vow as 'the essential gate for Birth under the twin Sāla trees'; he regarded it as the explicit teaching of the *Meditation Sūtra*.
2) The Twentieth Vow as 'the true gate for incomprehensible Birth'; he regarded it as the explicit teaching of the *Amida Sūtra*.
3) The Eighteenth Vow as 'the gate of universal salvation for inconceivable Birth;' he regarded the Eighteenth Vow, the teaching of the *Larger Sūtra of Eternal Life*, as the teaching implicit in the Nineteenth and Twentieth Vows.

In Shin Buddhism, this three-step process of development of religious consciousness is called 'the awakening of faith through the Three Vows' (三願転入 jp. *sangan tennyū*). First, the ethical consciousness is awakened through the Nineteenth Vow. Next, this develops into the ethico-religious consciousness expressed in the Twentieth Vow. Finally, the latter turns into the purely religious consciousness of the Eighteenth Vow.

What actually are these three vows? Let me quote these vows from the *Larger Sūtra of Eternal Life*[72] in order to better examine their content.

1) THE NINETEENTH VOW: "If, upon my attaining Buddhahood, all beings in the ten quarters, awakening their thoughts to Enlightenment and practising all deeds of virtue, should cherish the desire in all sincerity to be born in my Country and yet I, at the time of their death, should fail to appear before them surrounded by a large company, may I not attain Supreme Enlightenment."

2) THE TWENTIETH VOW: "If, upon my attaining Buddhahood, all beings in the ten quarters on hearing my name should cherish the thought of my Country and should plant the root of all virtues and turn it over in sincerity to being born in my Country, and if even so they should still not achieve that birth, may I not attain Supreme Enlightenment."

3) THE EIGHTEENTH VOW: "If, upon my attaining Buddhahood, all beings in the ten quarters, in all sincerity and joyous faith, aspiring to be born in my Country and pronouncing my Name (*nembutsu*) up to ten times, were not to be born there, then may I not attain Supreme Enlightenment. Excepted from this are those who have committed the five grave offences and those who slander the Right Dharma."

With regard to the Nineteenth Vow Shinran Shōnin says in the *Kyōgyōshinshō*:

> Hereupon, Śākyamuni Buddha revealed and expounded the Store of Virtue wherewith to lead the ocean of multitudinous beings; originally Amida Tathāgata had raised the [Nineteenth] Vow to guide the broad ocean of multitudinous beings. We already have the compassionate Vow. It is called (1) the Vow of performing virtuous deeds. It is also called (2) the Vow of the Buddha's appearing at deathbed, (3) the Vow of the Buddha's coming to lead the aspirant to birth [in the Pure Land], (4) the Vow of the Buddha's coming to receive us or (5) the Vow of sincere aspiration.[73]

Here you have the five descriptive names for the Nineteenth Vow, the first and the last names made by Shinran Shōnin himself and the other three by his predecessors. The first name emphasises the practice aspect of the Nineteenth Vow, the next three the benefit to be gained by the aspirant, and the last the aspirant's faith (*shinjin*).

As to the Twentieth Vow Shinran Shōnin said in the same work:

> Śākyamuni Buddha expounded the store of virtue, whereby he exhorted all sentient beings of the ten quarters in the corrupt times. Amida Tathāgata had originally raised the Vow of accomplishing ultimate salvation (i.e., the Twentieth Vow), whereby he guided all the multitudinous beings. The Compassionate Vow already exists. It is called (1) the Vow of planting the root of all virtues, (2) the Vow assuring the aspirant of ultimate birth, (3) the Vow of accomplishing ultimate salvation or (4) the Vow of sincere virtue-transference.[74]

Here you have the four descriptive names for the Twentieth Vow, the last given by Shinran Shōnin himself and the first three by his predecessors. The first name refers to the practice aspect of the Twentieth Vow, the next two to the benefit accruing to the aspirant, and the last to the aspirant's faith.

As to the Eighteenth Vow we find, again in the same work, the following passage:

> As I reverently reflect on virtue-transference in the outgoing phase, I see that there is the Great Faith. The Great Faith is the divine means for long life and no death, the excellent way of aspiring for the Pure Land and abandoning the defiled land, the honest mind endowed through the best-selected Original Vow, the deep and universal joyous faith endowed by Other Power, the true mind indestructible as a diamond, the Pure Faith for easy birth, which nevertheless

so few attain, the One Mind embraced and protected by Amida's mind-light, the rare and supreme Great Faith, the short way so difficult for the world to believe in, the true cause of realisation of the Great Nirvāṇa, the white path which so quickly enables one to attain complete and all-merging virtue, the sea of faith in the True Suchness of One Reality.

This mind originates from (1) the Vow of attaining birth [in the Pure Land] through the *nembutsu*. This Great Vow is called (2) the selected Original Vow. It is also called (3) the Vow of the three minds of the Original Vow, (4) the Vow of sincerity and joyous faith, and (5) the Vow of Faith in the outgoing phase.[75]

Here you have the five descriptive names for the Eighteenth Vow, of which the first two are traditional and the last three, referring to the faith aspect of the Eighteenth Vow, invented by Shinran Shōnin himself.

When interpreting the texts quoted above, it is most important for us never to forget that those Vows belong not to us but to Amida. In this respect everything is happening in the Buddha's world, whether it is implicit or explicit.

Ethics and the true and the provisional vows

In his Pure Land philosophy, Shinran Shōnin classifies Amida's Vows into the true 真 and the provisional 仮. With regard to the three Vows, the Eighteenth Vow is considered to be true, whereas the Nineteenth and Twentieth are considered provisional. Although they are all true in the sense that they originate from Amida Buddha, Shinran Shōnin regards the true meaning of the Nineteenth and Twentieth Vows to be implicit or hidden, and that the more obvious or explicit meaning of those Vows is not true but provisional. We are led to the true meaning via the provisional. More accurately, through the Nineteenth Vow we are led to the Twentieth and through the Twentieth, to the Eighteenth.

Those concerned with the Nineteenth Vow are at the ethical stage of development, at which the *nembutsu* is just one of a number of good deeds. At the existential stage represented by the Twentieth Vow, people have already despaired of moral and ethical life, and have abandoned all other good deeds to concentrate exclusively on the recitation of Amida's Name. Since all of their ethical efforts culminate in the pronouncing of the Name and since they are very aware of the Name being that of the Buddha, hence of it being completely religious, I call this stage the 'ethico-religious'.

The stage of development addressed by the Eighteenth Vow is the purely religious one which lies beyond all moral and ethical discrimination between good and evil. Its reality is pure faith in Amida Buddha, being awakened to Amida's love filling one's whole being just as one is. On attaining sincere faith in the Buddha one becomes full of joy, assured of salvation through the Buddha, and certain of attaining Enlightenment in his Pure Land.

Those who become deadlocked at this ethical stage of the Twentieth Vow are said
to be born in the Borderland, the realm of indolence and pride. All we can do is take
refuge in the Buddha, casting off all attachment to our own deeds and actions. This is
exactly what Amida wants us to do through our encounter with his Twentieth Vow,
called the Vow assuring the aspirant of ultimate birth [in the Pure Land] or the Vow of
accomplishing ultimate salvation. This peaceful awareness of Amida's great love and
compassion, which is attained at the stage of the Eighteenth Vow by going through the
stage of the Twentieth Vow, is what is known as true faith.

Shinran Shōnin said in one of his letters to his good friends:

> The depth of the Buddha's benevolence is such that even with birth in the realm
> of indolence and pride, the Borderland, the City of Doubt or the Womb Palace,
> such birth as is brought about only by the compassion revealed in Amida's
> Nineteenth and Twentieth Vows, we would still enjoy a happiness that goes
> beyond all our understanding, thus the depth of the Buddha's benevolence
> knows no bounds. However, with our birth into the true Land of Enjoyment
> and with our attainment of the enlightenment of supreme Nirvāṇa, how much
> more would we understand and appreciate the benevolence of the Buddha.
> This is not a matter that Shōshin-bō and I have decided amongst ourselves.
> Most certainly that is not the case.[78]

We should not materialise 'the Borderland.' To do so would be a great mistake. Just as
the Pure Land symbolises Enlightenment, so too does the Borderland, which is called
the realm of indolence and pride, stand for the unenlightened mind, the self-centred
world of delusion or the realm of self-power. Many people seem to be content to live
in that Borderland of self-power. However, Shin Buddhism teaches that this is not the
true world of religious life, and that we must undergo further spiritual development
before we can reach it.

Everyone Attains Enlightenment of the Highest Quality Equally and without Discrimination

Chapter 18

TRANSLATION

There are some people who assert that, depending on how big or small the size of one's donations to the Saṃgha, so one becomes a bigger or smaller Buddha [in the Pure Land]. This is utterly nonsensical, even ludicrous in fact.

First of all, is it not impossible to determine the size of a Buddha, to decide whether a Buddha is great or small? Even though the stature of Amida Buddha, the Supreme Teacher of the Pure Land, is described in the scriptures, such descriptions refer to the Dharmakāya of Amida Buddha in its manifested form. When one [becomes a Buddha], attaining the Enlightenment of Dharma-nature, one actually has no form, one is neither long nor short, square nor round, nor does one have any colour, neither blue, yellow, red, white nor black. How then can one's stature be determined at all?

It is stated [in Pure Land Sūtras] that, by pronouncing the *nembutsu*, one beholds a transformed Buddha (jp. *kebutsu*). Related to this it is also written [in the *Nichizō-bun* of the *Daijikkyō*] that with a big [voice pronouncing] *nembutsu* one sees a big Buddha and with a small [voice pronouncing] *nembutsu* one sees a small Buddha. The misinterpretation I have just been talking about may possibly have derived from some such a document.

Furthermore, offerings to the Saṃgha, should be regarded as the practice of the charity pāramitā (perfection). Nevertheless the offerings one will make to the Buddha or to one's teacher, however precious they may be, are actually meaningless if one lacks [pure] faith. If one entrusts oneself to Other Power and if one's faith is deep, even if one does not give a single sheet of paper or half a penny to the Saṃgha, still one will be in accord with the true intention of the Original Vow.

Do they seek to intimidate their fellow devotees, using the Buddha's teaching as a tool to fulfill their own selfish desires?

COMMENTARY

> "The chapter [that criticises the false conception] that
> the size of Buddha one becomes depends on the size
> of one's donations [to the Saṃgha]"
> — MYŌON-IN RYŌSHŌ —

This sort of distortion of a religious teaching is most unfortunate but I am sure you are aware of similar cases in many religious traditions throughout the world. Such distorted teachings are based on the worldly desires of those who live in religious orders. It is even claimed that what you become in the Pure Land or in Heaven is determined by how much you donate to the order you belong to. As Yuien said, "This is utterly nonsensical, even ludicrous in fact."

If people in religious orders really go to such extremes in this matter, you will be left wondering whether your donation is enough to ensure your passage to the Pure Land or Heaven. "Do they seek to intimidate their fellow devotees, using the Buddha's teaching as a tool to fulfil their own selfish desires?" This is totally wrong.

When we make a donation to a religious order, we do so out of gratitude to God or to the Buddha. We must be happy to do so, embraced by the Love or Compassion of our Lord and involved in the warm community of good friends. There is an important saying in Buddhism: 'Oneness of mind and matter.' Mind and matter are one and inseparable. It goes without saying that they should balance one another. Yuien's words found in the second paragraph from the end are properly based on this kind of Buddhist philosophy.

In Pure Land Buddhism a devotee is believed to attain Buddhahood when born in the Pure Land. A Buddha has no form and no colour in his Dharmakāya-in-itself or Dharma-nature. Yuien, therefore, is absolutely right in saying, "When one [becomes a Buddha], attaining Enlightenment of Dharma-nature, one has no form. One is neither long nor short, square nor round, and one has no colour, neither blue, yellow, red, white nor black. How then can one's stature be determined at all?"

The Supraindividual Individual:
The Person who Transcends
Selfish Attachment

TRANSLATION

ALL THE ERRONEOUS VIEWS discussed above must certainly have originated from some form of divergence from the true faith.

According to the talks of our late Master, Shinran Shōnin, in the time of Hōnen Shōnin while the latter was still alive, amongst his many disciples there were only a few whose faith accorded fully with that of Hōnen Shōnin himself. As a result of this situation there was a dispute between our late Master, Shinran Shōnin, and his fellow disciples under Hōnen Shōnin. The argument was occasioned by a pronouncement on the part of our Master, Shinran Shōnin, to the effect that his faith and that of his Master Hōnen Shōnin were one and the same. Fellow disciples such as Seikan-bō and Nembutsu-bō argued vehemently against this statement, asking, "How can your faith, Zenshin-bō (Shinran Shōnin's name at that time) be identical to that of Hōnen Shōnin?" To which Shinran Shōnin responded, "Hōnen Shōnin's wisdom and learning are immense and so I would certainly be mistaken if I claimed to be as great as Hōnen Shōnin in those respects. As far as faith (birth [in the Pure Land]) is concerned, however, there is no difference whatsoever. The Master's faith and mine are one and the same." This reply did not satisfy them, however. They remained dubious, asking how such a thing could be possible. So finally they all agreed to settle the question in the presence of Hōnen Shōnin and to see which side was right. When they explained the matter in detail, Hōnen Shōnin said, "My faith has been given by Amida, and so has that of Zenshin-bō [meaning Shinran Shōnin]. Therefore we are one and the same in faith. Those whose faith differs from ours will surely not go to the same Pure Land as I." Judging from this, it seems likely that there are some who are not one in faith with Shinran Shōnin even amongst our fellow followers who practice the *nembutsu* steadfastly and single-mindedly.

Although all these are but repetitions of things I have already mentioned, nevertheless I have written them all down again here. I feel the sum of my remaining days to be like a drop of dew on a withered blade of grass and so, not only have I been listening to my fellow followers talk about their uncertainties, but I have also been telling them all that I learned from my late Master, Shinran Shōnin. And yet I am afraid that, after my eyes close, there may arise great confusion about the teaching. For this reason, whenever you find yourselves confounded by people insisting on the views mentioned above, I advise you to study diligently those sacred writings the late Master used to read with such appreciation.

Generally speaking there is to be found in the sacred documents a mixture of teaching, that which is both true and real together with that which is provisional and expedient. It was because of our Master's true spirit that he adopted the true and set aside the provisional. You cannot be too careful when it comes to guarding against misunderstanding the sacred scriptures.

As evidence of the above I have selected some documents and appended them to this book as a set of criteria (*meyasu* in Japanese).

The Master was wont to say, "When I deeply reflect on the Vow of Amida, created through five kalpas of profound thought, I find the Vow is entirely meant for me, Shinran, alone. That is why I feel so grateful for the Original Vow in which Amida graciously resolved to save me, a person so heavily weighed down by [bad] karma." When I now ponder this expression of Shinran Shōnin's innermost feelings, I find that it is in perfect accord with the following golden passage from Shandao, "Know yourself to be an ignorant being, burdened with karmic evil, subject to birth-and-death, ever sinking, ever transmigrating from time immemorial, and with no possible lead to emancipation." It was the Master's merciful heart causing him to use himself as an example in an effort to awaken us to ourselves going astray without realising how deep our karmic evil is or how great is what has been done for us by [Amida] Tathāgata.

Indeed I myself and others prattle away about good and bad, proclaiming this to be good, that to be bad, and paying no heed to what the Tathāgata has done for us. The Master on the other hand said, "As to whether things are good or bad, I am in complete ignorance. The reason is this: if I knew what was good as completely as Amida Tathāgata knows, then I might be allowed to say I know what is good. Or again if I knew what was bad as completely as the Tathāgata knows, then I might be allowed to say I know what is bad. But amongst us ignorant beings, weighed down by blind passions in a world of impermanence, a world that is like a burning house, all is vain, all is empty, there is nothing true. Only the *nembutsu* is true."

All of us, including me, are in the habit of talking about utterly vain concerns, and one custom in particular is truly deplorable. I refer to the tendency, when we are talking about faith in the context of pronouncing the *nembutsu* or trying to explain faith to others, of ascribing to Shinran Shōnin passages he himself has never ever spoken, and this simply in order to silence others, or to gain the upper hand over our opponents. Such a practice is indeed both shameful and deplorable. I would like you to look into this matter very carefully and be utterly clear about it in your minds.

Although these are far from being my own words, they may appear somewhat awkward, since I myself am not familiar with the Sūtras and commentaries and have no deep understanding as to the meaning of the scriptures. Nevertheless, recalling a fraction, a hundredth part perhaps, of all that our Master, Shinran Shōnin, taught, I have put those fragments down in writing. How sad it would be if those fortunate enough to say the *nembutsu* were not to be born immediately into the Land of Enjoyment (the true Pure Land) but were forced to tarry in the Borderland.

I have taken up my brush in tears and have written all this down in order that there be no difference of faith amongst my fellow followers gathered in a single room. Let this writing be entitled *Tannishō, A Record of Lament over Divergence*. It is not to be shown to outsiders.

COMMENTARY

Shinran Shōnin's words, as quoted by Yuien in this concluding part of the work, reveal the fundamental standpoint of Shinran Shōnin's religious philosophy and constitute one of the most important parts of the whole text.

The Postscript starts with the story of a debate that Shinran Shōnin had with his Dharma friends concerning the quality of his faith. Shinran Shōnin was absolutely confident of the oneness of his own faith with that of Hōnen Shōnin, because faith is the right cause for birth in the Pure Land. His fellow followers disagreed. Hōnen Shōnin himself, however, brought the dispute to an end by saying, "My faith has been given by Amida, and so has that of Zenshin-bō (meaning Shinran Shōnin). Therefore we are one and the same in faith. Those whose faith differs from ours will surely not go to the same Pure Land as I."

There are several crucial points to be considered here:

1) Faith is the cause of birth in the Pure Land.
2) Faith is a gift from Amida.
3) We are one in faith.

I would prefer to focus on the third point rather than on the first two, because they have already been discussed in previous chapters.

Hōnen Shōnin's saying "We (Shinran Shōnin and Hōnen Shōnin) are one and the same in faith," is remarkable. At that time Shinran Shōnin was quite a young priest, some forty years younger than Hōnen Shōnin. He must have been overjoyed to receive such confirmation from his Master. Faith is usually thought to be a narrow path. It seems so not only for outsiders but also for those who seek to attain it. Once attained, however, it opens up a vast and single way of no hindrance.

The *nembutsu* is the single path that knows no obstruction. This is because the gods of heaven and earth bow down in reverence before one who practices the *nembutsu* with pure faith. No *māra*s (demonic beings) or heretics (non-Buddhists) can obstruct such a person. No evil deed can bring upon him karmic retribution, nor can any form of good equal his *nembutsu*. Therefore it is called the single path that knows no obstruction. (Chapter 7)

Let us return now to Hōnen Shōnin's words, "We are one and the same in faith."

We are one and the same in faith

Faith is an individual's personal experience. In this respect every individual returns to his or her own self in order to attain faith. In other words, religious faith divides people into individuals. To attain true faith one needs to be absolutely oneself, standing alone as an independent individual. If the individuality of faith ends up isolated and alone, however, such religious faith tends to be fanatical and will be accompanied by a sort of insanity caused by their separation from others.

As you know, there is no eternal entity in Buddhism. Everything is always changing, interrelated, and interdependent. Therefore, there is nothing that accords with the notion of the individual as conceived in Western philosophy. When I say 'individual,' the meaning of the word is quite different from its Western implication. By an individual I mean someone who is aware of themselves (or of their reality). Because everyone has their own karmic conditions that differ from everyone else's, everyone is a unique individual. In this context individuality means one's awareness of self (the reality of one's karmic condition), or one's relationship to oneself.

According to Buddhist philosophy, if you are truly awakened to your reality, that is, if you attain your own individuality, you will come to realise how closely you are related to others. Through your individuality, you arrive at the universal. Such awakening or faith makes you become one with others, breaking through your self-centred framework of consciousness (the illusory world).

"We are one and the same in faith" means not only that Shinran Shōnin's faith is one and the same as Hōnen Shōnin's in regard to quality, but also that the two persons are united in faith. Buddhist faith, or awakening, makes this possible. Faith is as vast as the ocean. D. T. Suzuki states in his book *Japanese Spirituality*, "It is possible to see both Hōnen Shōnin and Shinran Shōnin as one person."[77] When first I came across this passage I was rather surprised. As a researcher in Western philosophy I actually thought it somewhat absurd, for my way of thinking at that time was too heavily influenced by Western thought. I regarded faith to be strictly a matter of each individual and that two individuals could not be seen as one person. But now I see I was wrong.

It goes without saying that both Hōnen Shōnin and Shinran Shōnin were eminent individuals. Each having developed himself fully in his own way, they were individuals with extremely strong characters.

The supraindividual individual

According to D. T. Suzuki, Shinran Shōnin was 'a supraindividual individual' (超個の個 jp. *choko no ko*), that is, a person who has transcended selfishness. The 'supraindividual individual' well corresponds to what I mean by 'individuality' in Shin Buddhism. The supraindividual individual refers to one who has broken through the usual concept of the individual; that is, in the process of individuation we apply the principle of divide and conquer as we make an effort to distinguish ourselves from others. By contrast, the supraindividual individual means a person who reverses that process; this signals a return to the whole wherein we are reunited with others in gratitude and humility. In Shin Buddhist terms, the supraindividual individual is thus a person who goes beyond the individuality of self-power and returns to the totality of Other Power.

D. T. Suzuki's term was coined in connection with Shinran Shōnin's saying, "When I deeply reflect on the Vow of Amida, created through five kalpas of profound thought, I find the Vow is entirely meant for me, Shinran, alone. That is why I feel so grateful for the Original Vow in which Amida graciously resolved to save me, a person so heavily weighed down by [bad] karma." Commenting on Shinran Shōnin's statement that "I find the Vow is entirely meant for me, Shinran, alone," with reference to the expression 'for me, Shinran, alone' (親鸞一人がためなりけり), D. T. Suzuki says it shows Shinran Shōnin's 'supraindividual individuality'.[78]

The passage quoted above is a confession of faith. As I mentioned previously, Shin Buddhist faith has two aspects: 1) awakening to oneself and 2) awakening to Amida. This confession of faith shows that Shinran Shōnin is fully awakened to himself and at the same time to Amida. Shinran Shōnin accepts Amida's Original Vow with gratitude, realising it is entirely for himself alone. These two aspects become one in his pure faith. In his faith Shinran Shōnin is united not only with Amida and but also with Hōnen Shōnin. For Shinran Shōnin Hōnen Shōnin is the very embodiment of the Original Vow.

Furthermore, the expression, 'for me, Shinran, alone,' indicates the absolute passivity of the Shin Buddhist faith. In this absolute passivity one becomes a selfless recipient, through whom the great working of the Buddha can manifest itself freely. When one's individual self transcends the individual self, one becomes selfless and attains to the totality of oneness with others as a supraindividual individual. Although one is selfless and in a state of absolute passivity, one is clearly aware of the dynamics of one's karmic condition.

According to my understanding this awareness of one's unique existence is the reality of one's individuality. This Shin Buddhist notion of individuality is different from the Western interpretation of the individual self. What I refer to by 'individuality' is not the notion of an inherently existing self but to an awareness of oneself in light of one's interdependent karmic condition wherein one is linked karmically to all other things.

Awakening to oneself

When Shin Buddhists speak of 'awakening to oneself,' what do they mean by it? Yuien was very careful concerning this point and showed this by quoting from Shandao. Yuien said: "When I now ponder this expression of Shinran Shōnin's innermost feelings, I find that it is in perfect accordance with the following golden passage from Shandao, 'Know yourself to be an ignorant being, burdened with karmic evil, subject to birth-and-death, ever sinking, ever transmigrating from time immemorial, and with no possible lead to emancipation.' It was the Master's merciful heart causing him to use himself as an example in an effort to awaken us to ourselves going astray without realising how deep our karmic evil is or how great is what has been done for us by [Amida] Tathāgata."

When we use the expression 'awakening to oneself' in the Shin Buddhist context, 'awakening to oneself' means awakening to the unsavable reality of our existence. In other traditions, however, the same expression can have different connotations. For example, in Zen Buddhism it refers to the realisation of the true self or the Buddha-nature. As many people from various backgrounds have different understandings of this term, I feel I should clarify its specific meaning in Shin Buddhism.

As mentioned before, 'awakening to oneself' and 'awakening to Amida' are the two sides of the same coin of the true faith-experience. Through this faith we find our unsavable self is actually saved in the great embrace of Amida Buddha; in other words, one's self becomes one with Amida Buddha. In the absolute passivity of faith to entrust oneself entirely to Amida Buddha, one attains oneness with the Buddha. This oneness between the self and the Buddha as the reality of the Shin Buddhist faith is an inconceivable experience, totally freed from the prison of self-centered consciousness in our daily life. Quite paradoxically through the awareness of our unsavability, we are saved. 'The supraindividual individual' thus refers to a person of true faith freed from the selfish attachment to their own world.

If we realise through faith how deep our karmic evil is, then we will naturally be led to realise how grateful we are to Amida for his unconditional love embracing all beings without any discrimination. This is the key-point of Shin Buddhist philosophy. To reach and understand this point we need a good teacher. This is another essential aspect of Shin Buddhism.

In conclusion let me quote a passage from the Postscript, a passage which my own late father often quoted in his sermons.

As to whether things are good or bad, I am in complete ignorance. The reason is this: if I knew what was good as completely as Amida Tathāgata knows, then I might be allowed to say I know what is good. Or again if I knew what was bad as completely as the Tathāgata knows, then I might be allowed to say I know what is bad. But amongst us ignorant beings, weighed down by blind passions in a world of impermanence, a world that is like a burning house, all is vain, all is empty, there is nothing true. Only the *nembutsu* is true.

Part Three

THE DOCUMENTS
APPENDED TO
THE TANNISHŌ

後鳥羽院之御宇法然聖人他力本
願念佛宗ヲ興行ス于時興福寺
僧侶敵奏之上御弟子中狼藉
子細アルヨシ无實風聞ニヨリテ
罪科ニ處せラルヽ人數事
一法然聖人并御弟子七人流罪又
御弟子四人死罪ニオコナハルヽナリ聖人ハ
土佐國番多ト云所ヘ流罪ニ名
藤井元彦男ニテ生年七十六歳ナリ
親鸞ハ越後國罪名藤井善信云
生年三十五歳ナリ
淨聞房　　　備後國
澄西禪光房　伯耆國

好覺房　伊豆國　行空法本房　佐渡國
幸西成覺房善惠房二人同遠流
サレヲ 无動寺之善題大僧正
コレヲ申アヅカルト云
遠流之人々已上八人ナリト云
被行死罪人々
一番　西意善綽房
二番　性願房
三番　住蓮房
四番　安樂房
二位法印尊長之沙汰也
親鸞改僧儀賜俗名仍非僧非俗
然間以禿字爲姓被經奏聞畢
彼御申状于今外記廳ニ納ト云々
流罪以後愚禿親鸞令書給也

Tannishō, Historical Endnote A (*above*), B (*below*)

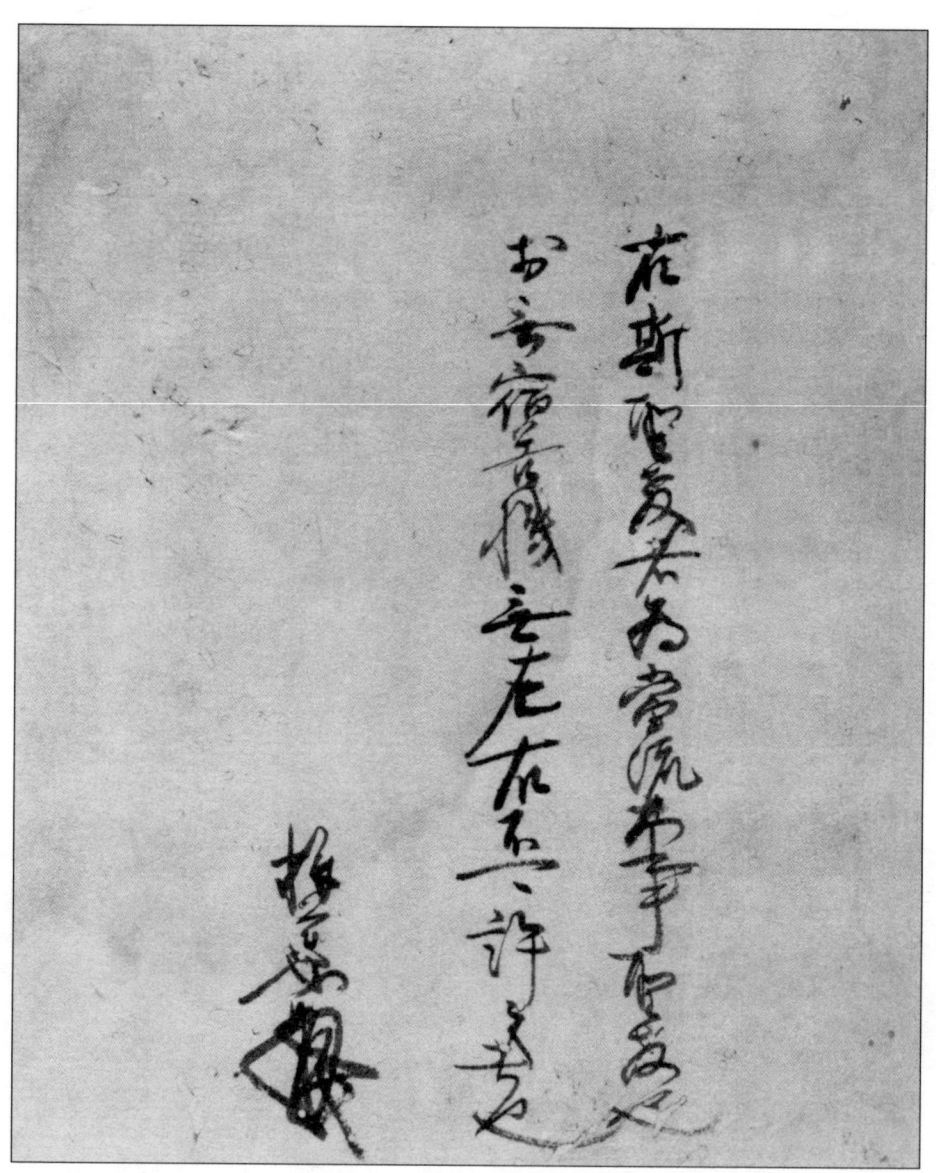

Rennyo Shōnin's Note and Signature

The Historical Endnote and Rennyo Shōnin's Note

TRANSLATION

Historical endnote on the persecution of Pure Land Buddhism in 1207

It was during the reign of Gotoba-in that Hōnen Shōnin founded the *Nembutsu* School, based on the teaching of Other Power, the Power of the Original Vow [of Amida Buddha]. However, the monks of the period from Kōfukuji Temple started accusing Hōnen Shōnin of being an enemy of the Buddha-dharma, and actually lodged a report with the Imperial Court to the effect that there was evidence of lawless misconduct amongst Hōnen Shōnin's disciples. As a result of all these groundless rumours a number of people were found guilty and punished.

Hōnen Shōnin and seven of his disciples were sent into exile and four other disciples were executed.

[Hōnen] Shōnin, himself, was exiled to Hata in Tosa province. His secular name as a branded criminal was 'Fujii no Motohiko, male.' He was seventy-six years old at the time.

Shinran was exiled to Echigo province. His name as a declared criminal was 'Fujii no Yoshizane.' He was then thirty-five years old.

Jōmon-bō was exiled to Bingo province; Chōsai Zenkō-bō, to Hōki province; Kōkaku-bō, to Izu province; Gyōkū Hōhon-bō, to Sado province.

It was likewise determined that both Kōsai Jōkaku-bō and Zenne-bō were also to be banished to remote areas, but finally the Great Abbot [Jien], Former Head of Mudōji, was asked to take custody of them.

Those who were sentenced to banishment were the eight men listed above.

Those who were sentenced to death were:

1) Saii Zenshaku-bō
2) Shōgan-bō
3) Juren-bō
4) Anraku-bō

These sentences were carried out by Dharma-seal Sonchō of the second Imperial Rank.

Shinran was laicised and given a secular name. Consequently he was neither monk nor layman. He decided, therefore, to take the word 'toku' (baldhead) as his surname and applied to the Imperial Court for permission to do so. His letter of application is said to be still stored in the Record Office.

After his banishment he would regularly sign his name Gutoku (baldheaded ignoramus) Shinran.

Rennyo Shōnin's Note

This sacred document is a teaching of great importance in our tradition. It should not be shown indiscriminately to anyone without past good karma.

COMMENTARY

These two documents are both appended to the *Tannishō*. I would contend that they were already appended when Rennyo Shōnin (1414–1499) made a copy of the book, his being the oldest of the six earliest copies. As for Rennyo Shōnin's Note, no one disputes the historical claim that it was added to the text by Rennyo Shōnin himself, for the writing is clearly his own, executed when he was aged sixty-five or so. I will discuss the meaning of this short note later.

Who appended the historical endnote and why?

With regard to the historical endnote on the Persecution of Pure Land Buddhism, starting from the Edo Period right up until the present day, famous scholars of the Shin Buddhist tradition have held a variety of different opinions. Most scholars, however, think that this part is an addition not by Yuien, the compiler of the *Tannishō*, but by someone else who lived at a later period. Furthermore they do not consider this note to have any intrinsic relationship with the contents of the book.

I myself have never been quite comfortable with the views expressed by traditional Shin Buddhist scholars. I have always entertained somewhat positive feelings towards the historical endnote, based on my own intuition that it was closely related to the important spiritual development that Shinran Shōnin, along with his master, Hōnen Shōnin, underwent when they were separated and banished to remote provinces by the government of the day. Shinran Shōnin's spiritual experience during and after that period of persecution, a time when his master was always on his mind, actually forms the core of his teaching in the *Tannishō*.

A challenge to the traditional views of the conservatives has appeared, in fact, from outside the Shin Buddhist tradition, in the form of a new study of the relevant part of the text by an eminent scholar named Takehiko Furuta. According to his book, *Shinran's Thoughts: A Critical Study of the Source Materials,*[79] the historical endnote on the persecution was originally attached to the *Tannishō* by Yuien himself at the time of its compilation. Accordingly it has to be of vital importance to the *Tannishō*.

Sadly, however, its importance has long been neglected. While the main text of the *Tannishō* is an oral tradition of Shin Buddhist teaching, the appendix is an historical document. It is the apparent difference in quality between the two texts that has led to the latter being considered merely as an historical document appended to the main book at a later date. Strange to say Shin Buddhist scholars during the Edo Period and even after the modernization of Japan have been far too interested in the dogmatic aspects of the text to become aware of the profound ties that exist between the historical facts and the essential aspects of the Shin Buddhist message.

Based on a detailed paleographical and philological study of the text, Furuta has confirmed that the main body of the *Tannishō* was copied by Rennyo Shōnin in his forties and that, at a later date, when aged around sixty-five, he transcribed the appended documents. Rennyo Shōnin copied the main document, written in the Kamakura Period, without any alteration of the original text in his possession. The way the Japanese language was written around that time, however, underwent a great many changes in subsequent eras, and consequently this Japanese text from the Kamakura Period would seem to include a large number of inaccuracies and mistakes when viewed by scholars of later times such as those in the Edo, Meiji, Taishō and Shōwa eras. Consequently they regarded Rennyo Shōnin's version as being of much less importance than they should have, whereas in actual fact, according to Furuta's research, Rennyo Shōnin's way of copying the text word for word was entirely accurate. By contrast, the annotated texts composed by later researchers may be correct from a contemporary point of view, but in actual fact differ widely from the original. Furuta's enormous research effort has made it clear that Rennyo Shōnin's version preserved the literary style of the Kamakura Period. In short Rennyo Shōnin's copy of the main text is the oldest existing one as well as the most accurate one.

Concerning the historical endnote, Furuta concludes that it has a close connection to a passage found in the Postscript to the *Tannishō* that reads, "As evidence of the above I have selected some documents and appended them to this book as a set of criteria (*meyasu* in Japanese)." According to Furuta's detailed analysis of the text, this passage refers to the historical endnote on the persecution appended to the whole text. Furuta's view is very different from the observations of other scholars such as Kōgatsuin Jinrei (1749–1817) and Myōon-in Ryōshō of the Edo Period, and subsequently those of Professors Daiei Kaneko, Shinryū Umehara, Raishun Taya and Toshihide Akamatsu who followed their lead. Kōgatsuin Jinrei, for example, states that the note on the persecution was originally attached to another text, and only appended to the *Tannishō* by mistake; Myōon-in Ryōshō holds that, although 'some documents as evidence' from the *Kyōgyōshinshō* or *The Letters* by Shinran Shōnin might have been attached to the text, the majority of the appendices were lost and only the record of the persecution remains; Professor Raishun Taya ventures a guess that the phrase 'some documents as evidence' points to two important sayings by Shinran Shōnin found in the Postscript to the *Tannishō*: "When I deeply reflect on the Vow of Amida, created through five kalpas of profound thought, I find the Vow is entirely meant for me, Shinran, alone..." and "As to whether things are good or bad, I am in complete ignorance... Only the *nembutsu* is true." He concludes that the actual historical document on the persecution was added by someone else at a later date. Takehiko Furuta's research shows that their views are not well grounded.

Through his critical study of source materials, Furuta has shown that the historical document on the persecution, appended to Rennyo Shōnin's copy of the text, is written in the legal style of the Kamakura Period. This means Rennyo Shōnin must have made an exact copy of the original, just as it was, and that it was one of the 'documents as evidence' that Yuien himself appended to the text. According to Furuta's observations, Yuien must have originally selected certain documents as evidence and appended them to the *Tannishō* as a set of criteria (*meyasu*) to be used as a possible petition to the government in order that the Shin Buddhist community might be able to protect their Dharma friends in legal matters. When he copied the *Tannishō* in his forties, Rennyo Shōnin had those legal documents on hand as evidence. Years later, realising that the historical document on the persecution of Hōnen Shōnin and his disciples, one of the legal documents appended by Yuien, was of vital importance to the Shin Buddhist tradition, Rennyo Shōnin copied the document and attached it to the main body of the *Tannishō*. At that time he would have been around age sixty-five, judging from his handwriting. As oppression of the *nembutsu* followers continued sporadically throughout the Kamakura Period, Yuien must have felt this document important then and for the future should need arise to prepare a possible petition, based on past legal cases he had conducted on behalf of his Dharma friends.

There is a problem, however, in Furuta's way of interpreting the word *meyasu* solely as a legal term. As the word *meyasu* was already used as a set of itemised statements of legal petition in the Kamakura period, Furuta would insist that we can interpret 'the historical endnote on the persecution of Pure Land Buddhism' as a legal document. But according to the relevant statement found in the Postscript, the term 'documents as evidence (*shōmon-domo*)' would indicate that there is more than one document. This is very clearly indicated by the plural suffix *-domo*, which is used to show the plural form of the noun to which it is affixed. In addition, long before the Kamakura Period the word *meyasu* (criteria) has been used in a broader sense simply to mean a document consisting of itemised statements. This is followed by the fact that it cannot be determined whether all the other documents were exclusively legal statements or not. Furuta discusses the matter simply by assuming that all the lost 'documents as evidence' must have been legal statements. Furuta's ability to analyse historical documents is sufficiently high to prove the 'historical endnote on the persecution' was a legal document but I have my doubts as to whether his assertion that all the lost 'documents as evidence' were legal statements is well grounded.

Regarding this aspect, I think Myōon-in Ryōshō is right in stating that the historical endnote on the persecution of Pure Land Buddhism is one of the lost documents appended to the main text by Yuien himself, in which case it is highly likely that the other documents might have included doctrinal teachings as well. According to Myōon-in Ryōshō, 'the documents as evidence' must have been something similar to the *Kechimyaku monjū* (血脈文集), which includes essential documents of Shinran Shōnin's teaching and also a similar historical endnote on the persecution of Pure Land Buddhism. The reason that I cannot fully agree with Furuta but feel sympathetic with Myōon-in Ryōshō is simply because I feel that it is not right for us to solve the actual problems of the world simply by resorting to legal methods. It is only by the process of attaining true faith or with the resultant peaceful awareness it ushers in, that we can arrive at a lasting solution to all the actual problems of this world, legal ones included. In Shin Buddhism the true solution of our problems is always accompanied by the attainment of true faith. I would thus contend that 'the documents as evidence' originally appended to the main text must have contained doctrinal documents based on Shinran Shōnin's writings, such as letters or sayings, rather than more legal documents.

Shinran Shōnin himself states in a postscript to his main writing the *Kyōgyōshinshō*,

> The Emperor and his ministers, acting against the Dharma and violating human justice, were stirred to anger and filled with hatred. As a result the Dharma Master Genkū (Hōnen Shōnin), the Great Patriarch who founded and promoted the true teaching, and a number of his followers, without receiving any deliberation of their 'crimes', were sentenced to death for no reason at all, or were deprived of their priesthood, given secular names and exiled to remote areas. I was amongst the latter. Thus I am now neither priest nor layman.[80]

Shinran Shōnin's actual words convey to us his infinite sorrow at the persecution of the *nembutsu* followers. After only six years of sharing with them the joy of attaining faith in the *nembutsu*, he was forced to part from his master and Dharma friends, as they were all banished or condemned to death. This experience of religious persecution had an incredibly important effect on his *nembutsu* life thereafter as he slowly began to understand and digest the true meaning of his encounter with Hōnen Shōnin, which he went on to do for the rest of his life. His sorrow at the persecution was not apart from his true faith or peaceful awareness that "I am now neither priest nor layman." This statement is his spiritual internalisation of these historical events in the light of pure faith.

Rennyo Shōnin's Note and the danger of misunderstanding the Tannishō

After adding the document describing the persecution to the main text of the *Tannishō*, Rennyo Shōnin wrote his own note: "This sacred document is a teaching of great importance in our tradition. It should not be shown indiscriminately to anyone without past good karma." It can be said that this means not only did Rennyo Shōnin recognise the *Tannishō* as 'a teaching of great importance in our tradition', but also that he saw the historical document on the persecution as being substantially related to the sacred text. Although there are many different opinions about the latter part of Rennyo's Shōnin's Note, I myself believe there is a connection with the persecution experienced by the Shin Buddhist Saṃgha. Because of the radical and paradoxical nature of the teaching of the *Tannishō*, if the public is exposed to the *Tannishō* without proper explanation, there is the real danger for misunderstanding and consequent antagonism, especially in the case of those who are spiritually immature and not ready to accept the teaching. The expression 'past good karma' that appears repeatedly in Rennyo Shōnin's writings means one's involvement in the teaching of Amida Buddha through various karmic conditions. There are some who think Rennyo Shōnin's statement, "It should not be shown indiscriminately to anyone without past good karma," demonstrates a somewhat autocratic attitude. But if you understand the good relationship that existed between the Master and his followers in the Saṃgha, it will be easy for you to see that Rennyo Shōnin's words sprang from the great love and compassion he felt for his dear Dharma friends.

EPILOGUE

In the subtitle of this book I have emphasised that the essence of the *Tannishō* lies in the pure encounter between master and disciple. Thanks to this gift left to us by Yuien we are able to glimpse the dynamic reality of daily *nembutsu* life as exemplified in the relationship between Shinran Shōnin and Hōnen Shōnin. If you have this kind of encounter in your own life you will find yourself surrounded by the world of 'all Buddhas' (jp. *shobutsu*) and receive diamond-like faith.

In this life, of course, even after the attainment of faith, you will still have many problems to confront but, just as Shinran Shōnin taught Yuien in Chapter 9, encountering the reality of our karmic existence becomes itself the impetus for us to return again and again to that first moment of receiving pure faith and realising Amida Buddha's constant and unconditional love. In this way our karma, which seemed such a burden, is transformed into 'good from the past' (jp. *shukuzen*) through Amida Buddha's Infinite Light made manifest in our daily lives.

In other words everything, according to the teaching of the Buddha, is in flux and there are no permanent entities, so our liberation cannot come about through some fixed idea but only through awakening to the reality of existence which is ever changing. As I said in my commentary, the way of life of a person of true faith is never stagnant and even the obstacles we meet will help us go forwards. For us to realise our original [Buddha] nature (jp. *kenshō*) or receive pure faith (jp. *shinjin*), awakening is the key. In Zen we need to be awakened from *samādhi* (deep concentration), in Shin Buddhism faith is seen as a simultaneous awakening both to the reality of our karmic existence and to the working of Amida Buddha's Original Vow. With this first experience of awakening as the foundation of our later lives, we find the working of Amida's unconditional love through everything and everybody that we meet in everyday life.

One day Daisetsu Sensei (D. T. Suzuki) took up his brush and executed a piece of calligraphy for my late master, Dharma-mother Ekai-ni. It read 無量寿 *Muryōju*, or Eternal Life, meaning Amida Buddha. As I was admiring it in my quarters at Engakuji Temple, it occurred to me that if I simply took it back to Shōgyōji Temple as it was, without any accompanying comment from Daisetsu Sensei, Ekai-san might be disappointed. With this in mind I went to see Daisetsu Sensei and asked him what the phrase meant: "Sensei, regarding the calligraphy you made for Ekai-san, what do the words '*Eternal Life*' mean?" "Well," he replied, "see that cat prowling around over there and those daffodils blooming in the garden? All of them are Eternal Life. Yes, everything is the working of Eternal Life." Dharma-mother Ekai-ni was extremely pleased to hear Daisetsu Sensei's comment. Though at the time I did not have eyes to see it, Sensei was actually living in a world filled with light, where, yes, everything was indeed the working of Eternal Life, of Amida Buddha.

Every day at the Three Wheels Temple here in London where I now live, I enjoy encounters and re-encounters with all kinds of people, both Japanese and Western. My role is to present Buddhism in English, a task that has become no easier now that I have reached my seventies. Almost every time I begin preparing my lectures, I come upon something for which I can find no adequate English expression. At that point I sit myself down before a small shrine dedicated to Daisetsu Sensei and talk to him. And he never fails to answer me, saying, "All you need do is simply become Namu-Amida-butsu itself; yes, everything's the working of Eternal Life." *Namu-Amida-butsu, Namu-Amida-butsu.*

The most precious feature of the *Tannishō* as a sacred document of our tradition is the way Yuien describes the richness of Jōdo Shinshū life, including the many challenges that confront the *nembutsu* followers and the way to go beyond these difficulties. If you read any chapter with a clear awareness of your own problems, you will find the solution to those problems right there in its pages. Reflecting upon this, I recall that once the Venerable Soga Ryōjin, asked by a student to name him the best commentary on the *Tannishō*, replied that the best commentary on the *Tannishō* was the *Tannishō* itself. As a record of the pure encounter between master and disciple it transmits to us both the teaching and the spirit of deep hearing. To study the *Tannishō* in depth, please just listen to it repeatedly.

Namu-Amida-butsu

APPENDIX

BIBLIOGRAPHY

Asahara, Saichi 浅原才市 (1850–1932), *Asahara Saichi shū* 妙好人浅原才市集, ed. Suzuki Daisetsu (1870–1966) [and Satō Taira], Tokyo: Shunjūsha, 1967. Posthumously published, the work was seen into print by a youthful Satō Taira, then in his late twenties, who did the bulk of the editing.

Bloom, Alfred, *Strategies for modern living*: a commentary with the text of the *Tannishō*, Berkeley, CA: Numata Center for Buddhist Translation and Research, 1992.

Dōgen (1200–1253), *Shōbōgenzō zuimonki: Dōgen goroku* 正法眼蔵随聞記: 道元語録, Tetsurō Watsuji (1889–1960), ed., Iwanami shoten, 1983, p. 93. Originally published in 1929.

Fromm, Erich, 'Memories of D. T. Suzuki, *The Eastern Buddhist* N.S. vol. 2, 1967, pp. 86–89.

Fujishima, Tatsurō 藤島達朗 (1907–1985), *Eshin-ni-kō: Shinran no tsuma* 恵信尼公: 親鸞の妻, 1984, Kyoto: Hōzōkan. Originally published under the same title by the Eshin-ni-kō Itoku Kenshōkai Jimukyoku, Arai: 1956.

Furuta, Takehiko 古田武彦 (1926–), *Shinran shisō: sono shiryō hihan* 親鸞思想: その史料批判 Shinran's Thoughts: A Critical Study of the Source Materials, Tokyo: Toyama-bō, 1975.

Kanamatsu, Kenryō, *Naturalness: A classic of Shin Buddhism*, Bloomington, IN: World Wisdom, 2002, pp. 116–117. Originally published in 1949.

Kurata, Hyakuzō 倉田百三 (1891–1943), *Shukke to sono deshi* 出家とその弟子 [A Priest and His Disciple], Tokyo : Iwanami-shoten, 1917.

Kurata, Hyakuzō, *The priest and his disciples: a play*, trans., Glenn W. Shaw, Tokyo: Hokuseido, 1922.

Myōon-in Ryōshō, 妙音院了祥 (1788–1842), *Tannishō monki* 歎異抄聞記, Kyoto: Hōzōkan, 1972. First published in 1908 by the Hōwakai shuppanbu, Tokyo.

Otto, Rudolf, *India's religion of grace and Christianity compared and contrasted*, Frank Hugh Foster, trans., New York: Macmillan, 1930.

Rogers, Minor L. and Rogers, Ann T., *Rennyo: The Second Founder of Shin Buddhism*, Berkeley, CA: Asian Humanities Press, 1991.

Sasaki, Ruth F. (1892–1967), trans., *The Record of Lin-chi*, Kyoto: The Institute for Zen Studies, Hanazono College, 1975.

Sasaki, Ruth F., trans., *The Record of Linji*, ed. Thomas Yūhō Kirchner, Honolulu: University of Hawai'i Press, 2009.

Satō, Taira (*b*. 1939), and Minakami, Tsutomu, eds., *Myōkōnin* 妙好人, *Daijōbutten: Chūgoku-Nihon hen:* vol. 28, Tokyo: Chūōkōron, 1987, p. 153.

Shinran Shōnin, *The Collected Works of Shinran*, Gadjin M. Nagao, ed., two volumes, Kyoto: Jōdo Shinshū Honganji-ha, 1997.

Shinran, Gutoku Shaku, *The Kyōgyōshinshō: The collection of passages expounding the true teaching, living, faith, and realizing of the Pure Land*, D. T. Suzuki, trans., Kyoto: Shinshū Ōtani-ha, 1973.

Shinshū shōgyō zensho 真宗聖教全書, Shinshū shōgyō zensho-hensansho, Kyoto: Ōyagi Kōbundō, 1964. A five volume series originally published under the same title by Kyoto: Kōkyō shoin, 1941–64.

Shōwa shinshū Hōnen Shōnin zenshū 昭和新修法然上人全集, Kyōdō Ishii, ed., Kyoto: Heirakuji-shoten, 1995. First published by Risōsha, Tokyo, and the Jōdoshumusho, Tokyo, in 1955.

Soga, Ryōjin 曽我 量深 (1875–1971), *Tannishō chōki* 歎異抄聴記, Kyoto: Chōjiya, 1948.

Suzuki, D. T., *Buddha of Infinite Light*, Taitetsu Unno, ed., 1998, Shambhala in association with the American Buddhist Academy, 1998, pp. 55–57.

Suzuki, D. T., *Collected Writings on Shin Buddhism*, ed., The Eastern Buddhist Society, Kyoto: Shinshū Ōtani-ha, 1973.

Suzuki, D. T., *Japanese Spirituality*, N. Waddell, trans., Tokyo: Japan Society for the Promotion of Science, 1972.

Suzuki, D. T., *Mysticism: Christian and Buddhist*, New York: Harper & Brothers, 1957.

Suzuki, Daisetsu, *Nihonteki reisei* 日本的霊性, *Suzuki Daisetz zenshū*, vol. 8, Iwanami-shoten, 1968. Originally published in 1944 by Daitō shuppan, Tokyo.

Suzuki, D. T. , *Shin Buddhism*, New York: Harper & Row, 1970.

Suzuki, Daisetsu, *Suzuki Daisetsu Shinshū nyūmon* 鈴木大拙真宗入門, Taira Sato, trans., Tokyo: Shunjūsha, 1983.

Takehara, Chimyo 竹原智明, *Shōshinge-eza* 正信偈会座, Futsukaichi, Fukuoka: Shōgyōji, 2005.

Takehara, Reion 竹原嶺音 (Daigyōin, 1876–1951), *Gushikō* 遇斯光, two volumes, Futsukaichi, Fukuoka Pref.: Shōgyōji, 1963. Originally published from 1953 on.

White, John (*b.*1924), *The Breath in the Flute* 笛の息, Taira Sato, trans., Tokyo: Shunjūsha, 2001.

CHRONOLOGY OF EVENTS

The encounter between Hōnen Shōnin and Shinran Shōnin

1133   Hōnen Shōnin is born.

1173   Shinran Shōnin is born.

1175   At the age of 43 Hōnen Shōnin takes refuge in Amida Buddha.

1181   At the age of 49 Hōnen Shōnin is asked to spearhead the reconstruction of the Tōdaiji temple. He refuses, however, and instead recommends one of his friends, Chōgen (1121–1206).

1184   Hōnen Shōnin administers the precepts of Buddhism to a warrior, Taira no Shigehira, after teaching him about Pure Land Buddhism.

1186   Hōnen Shōnin engages in a large open debate on Buddhism with the most eminent scholar-priests of the time.

1189   Hōnen Shōnin preaches to then Regent Kujō Kanezane about Pure Land Buddhism and administers the Buddhist precepts to him.

1190   At the request of Chōgen, Hōnen Shōnin preaches on the three Sūtras of Pure Land Buddhism at the Tōdaiji temple. In that year too Shōkū (1177–1247) becomes Hōnen Shōnin's disciple.

1193   A warrior, Kumagai Naozane (*d.* 1208) becomes Hōnen Shōnin's disciple.

1195   Another warrior, Tsunoto no Saburō Tamemori (1163–1243) visits Hōnen Shōnin and in the same year Genchi (1183–1238) becomes his disciple.

1197   Benchō (1162–1238) becomes Hōnen Shōnin's disciple.

1198   At the age of 66, as censure of his Pure Land School began to gather strength, Hōnen Shōnin sets out to write the *Senchaku hongan nembutsu shū* at the request of the Regent Fujiwara Kanezane to be read by only a few of his closest disciples. Divided into sixteen sections, this work elucidates Amida's Original Vow in which the practice of the *nembutsu* is specifically chosen as the right practice for all human beings. It centres on the idea of faith, found in Shandao's *Exposition on the Meditation Sūtra*. In this same year, Kōsai (1163–1247) becomes one of his disciples.

1199   Hōnen Shōnin gives Benchō a copy of the *Senchaku hongan nembutsu shū*.

1201   When Hōnen Shōnin was 69, Shinran Shōnin (1173–1262) becomes his disciple and Gishūmonin, Kanezane's daughter, enters the priesthood under Hōnen Shōnin's instruction.

1202   Kanezane himself enters the priesthood under Hōnen Shōnin's tutelage and Chōsai (1184–1227) becomes a disciple.

1204   Hōnen Shōnin gives Ryūkan (1148–1227) a copy of his *Senchaku hongan nembutsu shū*.

1205   Hōnen Shōnin allows Shinran Shōnin to copy the *Senchaku hongan nembutsu shū*.

1204–
1207   During this period Hōnen Shōnin's teaching comes under strong criticism from the representatives of the established sects of Nara and Mount Hiei and is subsequently

proscribed (1207). Despite Kanezane's desperate efforts to save them, four of Hōnen Shōnin's followers are executed on the banks of the River Kamo, and Hōnen Shōnin himself is banished to Tosa on the island of Shikoku. At least seven of his chief disciples are also each exiled separately to remote parts of Japan. Shinran Shōnin is exiled to Echigo, on the remote north shore of Japan's main island.

1207   In December of this year, however, Hōnen Shōnin is acquitted by Imperial decree and at the age of 79, in 1211, returns to Kyoto.

1211   Shinran Shōnin is reprieved by Imperial decree but does not return to Kyoto.

1212   Hōnen Shōnin finally passes away.

1214   Shinran Shōnin moves to Hitachi, north of present day Tokyo.

1262   Shinran Shōnin passes away.

1300   Kakunyo Shōnin begins to compile his *Life of Shinran Shōnin* and soon afterwards his *Life of Hōnen Shōnin*, that later became two famous picture scrolls of that period.

1480   Around this time Rennyo Shōnin (1414–1499), the eighth hereditary leader of the Honganji lineage, copies the *Tannishō*, now regarded as the earliest existing copy.

The encounter between Shinran Shōnin and Yuien

1173   Shinran Shōnin is born.

1182   Eshinni is born, later to be Shinran Shōnin's wife.

1214   Shinran Shōnin moves to Hitachi, north of present day Tokyo.

1216   Jishin-bo Zenran is born, Shinran Shōnin's eldest son.

1222   Yuien is born in Kyoto, fathered by Onomiya Zennen. Receives an education.

1224   Kakushin-ni is born in Hitachi, the youngest of Shinran Shōnin's daughters.

1234   At the age of 62 Shinran Shōnin moves with family to Kyoto.

1240   *Yuien meets Shinran Shōnin and becomes his disciple, learning the teaching from him. It is possible that Shinran Shōnin assigned him to be an advisor in the strategic Hitachi area, where Yuien founds the Senkeiji dojo next to a heart-shaped pond. He is known as Yuien of Kawada, to distinguish him from another person of the same name.

1243   Kakushin-ni gives birth to Kakue, fathered by first husband Hino Hirotsuna.

1249   Kakushin-ni's first husband dies, leaving her with a seven-year-old son.

1250   Around this time Jishin-bo Zenran is causing problems in the eastern sector (present day Tokyo area) by turning his back on the teaching of his father Shinran Shōnin.

1253   Kakushin-ni gives birth to Yuizen, fathered by Onomiya Zennen, who is also Yuien's father.

1256   Around this time a group of key disciples in the Kantō district makes the long journey from Hitachi to call on Shinran Shōnin in Kyoto to discuss the growing Samgha problems caused by Jishin-bo Zenran within the community. Consequently Shinran Shōnin disowns his own son. Yuien is amongst the members of the entourage, although technically speaking he is not one of the twenty-four key disciples per se but holds a separate status.

1262   Shinran Shōnin dies.

1268   Eshinni dies.

1270   Kakunyo Shōnin is born, third hereditary leader of the Honganji lineage, Shinran Shonin's great grandson.

1274   Estate left to Kakushin-ni by Onomiya Zennen. Yuien returns to the capital Kyoto, at length moving to Yoshino, in Nara, where he lives at Ryūkōji temple.

1275   Onomiya Zennen dies leaving Kakushin-ni as the caretaker of the Shinran Shōnin mausoleum.

1283   Kakushin-ni dies.

1286   Jishin-bo Zenran dies.

1288   Yuien is asked to instruct his grandnephew Kakunyo Shōnin (1270–1351) on Shinran Shōnin's teaching. It is possible that he composed the *Tannishō* for this occasion.

1289   *Yuien dies in Shimoichi, Nara.

1294   Kakunyo Shōnin composes the eulogy for the thirty-third memorial service for Shinran Shōnin and compiles *The Life of Shinran*, the first of many documents.

*The information for some entries based on the early Shin Buddhist chronology compiled by Senkei Ryōga, titled *Ōtani iseki roku*, published in 1779.

DESCRIPTIVE CHAPTER TITLES

Chapter 1	弘願信心章	The chapter on faith in the Vow of Universal Deliverance
Chapter 2	唯信念佛章	The chapter on pure faith in the *nembutsu*
Chapter 3	悪人正機章	The chapter on the persons with bad karma as the right object [of the Original Vow]
Chapter 4	慈悲差別章	The chapter on the difference in compassion between the Path of Sages and the Path of the Pure Land Buddhist
Chapter 5	念佛不廻章	The chapter on the *nembutsu* of no virtue-transference
Chapter 6	誠諍弟子章	The chapter on the admonition against engaging in disputes over disciples
Chapter 7	念佛無碍章	The chapter of the *nembutsu* of no hindrance
Chapter 8	非行非善章	The chapter on non-practice and non-good
Chapter 9	不喜不快章	The chapter on no joy and no happiness
Chapter 10	無義為義章	The chapter on the meaning of no meaning
Chapter 11	誓名別信章	The chapter on the erroneous view that makes a distinction between believing in the inconceivability of the Original Vow and believing in the inconceivability of the Name
Chapter 12	學解念佛章	The chapter that deals with the problem of trying to understand the *nembutsu* by learning
Chapter 13	禁誇本願章	The chapter that deals with the problem of prohibiting people from relying too heavily on the Original Vow
Chapter 14	一念滅罪章	The chapter [that criticises the misleading belief] that one can eradicate evil karma through a single utterance of the *nembutsu*
Chapter 15	即身成佛章	The chapter [that criticises the misconception] that one can become a Buddha in one's own earthly body
Chapter 16	自然廻心章	The chapter [that criticises the misconception] that as a matter of course [in order to attain birth in the Pure Land] one should be reforming oneself continuously
Chapter 17	邊地堕獄章	The chapter [that criticises the false message] that anyone born in the Borderland will ultimately descend into hell
Chapter 18	施量分報章	The chapter [that criticises the false conception] that the size of Buddha one becomes depends on the size of one's donations [to the Saṃgha]

Source: Myōon-in Ryōshō, *Tannishō monki* 歎異抄聞記, 1908.

GLOSSARY

Ānanda. Śākyamuni Buddha's faithful disciple and constant attendant. Ānanda's humble and sincere question on noticing one day the extraordinary brilliance of the Buddha's features is said to have provided the impetus for the Buddha's delivery of *The Larger Sūtra of Eternal Life* (jp. *Daimuryōjukyō*, skt. *[Larger] Sukhāvatīvyūha Sūtra*).

As-it-is-ness (jp. *sonomama*). A term coined by D. T. Suzuki to express the highest reality. He also applied it to Zen satori and Shinto spirituality, as well as Pure Land's naturalness (*jinen*).

Avalokiteśvara (jp. *Kannon, Kanzeon*). One of Amida Buddha's two attendant bodhisattvas who embodies the activity of great love and compassion. The Sanskrit word *Avalokiteśvara* means 'one who is sensitive to sound in the world', thus Bodhisattva Avalokiteśvara is the bodhisattva who saves all sentient beings upon hearing their request. Paired with Bodhisattva Mahāsthāmaprāpta, the bodhisattva of great wisdom, Avalokiteśvara is worshipped as the bodhisattva of great compassion throughout the Far East. Interestingly, it is believed that Shinran Shōnin saw his wife as a manifestation of Bodhisattva Avalokiteśvara.

Avataṃsaka Sūtra (jp. *Kegon-gyō*). Also known as *The Garland Sūtra*. Amongst other things this sūtra teaches the doctrine of unimpeded, free interpenetration of phenomena (jp. *jiji muge-hokkai*).

Awakening of Faith. The essence of Shin Buddhist faith (jp. *shinjin*) lies in an instantaneous awakening of two kinds: awakening to oneself and awakening to Amida Buddha's unconditional love. This instantaneous awakening of faith is referred to in the Shin Buddhist tradition as the one-thought moment of the awakening of faith (jp. *ichinen no shinjin*), or as faith attained in the one-thought moment of taking refuge [in Amida Buddha] (jp. *ichinen kimyo no shinjin*), when Pure Land birth becomes assured and a living awareness of the Dharma dawns in the consciousness of the *nembutsu* follower.

Awakening of Faith through the Three Vows (jp. *sangan tennyū*). Awakening to the truth of the Original Vow. In this process of spiritual development clarified by Shinran Shōnin, the Nineteenth and Twentieth Vows primarily serve as devices that help to direct us to the ultimate truth of the Eighteenth Vow, which he refers to as the Original Vow. Shinran Shōnin's ability to articulate such an insight stems from his own religious experience of having entrusted himself to the Original Vow as a result of his encounter with his master Hōnen Shōnin. As such, *sangan tennyū* lies at the critical core of Shinran Shōnin's religious thought and plays an important role in his masterful presentation of the Pure Land Buddhist teaching in his main work the *Kyōgyōshinshō*.

Birth in the Pure Land (jp. *ōjō*). In Shin Buddhism there are two kinds of 'birth in the Pure Land'. One meaning is to go beyond transmigration (birth-and-death) and is synonymous with Nirvāna; therefore it is also called 'the birth of no-birth' (and no-death). The second meaning is that if a person attains pure faith in the Buddha their new life is embraced by, and to some extent participates in, the Light of the Pure Land while remaining within the limitations of this world. The attainment of faith in this world, that is, birth in the Pure Land in the latter sense, assures the ultimate attainment of Nirvāna, birth in the Pure Land in the former sense.

Blind Passions (skt. *kleśa*, jp. *bonnō*). Delusion, afflictions, etc. As human beings we reconstruct our experience of this world through our intellect (mind) and our five senses (body). The world-view we thus form is entirely self-centred because we are not fully aware of the limitations of our intellect and sense organs. Usually we consider that our views represent the truth and that this truth is absolute and eternal and we remain strongly and selfishly attached to our views. Yet such an attitude, unless we become aware of it, leads to untold suffering and afflictions in our lives.

Borderland (jp. *henji*). A symbol of the self-centred world of illusion, the realm of attachment to self-power and the unenlightened, doubting mind of those followers who remain unable to attain true faith because of their doubt, pride, and indolence. Other epithets such as Realm or Land of Indolence and Pride (jp. *kemangai, kemangoku*) and the Womb Palace of the Castle of Doubt (jp. *gijō taigū*) allude to the mental state of those that are obliged to tarry in the Borderland for lack of faith and are used as synonyms for it. With regard to the Womb Palace of the Castle of Doubt, the original term *gijō taigū* can be broken down into its elements as 'Castle of Doubt' and 'Womb Palace.' In the present work, however, the combined use of the two elements has been selected to express the traditional interpretation that the Castle of Doubt is the cause of birth in the Borderland and the Womb Palace its result. The term derives from *The Larger Sūtra of Eternal Life*.

Daijikkyō. *The Great Collection of Sūtras*, a sixty-fascicle Mahāyāna sūtra collection especially notable for its inclusion of a discussion of the Right-, Semblance-, and Last Dharma Ages.

Dharmakāya, Dharma-body (jp. *hosshin*). The formless, ultimate truth of the Buddha-dharma or the absolute nature of the Buddha's Enlightenment which no words can express. The Buddha's Dharmakāya exists beyond his *rūpakāya* (jp. *shikishin*) or corruptible physical form.

Difficult Practice [Way] (jp. *nangyō*). *See* 'Path of Sages.'

Direct Way to Awakening. This refers to the teaching of sudden awakening (jp. *tongyō*). *See* 'Leaping over Crosswise.'

Easy Practice [Way] (jp. *igyō*[*dō*]). *See* 'Path of the Pure Land Buddhist.'

Essentials of Faith Alone. A work by Seikaku Hōin (1167–1235), one of Shinran Shōnin's closest Dharma friends, who also followed Hōnen Shōnin's teaching.

[Amida Buddha] Embraces All Beings, Forsaking None (jp. *sesshu fusha* 摂取不捨). A famous phrase from *The Meditation Sūtra*, which describes the working of the infinite light of Amida Buddha that embraces all beings forsaking none, indicating the all-encompassing and nondiscriminating nature of Amida's great compassion.

Evil Karma (jp. *akugō*). The negative karma that emburdens living beings and forces them to remain in their unenlightened state. Shinran Shōnin regarded all his self-powered actions, even ostensibly 'good' ones, as coloured by the three poisons of greed, anger, and ignorance, and indeed saw them as rooted in habitual (karmic) behaviours whose origins stretched so far back into the past as to defy comprehension. At the same time, such karma forms no hindrance to the inconceivable working of Amida Buddha's love and wisdom that has vowed to deliver all beings to the Pure Land.

Exposition on The Meditation Sūtra (jp. *Kanmuryōju-kyō sho, Kangyō-sho;* ch. *Guanjingshu* 観経疏). A Tang Dynasty commentary on *The Meditation Sūtra* by Shandao.

Gratitude [for the Buddha's benevolence]. Once we become aware of Amida Buddha's unconditional love through the acquisition of true faith (the state of mind which has no doubt), the *nembutsu* that issues from our mouths is an expression of our supreme gratitude. On attaining pure faith we become grateful not only to Amida but to everyone and everything that has helped us encounter Amida.

Hearing that Name. 'Hearing that Name' is the literal translation of the phrase 聞其名号 (jp. *mon go myōgō*), from the passage on the fulfilment of the Eighteenth Vow in *The Larger Sūtra of Eternal Life*. Here, the Name that is being heard refers to Amida Buddha's statement in the Seventeenth Vow: that, unless all Buddhas pronounce his Name in universal praise, he would choose to defer attaining Supreme Enlightenment. The world of Enlightenment is here being described in terms of the Name that is being heard and the Name that is being pronounced. The deeper significance of these passages as the Shin Buddhist faith-experience is brought out by Rennyo Shōnin who writes: 'Hearing that Name actually means that when we meet a good teacher, receive his teaching and entrust ourselves to the Name that he recites, then Amida Buddha saves us without fail' (*The Letters* by Rennyo Shōnin, Fascicle 1, fifteenth letter).

Hymns on the Pure Land (jp. *Jōdo Wasan*). Shinran Shōnin left more than five hundred *wasan* (lit., hymns in Japanese), which are compiled into several works such as *Hymns on the Pure Land*, *Hymns on the Pure Land Masters*, *Hymns on the Right-, Semblance- and Last Dharma-Ages* and *Hymns in Praise of Prince Shōtoku*. They are all beautiful expressions of the Shin Buddhist faith-experience and teachings. Shin Buddhist followers chant them at daily services.

Hymns on the Samādhi of All Buddhas' Presence. Shandao's *Banzhouzan* 般舟讚. The *samādhi* in question is that expounded in the *Pratyutpanna Sūtra*, one of the earliest Pure Land texts, and refers to the experience of viewing all Buddhas through the practice of pronouncing the Name of Amida Buddha.

Inconceivability. The original Sanskrit term *acintya* means 'beyond thinking.' Shinran Shōnin's acute awareness of the irredeemable nature of his own existence often makes him refer to the Original Vow as something inconceivable because it saves the unsavable, even the wicked and evil, with an all-embracing love that knows no discrimination.

Kechimyaku monjū. A collection of five of the letters written by Shinran Shōnin to his followers, as well as an historical note on the persecution of Pure Land Buddhism that is similar in content to the historical endnote appended to the *Tannishō*. For a partial English translation, see 'Letters of the tradition', *The Collected Works of Shinran*, I, 575–578 (documents no. 2, 4), 525–527 (1), 571-572 (3), 528 (6); the historical note (document no. 5) is the one item that is not included.

Kyōgyōshinshō (A Collection of Passages Expounding the True Teaching, Practice, Faith, and Realisation of the Pure Land). Shinran Shōnin's major work; a compilation of selected Pure Land writings arranged with commentaries representing his reinterpretation of the essential teachings firmly based on his own experience. For a partial English translation, see D. T. Suzuki, trans., the *Kyōgyōshinshō*, 1973. For a complete translation see G. M. Nagao, ed., *The Collected Works of Shinran*, I, Jōdo Shinshū Hongwanji-ha (Nishi Hongwanji), 1997.

Lamp for the Latter Age (jp. *Mattōshō*). A collection of Shinran Shōnin's letters to various followers and congregations.

Land of Enjoyment (jp. *hōdo*). *See* 'Pure Land'.

Land of Happiness (jp. *anraku-koku*). See 'Pure Land'.

Land of Utmost Bliss (jp. *gokuraku*). *See* 'Pure Land'.

Leaping over Crosswise (jp. *ōchō*). A technical term that indicates the way in which true faith in the *nembutsu* is imparted by Other Power, resulting in the severing of the roots of illusion and ultimately in the attainment of Buddhahood in the Pure Land.

The Letters [by Rennyo Shōnin] (jp. *Ofumi* or *Gobunshō*). Rennyo Shōnin (1414–1499), Restorer of the Honganji Temple, left more than two hundred letters addressed to his followers. Venerable Ennyo (1491–1521), one of his grandsons, is said to have compiled eighty of them into a formal edition known as *The (Five Fascicle) Letters*. The fifty-eight letters of Fascicles 1 to 4 are in chronological order, while the twenty-two letters of Fascicle 5 are all undated.

Mahāsthāmaprāpta (jp. *Seishi*). One of Amida Buddha's two attendant bodhisattvas. The original Sanskrit *Mahāsthāmaprāpta* means 'one who has attained great strength' and is associated with the great working of wisdom. The name refers to the bodhisattva's power to illumine the world of illusion and break the bonds of karmic suffering.

Myōon-in Ryōshō (1788–1842). A Shin Buddhist priest and scholar of the Edo Period who devoted his whole life to the study of the *Tannishō*. It is thanks to him that we know the author of the *Tannishō* to have been Yuien, one of Shinran Shōnin's disciples. Myōon-in Ryōshō wrote many books such as *Tannishō monki* (*Notes Made While Listening to the Tannishō*) and *Igishū* (*Collection of Divergent Teachings*). *See also* 'Descriptive Chapter Titles by Myōon-in Ryōshō' in the Appendix.

The Name (jp. *Myōgō*). The Name refers to the words 'Namu-Amida-butsu', literally meaning 'I take refuge in Amida Buddha.' The Name expressed in this act of taking refuge in Amida Buddha is understood to be due entirely to the working of Amida Buddha. The moment we entrust ourselves to Amida Buddha we find the Name wells up from within. In other words, the Name is the activity of the Dharma entering our consciousness at the deepest and most intuitive level, allowing us to perceive a higher reality and to grasp its ultimate truth. As a formula expressed in words, the Name works for our salvation through our senses and intellect; at the same time, the Name goes beyond the limits of senses and intellect, as the inconceivable working of Amida Buddha.

Naturalness (jp. *jinen*). The working of Other Power.

Neither Priest nor Layman (jp. *hisō-hizoku*). Prompted by his exile to Echigo Province, Shinran Shōnin declared in his main writing, the *Kyōgyōshinshō*, 'Thus I am now neither priest nor layman.'

Nirvāna (jp. *nehan*). The Sanskrit word *Nirvāna* means 'to be extinguished', 'to be calmed', 'to disappear', or 'to be deceased.' In Buddhism it refers to 'tranquillity as the fruit of Enlightenment,' the state of mind in which all blind passions binding one to transmigration through birth-and-death have been extinguished. It includes characteristics such as the extinction of suffering, awakening to the truth of life, formless wisdom, utter tranquillity, inner peace and, ultimately, universal love or sympathy for all beings.

Original Vow (jp. *hongan*). Amida Buddha's Eighteenth Vow to save all sentient beings without discriminating amongst them. See Chapter 8.

Other Power (jp. *tariki*). The power of Amida's Original Vow.

Past Good Karma, or **Good from the Past** (jp. *shukuzen*). All the factors and conditions that have led to our encounter with the Buddha-dharma. Often these factors may actually consist of 'bad' or 'evil' karma at first. Such karma is transformed through our encounter with the working of the Buddha-dharma. On attaining the true faith of entrusting ourselves to the Original Vow, we rediscover with gratitude that everyone and everything has helped us reach this point. Once we awaken to Other Power faith, in the new light of awareness that comes about through our involvement in the Buddha-dharma everything in our life is affirmed in its totality and found to be 'good'.

Pāramitā (jp. *haramitsu*). The Sanskrit term *pāramitā* (lit., 'perfection') has been translated into Chinese as 'crossing over', 'reaching the infinite', or 'reaching the other shore.' It is by means of *pāramitā* practice that one leaves this shore of birth-and-death and reaches the other shore of Nirvāṇa. The original six *pāramitā* practices of Early Buddhism were the perfections of donation, observance of precepts, patience, endeavour, meditation and wisdom. Because of their altruistic concerns the Mahayanists added to the original six a further four: the perfections of skillful means, vows, strength, and transcendental knowledge. In Mahāyāna Buddhism *pāramitā* practice is understood as the practice of bodhisattvas in general, and in Shin Buddhism as that of Bodhisattva Dharmākara (Amida Buddha) in particular.

Past Karma (jp. *shukugō*). The karmically-formed causes and conditions that together have brought us to our present situation. Whether for good or evil, our past karma, stored in our present existence, will always influence our thoughts and actions, though we are often unaware of it.

Path of the Pure Land Buddhist (jp. *jōdo-mon*). Pure Land teaching, often rendered as the Pure Land Path. The Mahāyāna tradition based upon the Pure Land sūtras and characterised by reliance on the power of Amida Buddha.

Path of Sages (jp. *shōdō-mon*). Traditions other than Pure Land Buddhism which are based on the cultivation and purification of the mind and body by means of meditative and non-meditative self-power practices.

Peaceful Awareness (jp. *anjin*). In the Shin Buddhist tradition, the word *anjin* is used synonymously with *shinjin* 信心 or faith. Taking into consideration the actual use of the word *anjin*, it is a term describing a peaceful state of mind, an awareness of oneself resting in the great compassion of the Buddha; this state is only reached through one's personal attainment of true faith, or *shinjin*. The original word thus covers a broad range of meaning that includes the tranquillity, peacefulness, stability, firmness, effortlessness, and naturalness of true faith, or *shinjin*, attained by entrusting oneself absolutely to Amida Buddha.

The Person with Bad Karma [as the object of salvation] (jp. *akunin shōki*). According to Hōnen Shōnin and Shinran Shōnin the Pure Land teaching of Other Power is especially concerned with the salvation of those who are burdened with karmic transgressions. Indeed those who have a deep and sincere awareness of their own limitations are more able to entrust themselves to the working of Amida's Vow.

Prajñā (jp. *chie*). Transcendental wisdom; seeing reality just as it is, without the interference of our discriminatory consciousness. *Prajñā* constitutes one of the two main aspects of the Buddha, the other being *karuṇā* (jp. *jihi*) or unconditional love. Amida's unconditional love for all beings, which is the essence of his Original Vow, naturally issues from this transcendental wisdom.

Provisional Vows. The Nineteenth and Twentieth Vows, in contrast to the true Vow, Eighteenth Vow.

Pure Land (jp. *jōdo*). In Shin Buddhism birth in the Pure Land is called 'the birth of no birth' [and no death]. The Pure Land is the world of Enlightenment where there is no birth and no death. Thus the Pure Land is also said to be the equivalent of Nirvāṇa and birth in the Pure Land [at death] means attaining Buddhahood. The Pure Land is used synonymously with the Land of Utmost Bliss (jp. *gokuraku kokudo*), the Land of Happiness (jp. *anraku koku*) and the Land of Enjoyment (jp. *hōdo*); the latter is also rendered as the Land of Recompense or the Land of Fulfilment.

Pure Land School (jp. *Jōdo-shū*). The movement that developed in Japan in the Kamakura Period subsequent to Hōnen Shōnin declaring the Pure Land teaching as an independent Buddhist tradition in its own right. After his death a number of Pure Land sects were established by his main disciples, such as the Jōdo-shū Chinzeiha by Shōkō, the Jōdo-shū Seizanha by Shōkū, and the Jōdo-shinshū by Shinran Shōnin.

Pūrva-praṇidhāna. Sanskrit for 'Original Vow.

Realm of Indolence and Pride. See 'Borderland'.

Rennyo Shōnin Goichidaiki Kikigaki (A Record of the Venerable Rennyo's Sayings and Doings Throughout His Life). A collection of sayings mainly by Rennyo Shōnin (1415–1499), the eighth leader of the Shin Buddhist Honganji sect, and partly by some of his followers from the Shin Buddhist community of that time.

Right Practice (jp. *shōgyō*). Simply put, this term designates the '*nembutsu* only' teaching as the practice most appropriate for ordinary people living in the last Dharma Age. According to Shandao's categorical explanation, there are five right practices: 1) reciting the Pure Land sūtras, 2) meditating on Amida Buddha and his Land, 3) paying reverence to Amida Buddha, 4) pronouncing the Name of Amida Buddha, and 5) praising Amida Buddha's virtues and making offerings to the Buddha. These five right practices stand in contradistinction to all other forms of good which are collectively known as 'miscellaneous practices' (jp. *zōgyō*). Of the five right practices, the right practice of 'pronouncing the Name' (i.e., *nembutsu*) is to be further distinguished from the other four as 'the right practice that truly assures birth in the Pure Land' (jp. *shōjōgō*), relative to which the other four are merely 'supportive practices' (jp. *jogō*). The 'right practice' in its strict sense is thus restricted only to the practice of pronouncing the Name (*nembutsu*) as the right act that truly assures us of attaining birth in Amida's Pure Land.

Root of Virtues, Goodness. In this context this term refers to Amida's Name, i.e., Namu-Amida-butsu.

Samādhi (jp. *sammai*). A state of heightened mental concentration and absorption in which the mind becomes purified, calm, and luminous. Through their *samādhi* Buddhas are able to convey an intimation of the formless Dharma to beings without resorting to the use of words. In *The Larger Sūtra of Eternal Life*, for example, Ānanda encounters the reality of Amida Buddha through intuiting the *samādhi* of his teacher Śākyamuni Buddha.

Samsāra (jp. *shōji*). The Sanskrit word *saṃsāra* in Japanese is *shōji*, meaning the cycle of birth and death. It is also rendered into English as 'birth-and-death' or 'transmigration.' In other words *saṃsāra* means life as it is experienced within the bondage of karmic attachment and transmigration.

Self-power (jp. *jiriki*). Counting on one's efforts to save oneself and attain Enlightenment or birth in the Pure Land. When contrasted to Other Power, the word *jiriki* has a negative connotation and implies attachment to or undue reliance on the belief that we can save ourselves by our own efforts and consequently the failure to entrust oneself completely to Other Power. Thus *jiriki* means attachment to our own ethical or religious efforts and good deeds and as such prevents us from attaining the spiritual freedom of Other Power faith.

Senchaku hongan nembutsu shū, or Senchakushū (Passages on the Selection of the *Nembutsu* in the Original Vow). Hōnen Shōnin's major work, a collection of writings that formed a doctrinal manifesto for the foundation of an independent Pure Land movement in Japan.

Shichikajō no kishōmon. Hōnen Shōnin's seven-article pledge that his disciples would adhere to certain guidelines. Written in response to criticism from Enryaku-ji temple in 1204, it was signed by Hōnen Shōnin and his one hundred and ninety disciples, including Shinran Shōnin.

Shinjin. *Shinjin* (faith) is the key word of Shin Buddhist philosophy and refers to the spiritual awakening attained at the very moment of entrusting oneself to Amida Buddha. The profundity and subtlety of meaning of the Japanese term are such that in English translation the word is often merely transliterated. In the present work, however, faith is chosen as the closest English word. At the same time, it should be noted that in Shin Buddhism the essence of faith lies very much in awareness or awakening, and never in blind faith or unquestioning belief. In Shin Buddhism the term has various connotations, such as 'awakening,' 'entrusting,' 'instantaneous leap,' and 'purification of the mind.'

Spiritual Reformation (jp. *eshin*). Abandoning one's old ways of thinking and entrusting oneself to the Original Vow.

Stage of Non-retrogression (jp. *futaiten*). The original Sanskrit *avinivartaniya* means 'not falling back into the realm of illusion.' The stage of non-retrogression is identical to the stage of The Truly Assured (jp. *shōjōju*) of attaining birth in the Pure Land. *Shōjōju* is also translated as 'the truly settled.' *See* 'The Truly Assured.'

Stage of the Truly Settled. *See* 'Stage of Non-retrogression' and 'The Truly Assured.'

Suchness (jp. *shinnyo*). This stands for the Sanskrit term *tathatā*, variously translated as Suchness, Thusness or As-it-is-ness, indicating, on the one hand, the absolute truth of reality which transcends all the forms found in the phenomenal world and, on the other hand, the same absolute truth of reality which underlies and sustains all phenomenal existence. Suchness is also regarded as being identical with the Dharmakāya in Dharma-in-itself, the essence of Buddha's existence that is formless and beyond the scope of words.

Supportive Practices (jp. *jogō*). Four forms of *nembutsu* practice apart from pronouncing the Name: 1) reciting the Pure Land Sūtras, 2) meditating on Amida Buddha and his Pure Land, 3) paying reverence to Amida Buddha, and 4) making offerings to Amida Buddha and praising his virtues. Hōnen Shōnin saw these as unnecessary for birth in the Pure Land but admitted their possible role as supportive practices. In contrast to these supportive practices, the practice of pronouncing the Name is called the right act that truly assures birth in the Pure Land (jp. *shōjōgō*). *See* 'Right Practice'.

Supraindividual Individual 超個の個. One of several terms that D. T. Suzuki coined to express the person who has become selfless and lives in the totality of Other Power. The term appears in *Nihonteki reisei*, volume 8 of his *Collected Works*, in a discussion of Shinran Shōnin. In the English translation of this work, *Japanese Spirituality*, it appears in various renderings from p. 76 on, such as 'the Person of supraindividual personality' and so on. The term well expresses the awakened individuality of the Shin Buddhist follower.

Supreme Enlightenment (jp. *shōgaku*). The original Sanskrit term *anuttara-samyaksaṃbodhi* (lit. perfect Supreme Enlightenment) refers to the Buddha's Enlightenment or Wisdom. Although the attainment of the experience of Supreme Enlightenment may be called the ultimate purpose of Buddhism, it is from this experience of Enlightenment that the great love and compassion of the Buddha starts to work for the salvation of all sentient beings. The attainment of Great Wisdom is the point where Great Love starts to work. Pure Land Buddhism has its origin here at this point, the Buddha's attainment of Supreme Enlightenment, the fountainhead of his Great Love and Compassion.

Suzuki, D. T. (1870–1966). Leading Japanese Zen Buddhist thinker, Daisetsu Teitarō Suzuki lived in the West for extended periods and was well acquainted with Western culture and thought. He also nurtured a lifelong appreciation for Pure Land Buddhism. He edited an English translation of the *Tannishō* published in 1928 and discusses the portrayal of Shinran in the *Tannishō* as a supraindividual individual in his wartime work *Nihonteki reisei* (Japanese spirituality) in 1944. His 1958 talks in New York were published as a small but popular book called *Shin Buddhism*. In his final years he was commissioned to translate Shinran's *Kyōgyōshinshō*. *See also* 'As-it-is-ness.'

Tathāgata (jp. *Nyorai*). One of the ten epithets of a Buddha; lit., 'one who has thus come' or 'one who has thus gone'.

Transformed Buddha (jp. *kebutsu*). On rare occasions the Japanese word *kebutsu* refers to a *nirmānakāya* or manifest-body Buddha; however, it usually signifies the transformed Buddhas that a *nirmānakāya* (manifest-body) or *sambhogakāya* (enjoyment-body) Buddha makes appear by using their supernatural powers for the salvation of sentient beings. It is also used to refer to the transformed Buddhas that appear in the light-beams radiating from a *nirmānakāya* or *sambhogakāya* Buddha. Amongst the Pure Land sūtras *The Meditation Sūtra* passage describing the transformed Buddhas appearing in the innumerable light-beams radiating from Amida Buddha is well known.

True Vow In the concept of *sangan tennyū* (awakening of faith through the three vows), the true vow refers to the Eighteenth Vow, known as the Original Vow. Regarding Amida's forty-eight vows, Shinran Shōnin speaks of 'six true vows' and 'two provisional vows' in his main work the *Kyōgyōshinshō*. The Eighteenth Vow is one of the six true vows. According to Shinran Shōnin's interpretation, the volume on true teaching (*kyō*) of the *Kyōgyōshinshō* is based on *The Larger Sūtra of Eternal Life*, the volume on True Practice (*gyō*) on the Seventeenth Vow, the volume on True Faith (*shin*) on Eighteenth Vow, the volume on True Realisation (*shō*) on the Eleventh and Twenty-second Vows and the volume on the True Buddha-land (*shinbutsu-do*) on the Twelfth and Thirteenth Vows, while the volume on the Land of Transformation Body (*keshin-do*) is based on the two provisional vows, the Nineteenth and Twentieth Vows.

The Truly Assured (jp. *shōjōju*). The term *shōjōju*, or 'the Truly Assured,' means those who are rightly or truly assured of birth in the Pure Land through their attainment of true faith. The same word is sometimes translated as 'truly settled'. *See* 'Stage of Non-retrogression'.

Vaidehī (jp. *Idaike*). The queen of Magadha who was imprisoned by her son Ajātaśatru (jp. Ajase) and to whom Śākyamuni Buddha expounded the method of visualising the Pure Land and attaining birth there as described in *The Meditation Sūtra* (jp. *Kanmuryōjukyō* or *Kangyō*).

Womb Palace of the Castle of Doubt. *See* 'Borderland'.

NOTES

Notes to Introductory essay

1   *Shinshū shōgyō zensho* 真宗聖教全書, Vol. 1, Shinshū shōgyō zensho-hensansho, Kyoto: Ōyagi Kōbundō, 1964, p. 881.

2   *Shinshū shōgyō zensho*, Vol. 1, p. 729.

3   *Shinshū shōgyō zensho*, Vol. 1, pp. 537–538.

4   *Shinshū shōgyō zensho*, Vol. 2, p. 46.

5   *Shōbōgenzō zuimonki* 正法眼蔵隨聞記, Watsuji, Tetsurō ed., Iwanami Shoten, 1983, p. 93.

6   *Shinshū shōgyō zensho*, Vol. 2, p. 68.

7   Kakunyo, *The Life of Shinran Shōnin*, compiled in Daisetz T. Suzuki, *Collected Writings on Shin Buddhism*, ed., The Eastern Buddhist Society, Kyoto: Shinshū Ōtani-ha, 1973, pp. 173–174.

8   *Shinshū shōgyō zensho*, Vol. 1, pp. 537–538.

9   Gutoku Shaku Shinran, *The Kyōgyōshinshō: The collection of passages expounding the true teaching, living, faith, and realizing of the Pure Land*, Daisetz T. Suzuki, trans., Kyoto: Shinshū Ōtani-ha, 1973, p. 59; slightly adapted.

Notes to Translation and Commentary

1   Shinran, *The Kyōgyōshinshō*, D. T. Suzuki, trans., p. 338; adapted.

2   Fujishima, Tatsurō, *Eshin-ni-kō: Shinran Shōnin no tsuma* 親鸞の妻　恵信尼公, Kyoto: Hōzōkan, 1984, pp. 99–100.

3   *Shinshū shōgyō zensho*, Vol. 2, p. 202: (雑行を棄てて本願に帰す).

4   Shinran, *The Kyōgyōshinshō*, D. T. Suzuki, trans., p. 125; adapted.

5   Shinran, *The Kyōgyōshinshō*, D. T. Suzuki, trans., p. 125; adapted.

6   Suzuki, D. T., *Collected Writings on Shin Buddhism*, pp. 127–128; adapted.

7   Shinran, *The Kyōgyōshinshō*, D. T. Suzuki, trans., p. 130; adapted.

8   Shinran, *The Kyōgyōshinshō*, D. T. Suzuki, trans., p. 15; adapted.

9   *Shinshū shōgyō zensho*, vol. 2, pp. 157–158.

10 *Shinshū shōgyō zensho*, vol. 2, pp. 165–166.

11 *Shōwa shinshū Hōnen Shōnin zenshū* 昭和新修法然上人全集, Kyōdō Ishii, ed., Kyoto: Heirakuji Shoten, 1995, p. 454.

12 *The Collected Works of Shinran*, Gadjin M. Nagao, ed., Kyoto: Jōdo Shinshū Honganji-ha, 1997, p. 663; adapted.

13 *Shinshū shōgyō zensho*, vol. 1, p. 339.

14 *Shinshū shōgyō zensho*, vol. 2, p. 202.

15 *Shinshū shōgyō zensho*, vol. 2, p. 44.

16 *The Kyōgyōshinshō*, D. T. Suzuki, trans., p. 15; adapted. The word 'merit' in the translation has been replaced by 'virtue.'

17   *The Kyōgyōshinshō,* D. T. Suzuki, trans., p. 15; adapted.

18   *The Kyōgyōshinshō,* D. T. Suzuki, trans., p. 338; adapted.

19   *Shinshū shōgyō zensho,* vol. 1, p. 288.

20   *Shinshū shōgyō zensho,* vol. 2, p. 527.

21   *The Kyōgyōshinshō,* D. T. Suzuki, trans., p. 9; adapted.

22   *Shinshū shōgyō zensho,* vol. 2, p. 672. Reply to Kakushin-bo.

23   *Rinzairoku* 臨濟録 Article 3, Shaku Sōen, ed., Tokyo: Morie Shoten, 1918, pp. 4-5. The translation is my own.

24   Discourse 16, *The Record of Lin-chi,* Ruth F. Sasaki, trans., Kyoto: The Institute for Zen Studies, Hanazono College, 1975, p. 17. The present text is taken from the edited version of Ruth F. Sasaki, trans., *The Record of Linji,* Thomas Yūhō Kirchner, ed., Honolulu: University of Hawai'i Press, 2009, p. 16. Ghee is clarified butter (skt. *sarpir-manda* 醍醐 jp. *daigo*). The original text for the last sentence of the first paragraph is as follows: 隨処作主立処皆真.

25   *Daijōbutten: Chūgoku-Nihon hen: Myōkōnin,* vol. 28, 大乗仏典, 中国日本篇: 第二十八巻: 妙好人, edited by Minakami Tsutomu and Sato Taira, Tokyo: Chūō Kōron, 1987, p. 153.

26   See article 10 of "The Records of Shōma's Words and Actions," in *Daijōbutten: Chūgoku-Nihon hen: Myōkōnin,* vol. 28, p. 127.

27   *The Kyōgyōshinshō,* D. T. Suzuki, trans., p. 15; adapted.

28   *The Kyōgyōshinshō,* D. T. Suzuki, trans., p. 15; adapted.

29   *Shinshū shōgyō zensho,* vol. 2, p. 39. (法王はただ一法なり。一切無礙人は一道より生死を出でたまへり。一切諸仏の身、ただ是一法身なり、一心、一智慧なり.)

30   *The Kyōgyōshinshō,* D. T. Suzuki, trans., p. 64; adapted. *See also: Shinshū shōgyō zensho,* vol. 1, p. 346.

31   *Gushikō* 遇斯光, vol. 2, Futsukaichi, Fukuoka: Shōgyōji, 1963, p. 185.

32   John White, *The Breath in the Flute* 笛の息, Taira Sato, trans., Tokyo: Shunjūsha, 2001.

33   This verse was one that D. T. Suzuki was rather fond of and he cites it twice in *Daisetsu tsurezuregusa, Suzuki Daisetsu zenshū* (SDZ) 20. Unfortunately the original notebook that included this poem ("tariki ni wa / jiriki mo nashi / tariki mo nashi / tada ichimen no tariki nari / Namu Amida butsu, Namu Amida butsu") is now lost. A similar poem appears in *Asahara Saichi shū,* ed. Suzuki Daisetsu [and Satō Taira], Tokyo: Shunjūsha, 1967, p. 174.

34   I heard these remarks directly from D. T. Suzuki when he dictated to me an essay entitled *Anjin: Zen to Shin* ("Peaceful Awareness in Zen and Shin"), in which this poem was cited. See his *Collected Works,* SDZ vol. 20, pp. 392-400.

35   Rudolf Otto, *India's Religion of Grace and Christianity compared and contrasted,* Frank Hugh Foster, trans., New York: Macmillan, 1930.

36   D. T. Suzuki, *Buddha of Infinite Light,* Taitetsu Unno, ed., 1998, Shambhala in association with the American Buddhist Academy, 1998, pp. 55-57.

37   *The Eastern Buddhist* N.S. vol. II, 1967, pp. 88-89.

38   Kurata, Hyakuzō, *Shukke to sono deshi* 出家とその弟子 [*A Priest and His Disciple*], Tokyo: Iwanami Shoten, 1917. For an English translation, see *The Priest and his Disciples: a play,* Glenn W. Shaw, trans., Tokyo: Hokuseido, 1922.

39 *The Kyōgyōshinshō,* D. T. Suzuki, trans., p. 125.

40 *The Kyōgyōshinshō,* D. T. Suzuki, trans., pp. 126–127.

41 *Shinshū shōgyō zensho,* vol. 2, p. 44. Cf. *The Kyōgyōshinshō,* D. T. Suzuki, trans., pp. 76–77.

42 *The Kyōgyōshinshō,* D. T. Suzuki, trans., p. 140; adapted.

43 Shinran Shōnin's *Jinen hōni sho,* D. T. Suzuki, trans., *Mysticism: Christian and Buddhist,* New York: Harper & Brothers, 1957, pp. 154–155; adapted. The word 'Nyorai' refers to Amida Nyorai, or Amida Tathāgata.

44 *Shinshū shōgyō zensho,* vol. 2, p. 523.

45 *Shinshū shōgyō zensho,* vol. 2, p. 523.

46 D. T. Suzuki, *Buddha of Infinite Light,* Boston: Shambhala Publications in association with the American Buddhist Academy, 1997, pp. 46–47. This particular text has a long and interesting history. Originally a series of talks that D. T. Suzuki gave in the spring of 1958, it was later published as *Shin Buddhism,* New York: Harper & Row, 1970, and subsequently translated into several languages including German, Spanish, Italian, Dutch, and Chinese. I myself did the Japanese translation, *Suzuki Daisetsu Shinshū nyūmon* 鈴木大拙真宗入門, Tokyo: Shunjūsha, 1983.

47 Shinran, *The Kyōgyōshinshō,* D. T. Suzuki, trans., p. 338; adapted.

48 D. T. Suzuki, *Buddha of Infinite Light,* p. 48.

49 Kanamatsu, Kenryō, *Naturalness: A classic of Shin Buddhism,* Bloomington, IN: World Wisdom, 2002, pp. 116–117. Originally published as *Amitābha, the life of naturalness,* Kyoto: Ōtani, 1949; then as *Naturalness,* Los Angeles: White Path Society, 1956, and in a revised edition by the same title by Bunmeido, in Kyoto, 1956.

50 Kanamatsu, *Naturalness,* pp. 118–119.

51 *Shinshū shōgyō zensho,* vol. 2, pp. 658–659. (*Lamp for the Latter Age,* 2)

52 *Shinshū shōgyō zensho,* vol. 2, p. 712. (*A Collection of Letters,* 10)

53 Shinran, *The Kyōgyōshinshō,* D. T. Suzuki, trans., p. 338; adapted. *Shinshū shōgyō zensho,* vol. 1, p. 10.

54 *Shinshū shōgyō zensho,* vol. 2, pp. 669–670. A letter addressed to Kyōmyō-bo.

55 *Shinshū shōgyō zensho,* vol. 2, pp. 672–673. A letter addressed to Yūamidabutsu.

56 *Shinshū shōgyō zensho,* vol. 3, 1964, p. 423.

57 *Shinshū shōgyō zensho,* vol. 3, p. 551.

58 D. T. Suzuki, *Buddha of Infinite Light,* p. 22.

59 *The Collected Works of Shinran,* G. M. Nagao, ed., pp. 547–548; adapted.

60 *The Collected Works of Shinran,* G. M. Nagao, ed., pp. 551–552; adapted.

61 *The Collected Works of Shinran,* G. M. Nagao, ed., pp. 553–554; adapted.

62 *The Collected Works of Shinran,* G. M. Nagao, ed., pp. 554; adapted.

63 *Shinshū shōgyō zensho,* vol. 1, p. 65.

64 *Shinshū shōgyō zensho,* vol. 1, p. 24.

65 *Shinshū shōgyō zensho,* vol. 3, pp. 508–510. Translation my own.

66 *The Collected Works of Shinran,* G. M. Nagao, ed., p. 540; adapted.

67   *The Collected Works of Shinran*, G. M. Nagao, ed., pp. 541–542; adapted.

68   *The Collected Works of Shinran*, G. M. Nagao, ed., p. 549; adapted. In this selection, the meaning of the word *shinjin* [faith] has been indicated in brackets on each occurrence. While some readers may prefer the word *shinjin*, a great many others will have difficulty in understanding what it means. Even in recent translations from the same translators of *The Collected Works of Shinran*, the policy has changed and now the word *shinjin* has been replaced with 'entrusting mind'.

69   *Shinshū shōgyō zensho*, vol. 3 pp. 406–408.

70   *Shinshū shōgyō zensho*, vol. 2, p. 493.

71   *Shinshū shōgyō zensho*, vol. 2, p. 493.

72   The English versions of these three are taken from D. T. Suzuki, trans., *The Kyōgyōshinshō*, p. 338; adapted.

73   *Shinshū shōgyō zensho*, vol. 2, pp. 143–144.

74   *Shinshū shōgyō zensho*, vol. 2, p. 158.

75   *Shinshū shōgyō zensho*, vol. 2, p. 48.

76   *The Collected Works of Shinran*, p. 527, adapted.

77   *Nihonteki reisei*, SDZ, vol. 8, Tokyo: Iwanami Shoten, 1968, p. 134. For an English translation, *see* Daisetz Suzuki, *Japanese Spirituality*, Norman Waddell, trans., Tokyo: Japan Society for the Promotion of Science, 1972. In this English version the phrase is translated as 'Thus we may view them as one character.'

78   D. T. Suzuki makes this statement on pp. 112–113 of his Japanese work; in the English translation, see p. 116.

79   Furuta, Takehiko, *Shinran's Thoughts: A Critical Study of the Source Materials*, 古田武彦 著 親鸞思想: その史料批判, Tokyo: Toyama-bō, 1975.

80   *Shinshū shōgyō zensho,* vol. 2, pp. 201–202.

THE TANNISHŌ

Preface to the Tannishō

As I humbly compare, within the limits set by my own ignorance, the time when Shinran Shōnin was alive with the present, I cannot help but lament how much the present followers diverge from the true faith directly expressed by our late Master. I am afraid that those who come after us may thereby fall into doubt and confusion. If I had not had the fortune of meeting my good master, how could I have realised the teaching of Easy Practice? We should not confound the doctrine of Other Power with our own understanding. For this reason, I have committed myself to writing down some of the sayings of the late Shinran Shōnin, which still reverberate in my mind. My sole wish is to dispel any doubts held by our fellow believers regarding our faith.

Chapter 1

"At the very moment when the thought that moves you to pronounce the *nembutsu* is awakened within you, believing that your birth in the Pure Land is attained through the inconceivable working of Amida's Original Vow, you instantly receive Amida's compassionate benefit 'that embraces all, forsaking none.' You should realise that Amida's Original Vow never discriminates between old and young, good and bad, and that faith alone is what is essential; for the Vow was originally made for the purpose of saving all sentient beings burdened with the weight of karmic evil and burning with the flames of blind passions. Thus, when you entrust yourself to this Original Vow, no other form of goodness is required because there is no goodness that can surpass the *nembutsu*; nor need you fear any form of evil, because there is no evil powerful enough to obstruct the working of Amida's Original Vow."

Thus spoke my Master.

Chapter 2

"Having crossed the borders of ten provinces or more, each of you has come to see me at the risk of your life. Your purpose is solely to hear from me how to be born in the Pure Land. If, however, assuming that I know other ways of being born in the Pure Land apart from pronouncing the *nembutsu* or thinking that I may be acquainted with some Buddhist texts that teach those special ways, you are concerned to know some hidden truth, I am afraid you are making a great mistake. If that is indeed your concern, there are many eminent scholars in the Southern Capital [Nara], or on the Northern Mountain [Hiei], whom you would be better off visiting in order to inquire to your hearts' content about the essentials for birth in the Pure Land.

As for myself, Shinran Shōnin, there is nothing else involved apart from simple faith in the *nembutsu*, according to the instruction of my good teacher, 'Just say the *nembutsu* so as to be saved by Amida.'

I do not profess to know whether the *nembutsu* will really work as the seed that allows me to be born in the Pure Land or whether it may prove the karmic act for which I am condemned to hell. If, however, by pronouncing the *nembutsu*, I were ultimately to find myself misled by my Master Hōnen Shōnin and cast into hell, even then I would have no regrets.

The reason is this: if I were actually capable of attaining Buddhahood by my own endeavours while following other practices but nevertheless simply pronounced the *nembutsu* and so fell into hell, then indeed I would feel regret at having been deceived. But I am quite incapable of any other practice, so hell would have to be my abode in any case.

If the Original Vow of Amida is true, the teaching of Śākyamuni cannot be untrue; if the teaching of Śākyamuni is true, the commentaries by Shandao cannot be untrue; if Shandao's commentaries are true, the teaching of Hōnen Shōnin cannot be untrue; if the teaching of Hōnen Shōnin is true, how can it be possible for me, Shinran, to utter untruth? This being so, it is up to you to choose whether to believe in the *nembutsu* or to reject it."

Thus spoke my Master.

Chapter 3

"Even a good person can attain birth [in the Pure Land], how much more readily, then, the person with bad karma.'

Normally, however, people of the world would say: 'Even a person with bad karma can attain birth, how much more readily, then, a good person.' Although at first sight this latter view appears perfectly reasonable, actually it runs counter to the purport of the Original Vow, Other Power faith. This is because people who rely on doing good through their own self-power fail to entrust themselves to Other Power and are not, therefore, in accord with Amida's Original Vow. If, on the other hand, they discard their reliance on self-power and entrust themselves to Other Power, they will attain birth in the True Land of Enjoyment.

It is impossible for us, fully burdened with blind passions, to free ourselves from birth-and-death through the pursuance of any religious practices whatsoever. Full of sadness at this, Amida brought forth his Vow, the essential purport of which is the person with bad karma's attainment of Buddhahood. Hence those who are aware of their bad karma and so entrust themselves to Other Power are precisely the ones who possess the true key to birth.

Accordingly he (Hōnen Shōnin) said; 'Even a good person can be born [in the Pure Land], so it goes without saying for the person with bad karma'."

Chapter 4

"Concerning the practice of love (*jihi* 慈悲) there is a distinct turning point from the Path of Sages to the Path of the Pure Land Buddhist.

Love in the Path of Sages means pitying, loving and nurturing all beings. It is extremely difficult, however, to accomplish the work of saving others in exactly the way one wishes.

Love in the Path of the Pure Land Buddhist means quickly attaining Buddhahood by pronouncing the *nembutsu* so that, through the mind of Great Love and Compassion, one is able to save all beings in exactly the way one wishes.

However much love and pity you may feel for others in this life, it is hard indeed to save them in the way you would wish; hence such love can never be perfect. Only the pronouncing of the *nembutsu* can manifest the mind of great unconditional love."

Thus spoke my Master.

Chapter 5

"I, Shinran, have never recited the *nembutsu*, not even once, for the repose of my departed father and mother. The reason is that all sentient beings, without exception, have been my parents and brothers and sisters in their successive past lives, in various states of existence. On attaining Buddhahood at your next birth, you will be able to save every one of them.

If the *nembutsu* were something virtuous to be performed through your own power, then you could direct the virtue of *nembutsu* toward saving your father and mother.

But if, discarding all attempts at self-power, you quickly attain enlightenment in the Pure Land, then, by means of the miraculous powers which you acquire, you will be able to save first of all those you have the closest karmic relations to, however much they may be suffering due to their previous karma in the six realms through the four modes of birth."

Thus spoke my Master.

Chapter 6

"It is completely unreasonable for there to be quarrelling amongst our fellow followers reciting the *nembutsu* exclusively, with people saying that such and such are 'my disciples' while such and such are not. I, Shinran, have no disciples.

The reason is this: if a man by his own efforts makes others recite the *nembutsu*, then he may call them his disciples. But it is most presumptuous to claim as 'my disciples' those who recite the *nembutsu* solely as a result of Amida's working within themselves.

It is all due to the karmic condition of things that some follow one master while others leave him. This being so, it would be absurd to say that one who turns from one master to another will not attain birth in the Pure Land. Do people mean to take back the faith given to each person by Amida as if it were something of theirs? Such views are most decidedly unreasonable.

If one follows the truth of reality as it is, one will understand exactly how grateful to be to Amida, and how grateful to be to the master."

Thus spoke my Master.

Chapter 7

"The *nembutsu* is the single path that knows no obstruction. This is because the gods of heaven and earth bow down in reverence before one who practices the *nembutsu* with pure faith. No *māras* (demonic beings) or heretics (non-Buddhists) can obstruct such a person. No evil deed can bring upon him karmic retribution, nor can any form of good equal his *nembutsu*. Therefore it is called the single path that knows no obstruction."

Thus spoke my Master.

Chapter 8

"For the devotee, the *nembutsu* is neither a religious practice nor a good deed. Because the *nembutsu* is not a religious practice carried out intentionally, it is called 'non-practice,' and because the *nembutsu* is not a good act performed intentionally, it is called 'non-good.' Since the *nembutsu* comes entirely from Other Power and is quite beyond self-effort, the *nembutsu*, for the devotee, is neither a religious practice nor a good deed."

Thus spoke my Master.

Chapter 9

"Although I recite the *nembutsu*, I seldom feel like dancing for joy, nor do I desire to hasten to the Pure Land. Why is this so?' I asked.

My Master answered, 'I, Shinran, had the same doubts. O Yuien-bō, you have the same doubts just as I did! But when you reflect on the matter more deeply, you will find that your birth in the Pure Land is all the more assured just because you cannot rejoice at what should make you feel like dancing for joy on earth and in the air. It is the effect of blind passions lying heavy on one's heart and preventing one from rejoicing. Knowing this fact beforehand, the Buddha called us 'ignorant beings filled with blind passions.' Thus I realise that the Compassionate Vow of Other Power is for the benefit of such ignorant beings as ourselves and I find it all the more to be trusted.

Furthermore, not being desirous of hastening to the Pure Land, we feel very much dejected when we become ill, however mild the illness, at the thought of our possible death. This is likewise caused by the effect of blind passions. We feel reluctant to abandon this old home of pain and suffering, where we have been transmigrating from time immemorial right down to the present day, and we feel no longing for the Land of Peace and Happiness, where we have yet to be born. This is again due to our blind passions, so fierce and powerful. But when our karma in this *sahā* world expires and we have no choice but to leave it behind, then, however reluctant we may feel, we will nevertheless proceed to the Pure Land. Amida especially pities those who are not desirous of hastening to the Pure Land. When you consider all this, you may realise all the more clearly how trustworthy the Great Compassionate Vow is and how firmly your birth in the Pure Land is assured.

If, on the contrary, you felt like dancing for joy and wished to hasten to the Pure Land, you might wonder if you had any blind passions at all."

Thus spoke my Master.

Chapter 10

" 'As regards the *nembutsu*, no meaning is meaning, because it is immeasurable, indescribable and inconceivable.' Thus my Master [Hōnen Shōnin] taught me."

Preface to Chapters 11–18

Now, in days gone by, when our Master Shinran was still alive, those sharing one and the same faith and aspiring to the Land of Enjoyment, who journeyed to the distant capital with a common aim, all had the privilege of receiving our Master's instruction at firsthand. Lately, however, I have been informed that amongst the countless numbers of both young and old, who recite the *nembutsu* under the guidance of those older followers, there are now to be found a great many who are spreading erroneous views not taught by the Master himself. Such groundless views will be looked at in detail in the following chapters.

Chapter 11

There are some who, seeing illiterate people reciting the *nembutsu*, frighten them into confusion by asking whether they do so with faith in the inconceivability of the Vow or with faith in the inconceivability of the Name but without clarifying for them what these two kinds of inconceivability mean. This is a serious matter. To understand it clearly needs very careful thought.

By virtue of the inconceivability of the Vow, Amida Buddha devised the Name as something easy to retain and easy to recite and promised to welcome [to his Pure Land] all those who pronounced the *nembutsu*. Thus it is we come to recite the *nembutsu*, first and foremost in the belief that we will be delivered from birth-and-death by the inconceivability of Amida's Vow of Great Compassion. When we realise this, that it is all due to the Tathāgata's benevolent design that we are able to pronounce the Name, then our own way of thinking is not mixed with this at all. For this very reason we are, in accordance with the Original Vow, to be born in the True Land of Enjoyment.

If we have pure faith in the inconceivability of the Vow, then do we also in the inconceivability of the Name. The inconceivability of the Vow and that of the Name coalesce into one, allowing no difference between them.

Furthermore if a person makes a distinction between good and evil acts, imagining that the former help, and the latter hinder, birth in the Pure Land and brings his own way of thinking into the matter, such a person is failing to entrust himself to the inconceivability of the Vow. He is working for his birth in the Pure Land depending on his own mind and thinks pronouncing the Name is something he achieves by himself. Such a person does not entrust himself to the inconceivability of the Name either. In spite of his lack of faith, he will still be born in the Borderland, the realm of Indolence and Pride or the Womb Palace of the Castle of Doubt and will eventually attain birth in the True Land of Enjoyment by virtue of 'the Vow that those who have reached this stage may attain birth in the Pure Land.' This is all due to the inconceivable Power of the Name. Since this is also none other than the inconceivability of the Vow, these two are one and the same.

Chapter 12

Some followers hold that those who do not read and study the Sūtras and commentaries cannot be assured of birth in the Pure Land. This view could not be further from the truth.

All the sacred documents that expound the truth of Other Power clearly show that everyone who believes in the Original Vow and recites the *nembutsu* will become a Buddha [attaining birth in the Pure Land]. What need is there of further learning for birth [in the Pure Land]?

To be sure anyone who has doubts about their birth in the Pure Land should study hard to try and grasp the purport of the Original Vow, but it is a great pity that there are some who fail to understand the true meaning of the sacred texts despite their best efforts to read and study the Sūtras and commentaries.

Because Amida's Name can easily be recited by those who are unlettered and ignorant of what the Sūtras and commentaries mean, such practice is called the Easy Way. Those who consider learning essential belong to the order of the Path of Sages. Their practice is called the Difficult Way. As for those who engage in academic study, mistakenly looking for fame and wealth, there is an authoritative passage [from Shinran Shōnin's letter]: 'I am doubtful of their birth in the Pure Land after this life.'

At present those that follow the exclusive practice of the *nembutsu* and those that follow the Path of Sages are locked together in doctrinal dispute, each side insisting that its own doctrine is superior and the other inferior. This leads to the emergence of forces inimical to the Dharma and the slandering of the Dharma. Does it not amount after all to the slandering and destruction of one's own Dharma? Even if all the other schools join forces in attacking you and declare that the *nembutsu* is just for worthless people and that this teaching is shallow and vulgar, you should not try and answer their criticism but simply reply, "As we are convinced that foolish beings of inferior ability such as ourselves, who may not know a single letter of the alphabet, will be delivered through faith alone, this teaching is the supreme Dharma for us, though it may seem base to those of superior ability. No matter how wonderful another teaching may be, we cannot follow it, for it is beyond our capability. Since the basic intention of all Buddhas is simply to free everyone, not just the personal self but others too, from birth-and-death, please leave us alone to go our own way." If you respond to them in this way without any rancor, why should they harm you?

Moreover, there is an authoritative passage [in the *Shichikajō no kishōmon* 七箇条起請文] which reads, "Where there are disputes, all kinds of blind passions arise. A person would be wise to stay far away from such disputation."

The late Master also said, "The Buddha foretold that there would be some who trusted in this teaching and there would be also others who reviled it. I already have faith in the teaching and there are others who slander it. By this fact I know that what the Buddha taught is true. Therefore you should be confident that your birth in the Pure Land is all the more certain. If, by chance, there were none who reviled the teaching, then we would wonder why there were no slanderers whereas there were believers. I do not mean by this that the teaching should necessarily be slandered. I merely talk about the fact that the Buddha, foreseeing there would be believers and slanderers, foretold this so that his followers would not harbor doubts in the future."

Nowadays, however, there appear to be people who study the Buddha's teaching specifically to stop others from slandering it. Are they really content to dissipate their energies in argument and debate? The more one studies, the more clearly one should understand Amida's true intent and realise the boundlessness of his Compassionate Vow. Only if one becomes the kind of scholar who is capable of persuading people that the Original Vow does not discriminate between good and evil, pure and impure and that they are perfectly able to be born in the Pure Land despite their imperfections that might have made them doubt about their birth, only then will scholarly life take on any meaning.

If you insist that learning is essential for birth and consequently intimidate even those who happen to live the *nembutsu* selflessly in accordance with the Original Vow, your behaviour is nothing less than a diabolical obstruction of the Dharma and a hostile act against the Buddha. Those who insist on doing so not only lack faith in the Other Power but also confuse others with false thoughts.

You should humbly stand in awe [of the Buddha-dharma] lest you go against the teaching of the late Master and also lest you are in disaccord with the Original Vow of Amida Buddha.

Chapter 13

There are some people who insist that those who are not alarmed by their own evil because of [their reliance on] the inconceivable power of Amida's Original Vow are relying too heavily on the Original Vow and will definitely fail to be born in the Pure Land.

Such a view betrays a lack of trust in the Original Vow and a lack of understanding of the way good and evil deeds result from past karma. Good thoughts arise due to the effect of past good [karma] and evil thoughts do likewise under the influence of [past] evil karma.

The late Master said, "You should understand that even if it looks as insignificant as a speck of dust on the tip of a single hair from a rabbit's coat or a sheep's fleece, every evil you commit is nothing but the product of your past karma."

On another occasion he asked me, "O Yuien-bō! Would you believe whatever I told you?"

"Yes, Master, I would," was my reply.

"And are you sure you would not disobey me?"

"Yes, I am sure," I answered.

"Suppose," he went on, "you were asked to murder a thousand men on the understanding that your birth in the Pure Land depended on it."

"Even if it were you giving the order," I protested, "I still would not be able to kill a single person."

"In that case," replied my master, "why did you say you would never disobey my orders whatever they might be? You can see now from this that, if it really were in accordance with your karma and you were required to do so, you would indeed be able to kill a thousand people for the sake of birth in the Pure Land. You yourself would not kill, not because your thoughts are good but because you yourself do not have the karma to kill even one single person. And yet, though you may not wish to injure anyone, it is still possible you might be led to kill a hundred or a thousand people."

The point being made here is that, because we judge simplistically that thinking good thoughts is good for birth in the Pure Land and thinking evil thoughts bad, we are actually failing to realise that it is only the inconceivable power of the Original Vow that enables any of us to attain birth at all.

There was once a man who had fallen into a completely erroneous way of thinking. He taught that, because the Vow was made to save those who had committed evil, one should actually commit evil on purpose as a way of attaining birth. As rumours of this man's evil deeds spread, Shinran Shōnin wrote in one of the letters addressed to his followers, "Do not take poison just because there is an antidote." By this admonishment Shinran Shōnin sought to put a stop to people's erroneous attachment to such a belief. In no way did he mean that evil could obstruct birth in the Pure Land.

Shinran Shōnin also observed, "If the only way we could entrust ourselves to the Original Vow were through observing the moral precepts and upholding the rules of order, how could we ever free ourselves from birth-and-death?" Wretched beings that we are, it is only through our own personal encounter with the Original Vow that we are truly able to rely on it. Indeed how would we come to commit evil acts if there were not some karmic cause within ourselves?

"This holds true," the Master continued, "for those who gain their livelihood by casting nets or fishing in the seas and rivers, for those who support themselves by hunting beasts and fowl in the mountains and fields and for those who pass their lives conducting trade or cultivating the fields. If their respective karma has matured sufficiently they will commit any kind of act."

Despite the Master's statement there are some followers nowadays affecting to be 'seekers for Rebirth', who claim that only good persons are entitled to pronounce the Name. Indeed they sometimes even go so far as to put up notices at places of worship, saying that those who have committed such and such an act are prohibited from entering. Are these not the sort of people who 'while outwardly demonstrating how wise, good and diligent they are, inwardly remain false and deceitful'?

Evil acts committed by people relying too heavily on the Original Vow are also actually caused by their past karma. If we thus acknowledge that all good and evil deeds are the result of our past karma and if we put our trust instead in the Original Vow, then we will find ourselves in accord with Other Power. *The Essentials of Faith Alone* asks: "How can you fathom the extent of Amida's power and claim to see in yourself too much karmic evil to be saved?" It is actually because we are guilty of relying too heavily on the Original Vow that we finally come to attain the faith to entrust ourselves to Other Power.

If we were to attain faith in the Original Vow only after having extinguished all our karmic evil and blind passions, then there would be no need for us to rely on the Original Vow at all. But if we had been able to extinguish all our blind passions like this, we would already be Buddhas and if we were Buddhas, the Original Vow, the fruit of five kalpas of profound meditation, would be of no use to us.

Those who chastise others for relying too heavily on the Original Vow appear themselves to be filled with blind passions and impurities. Do not they rely on the Original Vow? What kind of evil-doing is caused by relying too heavily on the Original Vow and what kind of evil-doing is caused by not doing so? Is not all their criticism just so much childish talk?

Chapter 14

There are those who insist that one should believe that reciting the *nembutsu* just once is sufficient to eradicate the heavy burden of evil karma accumulated over eight thousand million kalpas.

Such a view relates to a person who, having committed the ten evils and the five grave offences during their lifetime, without ever once reciting the *nembutsu*, finally on their deathbed comes face to face with a good teacher for the very first time. This teacher tells them that if they recite the *nembutsu* just once, the evil karma of eight thousand million kalpas will be expunged and that if they recite it ten times, the heavy burden of evil karma of eighty thousand million kalpas will be eradicated and they will thus attain birth [in the Pure Land]. This passage [from *The Meditation Sūtra*] about reciting the *nembutsu* once or else ten times would appear to have been included in order to make us aware of the awesome gravity of the ten evils and the five grave offences. Such a way of thinking, while pointing to how beneficial the *nembutsu* is for the dissolution of evil karma, is nevertheless far removed from the tenets of our faith. The reason for this is that, at the very moment when we are truly awakened, having been illuminated by Amida's Light, we are endowed with Diamond-like Faith and join the company of those truly assured [of birth in the Pure Land]. Thus, when our lives reach their end, all our blind passions and evil hindrances are transformed into the recognition that there is no birth [and no death].

How could we, miserable wrongdoers, be delivered from birth-and-death were it not for Amida's Compassionate Vow? Bear this in mind and cherish the thought that the *nembutsu* you keep reciting throughout your life is entirely the expression of your gratitude to Amida Tathāgata for all he has done to save you through his Great Compassion.

To believe that every recitation of the *nembutsu* has the power to extinguish your evil karma will merely lead you to strive to wipe out your evil karma through your own efforts in order to attain birth in the Pure Land. In that case, given that every thought you have throughout the whole course of your life is a fetter binding you to birth-and-death (transmigration), you will only be able to attain birth in the Pure Land if you recite the *nembutsu* without ceasing right up until the very moment you die. We are, however, constrained by the effects of our past karma and so may very well die without dwelling in right-mindedness, for at any time we can meet with an unexpected accident or suffer the agonies of a serious disease. In such circumstances it would be very difficult for us to recite the *nembutsu*, but then how would we eradicate the karmic evil committed during the last fraction of our lives? And if it were not expunged, would it not be impossible for us to attain birth in the Pure Land?

It is quite possible that, through circumstances beyond our control, we may come to commit an evil act and die without ever being able to recite the *nembutsu* in our final hour. Even under such circumstances, if we have entrusted ourselves to Amida's Vow that vows to embrace all and abandon none, then we will still be able to attain Birth instantly in the Pure Land. Moreover, if the *nembutsu* wells up spontaneously as our time of attaining Supreme Enlightenment approaches, we will find ourselves placing more and more reliance on Amida Buddha and feeling more and more grateful to him for all he has done for us.

Those who desire to eradicate evil karma by reciting the *nembutsu* are relying on self-power. The fact that their basic intent is to maintain a state of right-mindedness when their lives end means they have no faith in Other Power.

Chapter 15

There are some who insist they have already attained Enlightenment even while still maintaining this earthly body full of blind passions. Such a view really is quite unacceptable. The attainment of Buddhahood while still in this earthly body is the essential teaching of the Shingon School of Esoteric Buddhism and is achieved, they say, by means of the Three Esoteric Practices. The Purification of the Six Senses is the teaching of the One Vehicle Lotus Sūtra and is said to be achieved through the Four Peaceful Practices. But these are all difficult practices, only to be followed by those of superior ability, with Enlightenment attainable only through perfect meditation. In contrast to this, in Pure Land Buddhism the essence of the teaching of Other Power is the attainment of Enlightenment in the next life, since this way to Enlightenment is realised through the establishment of faith [in Amida Buddha]. It is the Easy Way, the way to be followed by those of poor ability, the Dharma in which there is no discrimination between good and evil.

As it is extremely difficult to eliminate blind passions and evil hindrances in this life, even the holy monks who practice the Shingon and Tendai disciplines still pray for [the attainment of] Enlightenment in the next life. How much more so, then, should we who are of far lesser ability! Although in our case there is no observance of precepts nor realisation of wisdom to be found, nevertheless when once we have crossed the painful ocean of birth-and-death on board the ship of Amida's Vow and have attained the shores of the Pure Land, the dark clouds of blind passions will swiftly clear away and the moon of Enlightenment of Dharma-in-itself will immediately appear. Having become one with the Unimpeded Light that illuminates all the ten quarters, we will benefit all sentient beings. This is true Enlightenment.

Do those who claim to have already attained Enlightenment in this earthly body freely expound the Dharma to benefit all beings, as Śākyamuni did, by revealing themselves in various transformations of the Dharma-body, endowed with the thirty-two features and eighty characteristics [of the Buddha]? This is what is actually meant by the attainment of Enlightenment in this life. A hymn by Shinran Shōnin tells us:

At that moment when solid as a diamond
Faith is first established,
The Light of Amida's Heart enfolds and protects us
So that we are forever separated from birth-and-death.

This means that, because at the moment faith is established Amida embraces us never to let us go, we shall no longer transmigrate through the Six Realms of Existence. This is why 'we are forever separated from birth-and-death (transmigration).' But how can we confuse this awakening with 'Enlightenment'? How regrettable that there should be such a misunderstanding!

The late Master (Shinran Shōnin) said:

"I have learned that in the true teaching of the Pure Land (浄土真宗 jp. *Jōdo shinshū*) one entrusts oneself to the Original Vow in this present life and one attains Enlightenment in the Pure Land.'

Chapter 16

There are some people who insist that, whenever a follower of our faith becomes angry or does something wrong or has a dispute with his fellow-followers, then as a matter of course (*jinen* 自然, literally 'naturally') he should be sure to reform himself (*eshin* 廻心, literally 'to turn the mind').

Do they mean by this that we should eliminate evil and practice good [in order to attain birth in the Pure Land]? For those that follow the practice of the *nembutsu* exclusively and single-mindedly this spiritual reformation, known as *eshin* ('turning-of-mind'), occurs only once when a person, hitherto ignorant of the true teaching of the Other Power of the Original Vow, comes to realise, through the wisdom bestowed on him by Amida Buddha, that he cannot attain birth in the Pure Land with the thoughts and feelings he has been harbouring until now, and so abandons his old ways of thinking and entrusts himself to the Original Vow. This is what is meant [in our tradition] by *eshin*, 'spiritual reformation.' If it were necessary to reform oneself in every way morning and evening in order to attain birth in the Pure Land, Amida's Vow that embraces all and forsakes none would be proved useless: one might die before one ever had the chance to reform oneself and regain a tender and forbearing attitude, for life is so fragile it can end in an instant, between breathing out and breathing in.

There are some who claim with their lips that they trust in the power of the Original Vow, all the while thinking in their minds that, although Amida's Vow to save even those with bad karma is said to be inconceivably great, the Vow will still save all the good people in particular. Those who by thinking in this way betray their lack of trust in the effectiveness of Amida's Vow are also unable to entrust themselves to Other Power and are thus destined for birth in the Borderland of the Pure Land. How deplorable this is!

Since birth is brought about by Amida's benevolent design, it is obvious that, once faith has been established, there can be no room for our own way of thinking. The realisation that we are evil should make us revere the Power of the Vow all the more. Then quite naturally (*jinen* 自然) we will acquire a tender and forbearing attitude of mind.

Whatever actions we take in connection with birth in the Pure Land, we should never pretend to be wise but should remain reverential and mindful at all times of how deeply indebted we are to Amida Buddha. The *nembutsu* will then well up spontaneously. This is 'natural (*jinen*).' Not imposing our way of thinking is called 'natural.' This is Other Power.

To my regret, however, I have heard that there are those who speak knowingly about 'naturalness' as if there existed some other kind of 'naturalness.' How lamentable this is!

Chapter 17

There are some who maintain that anyone born in the Borderland will ultimately descend into hell.

Whatever kind of sacred documents are there that make such a claim? It really is quite deplorable that such a false view should have begun to circulate amongst people claiming to be scholars. In what strange way, I wonder, are such people studying the sacred books like the Sūtras and the commentaries?

I have learned [from my Master] that those who lack [pure] faith will indeed be born in the Borderland, because of their lack of faith in the Original Vow, and that after having atoned for their evil karma of doubt [by staying there], they will be born again in the Land of Enjoyment and thus ultimately attain Enlightenment.

Since devotees with pure faith are few in number, many people [who cannot attain pure faith] are led to the Land of Transformation (Borderland). To assert that their birth [in the Borderland] will ultimately prove to have been in vain, however, is tantamount to accusing the Buddha of having led them in the wrong direction!

Chapter 18

There are some people who assert that, depending on how big or small the size of one's donations to the Saṃgha, so one becomes a bigger or smaller Buddha [in the Pure Land]. This is utterly nonsensical, even ludicrous in fact.

First of all, is it not impossible to determine the size of a Buddha, to decide whether a Buddha is great or small? Even though the stature of Amida Buddha, the Supreme Teacher of the Pure Land, is described in the scriptures, such descriptions refer to the Dharmakāya of Amida Buddha in its manifested form. When one [becomes a Buddha], attaining the Enlightenment of Dharma-nature, one actually has no form, one is neither long nor short, square nor round, nor does one have any colour, neither blue, yellow, red, white nor black. How then can one's stature be determined at all?

It is stated [in Pure Land Sūtras] that, by pronouncing the *nembutsu*, one beholds a transformed Buddha (化佛, jp. *kebutsu*). Related to this it is also written [in the *nichizō-bun* of the *Daijikkyō*] that with a big [voice pronouncing] *nembutsu* one sees a big Buddha and with a small [voice pronouncing] *nembutsu* one sees a small Buddha. The misinterpretation I have just been talking about may possibly have derived from some such a document.

Furthermore, offerings to the Saṃgha should be regarded as the practice of the charity paramita (perfection). Nevertheless the offerings one will make to the Buddha or to one's teacher, however precious they may be, are actually meaningless if one lacks [pure] faith. If one entrusts oneself to Other Power and if one's faith is deep, even if one does not give a single sheet of paper or half a penny to the Saṃgha, still one will be in accord with the true intention of the Original Vow.

Do they seek to intimidate their fellow devotees, using the Buddha's teaching as a tool to fulfill their own selfish desires?

Postscript to the Tannishō

All the erroneous views discussed above must certainly have originated from some form of divergence from the true faith.

According to the talks of our late Master, Shinran Shōnin, in the time of Hōnen Shōnin while the latter was still alive, amongst his many disciples there were only a few whose faith accorded fully with that of Hōnen Shōnin himself. As a result of this situation there was a dispute between our late Master, Shinran Shōnin, and his fellow disciples under Hōnen Shōnin. The argument was occasioned by a pronouncement on the part of our Master, Shinran Shōnin, to the effect that his faith and that of his Master Hōnen Shōnin were one and the same. Fellow disciples such as Seikan-bo and Nembutsu-bo argued vehemently against this statement, asking, "How can your faith, Zenshin-bo (Shinran Shōnin's name at that time) be identical to that of Hōnen Shōnin?" To which Shinran Shōnin responded, "Hōnen Shōnin's wisdom and learning are immense and so I would certainly be mistaken if I claimed to be as great as Hōnen Shōnin in those respects. As far as faith in salvation (birth [in the Pure Land]) is concerned, however, there is no difference whatsoever. The Master's faith and mine are one and the same." This reply did not satisfy them, however. They remained dubious, asking how such a thing could be possible. So finally they all agreed to settle the question in the presence of Hōnen Shōnin and to see which side was right. When they explained the matter in detail, Hōnen Shōnin said, "My faith has been given by Amida, and so has that of Zenshin-bo [meaning Shinran Shōnin]. Therefore we are one and the same in faith. Those whose faith differs from ours will surely not go to the same Pure Land as I." Judging from this, it seems likely that there are some who are not one in faith with Shinran Shōnin even amongst our fellow followers who practice the *nembutsu* steadfastly and single-mindedly.

Although all these are but repetitions of things I have already mentioned, nevertheless I have written them all down again here. I feel the sum of my remaining days to be like a drop of dew on a withered blade of grass and so, not only have I been listening to my fellow followers talk about their uncertainties, but I have also been telling them all that I learned from my late Master, Shinran Shōnin. And yet I am afraid that, after my eyes close, there may arise great confusion about the teaching. For this reason, whenever you find yourselves confounded by people insisting on the views mentioned above, I advise you to study diligently those sacred writings the late Master used to read with such appreciation.

Generally speaking there is to be found in the sacred documents a mixture of teaching, that which is both true and real together with that which is provisional and expedient. It was because of our Master's true spirit that he adopted the true and set aside the provisional. You cannot be too careful when it comes to guarding against misunderstanding the sacred scriptures.

As evidence of the above I have selected some documents and appended them to this book as a set of criteria (*meyasu* in Japanese).

The Master was wont to say, "When I deeply reflect on the Vow of Amida, created through five kalpas of profound thought, I find the Vow is entirely meant for me, Shinran, alone. That is why I feel so grateful for the Original Vow in which Amida graciously resolved to save me, a person so heavily weighed down by [bad] karma." When I now ponder this expression of Shinran Shōnin's innermost feelings, I find that it is in perfect accord with the following golden passage from Shandao, "Know yourself to be an ignorant being, burdened with karmic evil, subject to birth-and-death, ever sinking, ever transmigrating from time immemorial, and with no possible lead to emancipation." It was the Master's merciful heart causing him to use himself as an example in an effort to awaken us to ourselves going astray without realising how deep our karmic evil is or how great is what has been done for us by [Amida] Tathāgata.

Indeed I myself and others prattle away about good and bad, proclaiming this to be good, that to be bad, and paying no heed to what the Tathāgata has done for us. The Master on the other hand said, 'As to whether things are good or bad, I am in complete ignorance. The reason is this: if I knew what was good as completely as Amida Tathāgata knows, then I might be allowed to say I know what is good. Or again if I knew what was bad as completely as the Tathāgata knows, then I might be allowed to say I know what is bad. But amongst us ignorant beings, weighed down by blind passions in a world of impermanence, a world that is like a burning house, all is vain, all is empty, there is nothing true. Only the *nembutsu* is true and real.'

All of us, including me, are in the habit of talking about utterly vain concerns, and one custom in particular is truly deplorable. I refer to the tendency when we are talking about faith in the context of pronouncing the *nembutsu* or trying to explain faith to others, of ascribing to Shinran Shōnin passages he himself has never ever spoken, and this simply in order to silence others, or to gain the upper hand over our opponents. Such a practice is indeed both shameful and deplorable. I would like you to look into this matter very carefully and be utterly clear about it in your minds.

Although these are far from being my own words, they may appear somewhat awkward, since I myself am not familiar with the Sūtras and commentaries and have no deep understanding as to the meaning of the scriptures. Nevertheless, recalling a fraction, a hundredth part perhaps, of all that our Master, Shinran Shōnin, taught, I have put those fragments down in writing. How sad it would be if those fortunate enough to say the *nembutsu* were not to be born immediately into the Land of Enjoyment (the true Pure Land) but were forced to tarry in the Borderland.

I have taken up my brush in tears and have written all this down in order that there be no difference of faith amongst my fellow followers gathered in a single room. Let this writing be entitled *Tannishō, A Record of Lament over Divergence*. It is not to be shown to outsiders.

Historical endnote on the persecution of Pure Land Buddhism in *1207*

It was during the reign of Gotoba-in that Hōnen Shōnin founded the *Nembutsu* School, based on the teaching of Other Power, the Power of the Original Vow [of Amida Buddha]. However, the monks of the period from Kōfukuji Temple started accusing Hōnen Shōnin of being an enemy of the Buddha-dharma, and actually lodged a report with the Imperial Court to the effect that there was evidence of lawless misconduct amongst Hōnen Shōnin's disciples. As a result of all these groundless rumours a number of people were found guilty and punished.

Hōnen Shōnin and seven of his disciples were sent into exile and four other disciples were executed.

Hōnen Shōnin, himself, was exiled to Hata in Tosa province. His secular name as a branded criminal was 'Fujii no Motohiko, male.' He was seventy-six years old at the time.

Shinran Shōnin was exiled to Echigo province. His name as a declared criminal was 'Fujii no Yoshizane.' He was then thirty-five years old.

Jōmon-bō was exiled to Bingo province; Chōsai Zenkō-bō, to Hōki province; Kōkaku-bō, to Izu province; Gyōkū Hōhon-bō, to Sado province.

It was likewise determined that both Kōsai Jōkaku-bō and Zenne-bō were also to be banished to remote areas, but finally the Great Abbot [Jien], Former Head of Mudōji, asked to take custody of them.

Those who were sentenced to banishment were the eight men listed above.

Those who were sentenced to death were:

1) Saii Zenshaku-bō
2) Shōgan-bō
3) Juren-bō
4) Anraku-bō

These sentences were carried out by Dharma-seal Sonchō of the second Imperial Rank.

Shinran was laicised and given a secular name. Consequently he was neither monk nor layman. He decided, therefore, to take the word '*toku*' (baldhead) as his surname and applied to the Imperial Court for permission to do so. His letter of application is said to be still stored in the Record Office.

After his banishment he would regularly sign his name Gutoku (baldheaded ignoramus) Shinran.

Rennyo Shōnin's Note

This sacred document is a teaching of great importance in our tradition. It should not be shown indiscriminately to anyone without past good karma.

MAP OF JAPAN

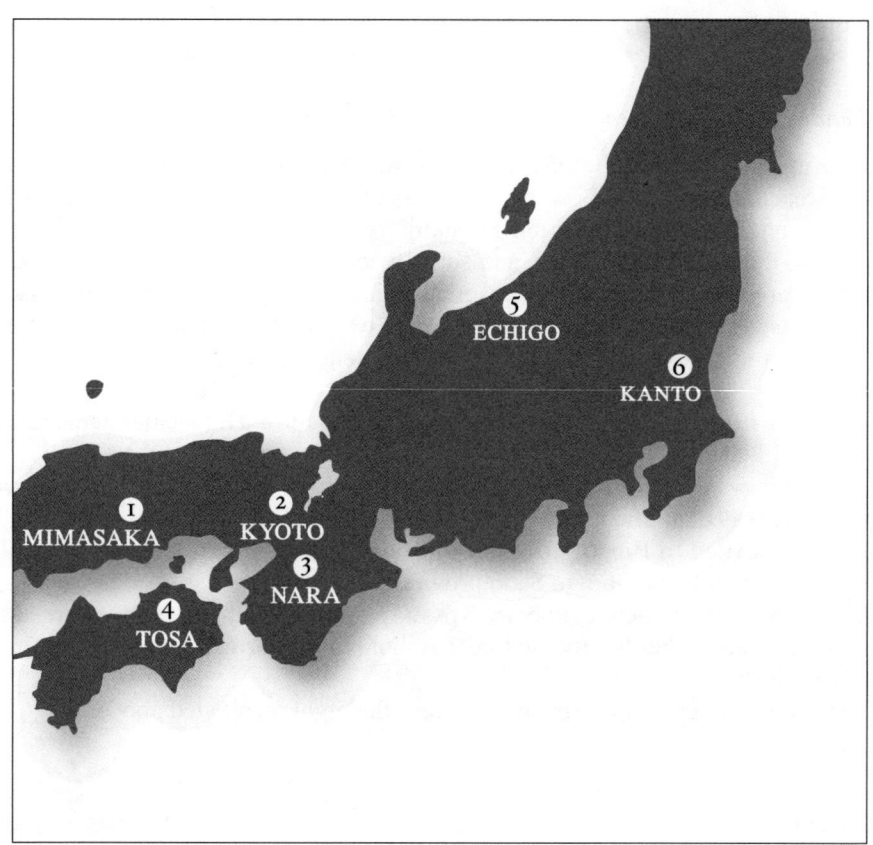

HŌNEN SHŌNIN

① Birthplace, Mimasaka, 1133

② Encounters the Original Vow, 1175

② Propagation, Kyoto

④ Exile, Tosa, revised to Sanuki, 1207

② Death, Kyoto, 1212

SHINRAN SHŌNIN

② Birthplace, Kyoto, 1173

② Encounters Hōnen Shōnin, 1201

⑤ Exile, Echigo, 1207

⑥ Propagation, Kanto

② Encounter with Yuien, 1240*

② Death, Kyoto, 1262

YUIEN

② Birthplace, Kyoto, 1222

② Encounters Shinran Shōnin, 1240*

⑥ Propagation, Kanto

❸ Composes the *Tannishō*, Nara, 1288*

❸ Death, Nara, 1289*

*Designations based on conjecture.

INDEX

GREAT LIVING by Reverend Kemmyo Taira Sato

AFTERWORD

At present the *Tannishō* is without question the most famous text associated with the Jōdo Shinshū (Shin Buddhist) faith. As such it is often perceived as a doctrinal primer through which one may gain a concise introduction to Shinran Shōnin's thought. As Reverend Kemmyo Taira Sato has detailed so carefully in this book, however, the origins and structure of the text are far more complex and challenging than one might first assume.

Before attaining its current celebrity status the *Tannishō* languished in obscurity for many years until it was reintroduced to the world by Reverend Manshi Kiyozawa (1863–1903) and his disciples. During their struggles to bring the Jōdo Shinshū teachings into the modern era these reformers came to feel that the *Tannishō*, with its emphasis on each person's individual awakening of faith, was the ideal vehicle to revitalise the tradition. This strongly existential aspect of the *Tannishō* is of course captured most famously in Shinran Shōnin's words, 'When I deeply reflect on the Vow of Amida, created through five kalpas of profound thought, I find the Vow is entirely meant for me, Shinran, alone'.

In one sense, Reverend Kiyozawa's intuition proved correct and the popularisation of the *Tannishō* was an epoch-making event which contributed to an energetic new flourishing of faith that flowed through and between many Jōdo Shinshū communities. Indeed, taking the Shōgyōji temple as an example, after his attainment of faith, our late head priest Venerable Reion Takehara (1876-1951) happened to encounter Reverend Kiyozawa's younger colleague Reverend Jōkan Chikazumi (1870-1941) and their lifelong friendship played an important part in nurturing the modern-day Shōgyōji faith-movement through various difficulties.

At the same time, however, the strongly individualistic bent that Reverend Kiyozawa's existential emphasis gave to Shinran Shōnin's thought was sometimes at the expense of the full breadth of his vision for the Shin Buddhist community, where the self must be transcended in order for the individual person to become whole again. This has often led modern interpreters to neglect the critical importance of the faith-transmission that takes place in the pure encounter of teacher and disciple, which Reverend Sato identifies at the heart of the *Tannishō*.

We should consider ourselves most fortunate that English translations of the *Tannishō* currently abound, from the 1928 version by Tosui Imadate (1855–1931) edited by D. T. Suzuki (1870–1966) through to the more recently published ones. Nonetheless, Reverend Kemmyo Taira Sato, through careful study of its historical and philological context, has been able to present us with a startlingly vivid new reading of the work, embellished with illuminating insights drawn from his own living encounter with the Dharma. Although there have been numerous detailed commentaries on the *Tannishō* published in Japanese, this is the first version in English attempted on such grand scale and with such spiritual depth. It therefore constitutes, we believe, a landmark work in the understanding of the *Tannishō* in the English-speaking world. It will, it is hoped, lead to further insights and still deeper understanding of this important Shin Buddhist document.

Being aware of these facts, those of us who have been studying at Three Wheels under Sato Sensei's guidance would like to offer our deepest gratitude for his great efforts to transmit the Jōdo Shinshū teachings to the Saṃgha in this country for over a decade. It is indeed a great honour for us to have been involved firsthand in the publication of this book presenting the faith-transmission of Shinran Shōnin's teaching to the world.

Namu-Amida-butsu.

Andy Barritt
Representative
The Three Wheels Circle of Dharma Friends

ACKNOWLEDGEMENTS

Towards the end of 1993 my master, the Venerable Chimyo Takehara, sent me to Great Britain to improve my language skills so as to better contribute to the ongoing spiritual dialogue taking place between members of University College London and Shogyoji Temple in Fukuoka, Japan. This book is the fruit of that spiritual exchange, as well as of the myriad other precious encounters I have shared with sincere people of many nationalities over the past fifteen years. The names of a few of those I would like to thank are as follows:

My master, the Venerable Chimyo Takehara, and his followers of the Shogyoji Saṃgha, for their enormous help and support in establishing the Three Wheels Shin Buddhist Centre and developing its various activities.

My dearest friend Professor John White, former Vice-Provost of UCL, who provided the initial impetus for this book by encouraging me to give these talks in English and who helped me so much with the editorial work by reviewing the original manuscript over and over again.

Mrs Etsuko Crellin whose request that I teach her daughter Ana-Marie about the Buddha-dharma inspired me to give these talks at Three Wheels.

Representatives of Birkbeck College, SOAS, The Buddhist Society and The Golden Buddha Centre who so generously gave me the opportunity to present my translations and commentary to earnest and challenging audiences.

Mrs Dilly Suzuma who read and reread all my drafts, and made wonderful suggestions as to how to improve and polish my English.

Mr Andy Barritt and Mr Andrew Webb for their critical comments and work on the notes and glossary, and all the other members of the Three Wheels Saṃgha for their support and encouragement.

Mr Wayne Yokoyama whose hard work and professional eye moulded my writings into a form fit for publication.

Last but not least I would like to thank my wife Hiroko without whose efforts to support and protect my practice I could not have completed this work.

With the deepest gratitude to all my friends for their encouragement.

Namu-Amida-butsu.

Kemmyo Taira Sato
Three Wheels, London

Three Wheels, Sanrin Shoja,
is a place
of journeying,
of coming together,
of spiritual adventure
and exchange.

It is a place
for young and old
to learn from each other.
It is a place to 'be'.

It is a physical symbol
of a spiritual ideal,
the concept of true service,
represented
by the Three Wheels
of the Giver, the Receiver,
and the Gift.

If the Gift itself is pure,
given solely
for the giving,
without thought
of reward or return
for the Giver,
of debt or obligation
in the Receiver,

then,
in their return,
the Receiver
can freely become the Giver,
the Giver
becomes the Receiver.

Then,
out of diversity
unity and harmony
are born.

The Three Wheels
are the one wheel
and the Great Wheel
turns.

This
is the meaning and purpose
of Sanrin Shoja.